OLLARS
for
BULLETS

THE STORY OF AMERICAN
RULE IN NICARAGUA

By HAROLD NORMAN DENNY

GREENWOOD PRESS, PUBLISHERS
WESTPORT, CONNECTICUT

Library of Congress Cataloging in Publication Data

Denny, Harold Norman, 1889-
    Dollars for bullets.

    Reprint of the ed. published by Dial Press, New York.
    Bibliography: p.
    Includes index.
    1. United States--Foreign relations--Nicaragua.
2. Nicaragua--Foreign relations--United States.
3. Nicaragua--Politics and government--1909-1937.
I. Title.
E183.8.N5D4 1980   972.85'05   79-25688
ISBN 0-313-22269-X

Reprinted with the permission of Gladys Denny Shultz

Reprinted in 1980 by Greenwood Press, Inc.
51 Riverside Avenue, Westport, CT 06880

Printed in the United States of America

10 9 8 7 6 5 4 3 2 1

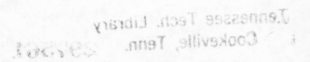

DOLLARS
for
BULLETS

"The diplomacy of the present administration has sought to respond to modern ideas of commercial intercourse. This policy has been characterized as substituting dollars for bullets. It is one that appeals alike to idealistic humanitarian sentiments, to the dictates of sound policy and strategy, and to legitimate commercial aims."—PRESIDENT TAFT *in a definition of "Dollar Diplomacy" in 1912.*

CONTENTS

ILLUSTRATIONS

FOREWORD

This volume is to a great extent the result of a six months' study of the situation in Nicaragua, made in that country during the critical period in the Winter and Spring of 1927–1928. That study has been supplemented by inquiries in Washington and the financial district of New York and by consultation of bankers' records, State Department documents and other pertinent material.

In Nicaragua the author visited every part of the Republic and came to know not only the chief figures in the many-sided struggle, but all classes of Nicaraguans of all shades of opinion, down to the hospitable Indians in the jungle. He learned in Nicaragua that the proceedings of the United States in that country in the past two years did not constitute an isolated and sporadic "adventure," but a sequence in a long train of events—a chapter in a continuing story—and could be understood only as they were viewed against the background of earlier chapters in the history of the Caribbean, and of the basic international and strategic principles of the United States. This volume is an attempt to make them so understood. To this end the author has endeavored to present the story objectively, with a minimum of interpretation, permitting the facts as far as possible to interpret themselves.

At many points the story reflects credit upon the Government of the United States. At others it reveals the Government as open to criticism. In dealing with incidents which might put the State Department in an unfavorable light, the author has excluded accusations by biased parties, except where necessary to give every side its say; in such cases he has depended for his material on publications of the State Department or other official American documents, on the statements of persons friendly to the American policy in Nicaragua, or on facts which he personally ascertained. Some of the material in this book was obtained from confidential personal sources which cannot be disclosed.

The author's journey to Nicaragua was made as a staff correspondent of *The New York Times,* from which he afterward resigned in order to complete the extensive research necessary to this work. The *Times,* of course, is in no way concerned in any statements in the present volume, for which the author alone is responsible.

New York,
February 10, 1929

DOLLARS
for
BULLETS

WHY THE UNITED STATES IS IN NICARAGUA

WHEN one studies the complex, contradictory, and still unfinished story of American activities in Nicaragua, he will come upon three phrases which may guide him to an understanding of the purpose and behavior of the United States.

These phrases are: "Manifest Destiny," "Dollar Diplomacy," and "Mutual Good Will."

They embody the motives which have governed the policy of the United States toward Nicaragua at three different periods. And, varied and conflicting though these motives are, they all are potent even now in the relations of the United States with that little country which has suffered so much and has cost America so dearly in trouble and blood and treasure.

"Manifest Destiny" was the slogan—almost an article of religious faith—of American pioneers in the period just before the Civil War. The United States had expanded its territories mightily, and with every gain it was greedy for more. Men of the sturdy, adventurous stamp who had crossed the plains and the Rockies to the gold fields of California felt that America must engulf the continent and round out its domains into one vast empire of the West. There was no limit to their ambition. There was nothing which Americans could not accomplish. It was a period of national adolescence.

And so fearless faith in the young nation's manifest destiny impelled American filibusters into Mexico and into Nicaragua to wage unsanctioned or half-sanctioned wars in an effort to add more territories to the already far-spread United States. It was purely and frankly selfish: an expression of the divine right of might and ambition.

"Dollar Diplomacy" is of our own era. The phrase came into general currency early in the present century, after America's bewildering success in the war with Spain had made it a world power over night, when the products of its rapidly developing industrial system had begun to rove the world for markets, and when the United States, whose economic expansion had been launched with money supplied by European investors, itself had become a lending nation. As the United States had become great and had taken its place in the society of nations, it also had become more sophisticated. "Manifest Destiny" no longer was heard. It had been swallowed up, incorporated, in "Dollar Diplomacy."

And dollar diplomacy was proclaimed quite as frankly as the belief in manifest destiny had been proclaimed.

President Taft stated it unabashedly in his message to Congress in 1912, at a time when his Government was involved in Nicaragua as intimately as can be conceived. United States marines had just played a deciding part in putting down a dangerous and disastrous rebellion and had given the lives of seven of their own men in doing it; and while factions in the United States and in Nicaragua were bitterly opposing every step, the United States had installed Wall Street bankers in the debt-ridden Republic in an effort to untangle its affairs and place the country on a sound and peaceful basis.

At the end of that nightmare year President Taft said:

"The diplomacy of the present administration has sought to respond to modern ideas of commercial intercourse. This policy has been characterized as substituting dollars for bullets. It is one that appeals alike to idealistic humanitarian sentiments, to the dictates of sound policy and strategy, and to legitimate commercial aims. It is an effort frankly directed to the increase of American trade upon the axiomatic principle that the Government of the United States shall extend all proper support to every legitimate and beneficial American enterprise abroad."

The President added that because modern diplomacy is commercial there had been a disposition in some quarters to attribute to it none but materialistic aims. But this, he said, was a mistake.

Philander C. Knox, Secretary of State under Taft and identified with dollar diplomacy more closely than any other statesman, avowed it quite as openly.

"True stability is best established not by military, but by economic and social forces," he remarked of Central America in 1910. And a few months later, discussing the State Department's fostering of loans by American bankers for the purpose of refunding previous loans made by European bankers to weak Caribbean countries, he said: "It is the fashion to style this 'Dollar Diplomacy,' the phrase being originally intended in a disparaging sense. It seems, on the contrary, to be a creditable and happy phrase. If the American dollar can aid suffering humanity and lift the burden of financial difficulty from States with which we live on terms of intimate intercourse and earnest friendship, and replace insecurity and devastation by stability and peaceful self-development, all I say is that it would be hard to find better employment. Anyhow, the State Department will always be glad to take advantage of the American dollar in furtherance of peace on earth and good will to fellow men."

"Mutual Good Will" was a phrase created, in relation to Nicaragua, by Charles Evans Hughes, but the concept itself was by no means new. The one-time Secretary of State used the phrase at the Pan-American Conference in Havana in January, 1928, when he listed it among the four pillars of Pan-Americanism. The other pillars, as Mr. Hughes saw them, were Independence, Stability, and Coöperation.

"We do not wish the territory of any American republic," Mr. Hughes said later at this same conference,

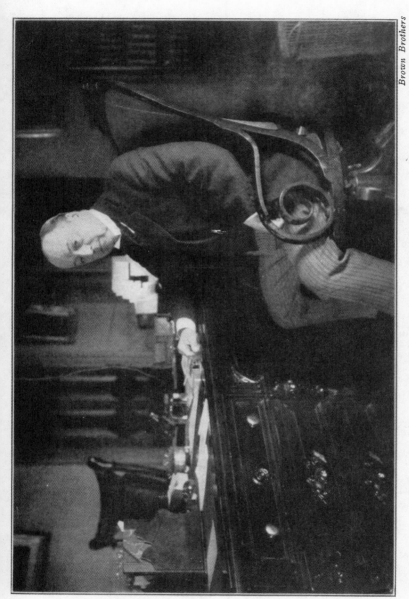

~ Philander Chase Knox ~
Chief Exponent of "Dollar Diplomacy"

when delegates of some of the Latin American states endeavored to bring up the matter of American intervention in Nicaragua, "We do not wish to govern any American republic. We simply wish peace and order and stability, and recognition of earnest rights properly acquired, so that this hemisphere may be not only the hemisphere of peace, but the hemisphere of international justice."

Nor can it be charged that Mr. Hughes was insincere, that these were merely pleasant words designed to lull Latin American neighbors. As will appear later in this narrative, Mr. Hughes, when Secretary of State, had demonstrated by deed the genuineness of his feeling for the independence of Latin American states. The revolution which followed closely on the carrying out of that honest purpose cost Nicaragua some thousands of lives and brought on the whole train of crises in Nicaragua and in Nicaragua's relations to the United States which just now have come to a seeming solution with the successful American supervision of Nicaragua's election.

This "good will" policy, although most completely exemplified by Mr. Hughes, already had been enunciated by Woodrow Wilson soon after he took office in 1913, when he proclaimed a new day for the Latin American states. But President Wilson took up the work in the Caribbean just where President Taft had left it, and the policy of his administration in relation to Nicaragua varied in no essential from that under Republican presidents.

The history of America's relations with Nicaragua well illustrates the truth that governments, no more than individuals, are all good or all bad in their characters and actions. It is as inaccurate history to picture the United States playing only a noble, or only an ignoble, rôle in Latin America and specifically in Nicaragua, as it is faulty art in fiction to portray villains and heroes in uncompromising black and white.

At times the United States has been a noble and unselfish hero to Nicaragua; at times it has been the villain who would let nothing thwart his purpose. And often it has been both hero and villain at once, as in its high handed, yet absolutely necessary, enforcement of American supervision of the last Nicaraguan election over the volubly expressed will of the Nicaraguan Congress. As is usual in life, the United States has been punished the most severely when it was acting the most altruistically.

No one was more regretful than the gentlemen in the State Department a little while ago at a concatenation of events which set the United States to interposing in a civil war, to bolstering, by virtue of its military power, a sagging Nicaraguan administration, to carrying on a sanguinary war against a portion of Nicaragua's people, and to struggling to put the conduct of a Nicaraguan national election under the absolute control of Americans.

But the United States has been involved in Nicaragua at intervals and to some extent ever since the Central American colonies broke away from Spain in

1821, and set out, with ill-founded optimism, to govern themselves. Its actual and continuing interference in Nicaragua began in 1909, however, and it is properly from that date that the situation of the past two or three years may be traced.

In that year the United States, under President Taft and Secretary Knox, threw its powerful weight on the side of a Conservative revolution against President Zelaya, sent him in flight from the country, forced his followers into political exile, virtually appointed a President to its own liking, and set about generally to run the country.

It really became an adventure then, although based on powerful and fundamental considerations, and it was an adventure in which the United States Government was not always happy. For, once in, it found that it could not get out. It tried to get out, and disaster struck Nicaragua and dragged it in again. To put it vulgarly but accurately, in 1909 the United States took a bear by the tail, and it has never been able to let go.

Few things in its history have brought more condemnation on the United States than has its career in Nicaragua. It has been violently attacked as the "Colossus of the North," the "Yankee peril," by first one faction and then another in Nicaragua, and when the political tables in that country have turned, it has been hailed as saviour by the very factions which had so bitterly denounced it. The course of the United States in Nicaragua arouses perennial fears in other

Central and South American countries. And in the United States it has inspired violent criticism of every administration under which the Nicaraguan problem has been acute.

Often the assertions of the critics have been true; often they have been baseless, or founded on misunderstanding.

Before entering on the story of Nicaragua and the relations of the United States to that country, it may be helpful to set down the principal counts in the indictment against the American Government.

The United States has been accused of stealing away Nicaragua's independence and making that country its satellite, while it loudly and piously declared its determination that all Latin American countries should enjoy complete freedom.

It has been accused of exercising this domination in order that American business interests might prosper.

Most seriously of all it has been accused of being the tool of Wall Street, of holding Nicaragua prostrate with the bayonets of American marines at its throat, while predatory bankers robbed and exploited the defenseless and poverty stricken republic at their will.

The United States, if it is honest, must plead guilty with extenuating circumstances on the first count. On the second count it can plead not guilty with a fair chance of acquittal. And as to the third count, it is justified in entering an indignant denial.

The United States has ruled Nicaragua during most of the past eighteen years more completely than the American Federal Government rules any state in the Union. It unquestionably has exercised a protectorate over Nicaragua, however spiritedly the State Department may disavow the word. It occupies the country with its armed forces and probably will continue to occupy it for some time to come. Even now, as a Liberal administration comes into office after eighteen years of Conservative rule, the United States may be expected to keep close watch over Nicaragua's affairs and to interfere in them whenever, or if ever, they run counter to what the United States considers to be its own fundamental interests.

At intervals in the past eighteen years the United States has chosen presidents for Nicaragua and upheld them by force of arms. It has dictated constitutional provisions for Nicaragua to adopt, and laws for its Congress to pass. And when Congress has balked it has written decrees for the President to sign, and thus attained its will.

The United States has taken away Nicaragua's army and disarmed its inhabitants—in the interest of peace and by Nicaragua's consent—and is building up a new army for the Republic, officered by American marines.

An American citizen, jointly chosen by the State Department and American bankers, collects Nicaragua's customs duties, half its total revenue, and pays out a portion of these monies to apply on Nicaragua's foreign debt before Nicaragua can touch a penny of it.

An American is manager of the National Bank of Nicaragua, and as such is comptroller of Nicaragua's currency.

American citizens have an indirect control over Nicaragua's internal as well as its customs taxation, and over its governmental expenditures.

American marines, under the leadership of an American army general endowed with dictatorial powers, have just conducted Nicaragua's presidential election, and incidentally have given that country the first free, fair, and honest ballot in its history.

These indeed are extraordinary measures; but as to the charge that they have been undertaken with the object of exploiting Nicaragua, for turning the little Republic over to American business interests to be plucked—that charge collapses under examination.

The bankers have not exploited Nicaragua. They have made comparatively little money in the country. Wall Street, far from using the State Department as its tool, has been employed by the State Department as an instrument for the carrying out of the established American policy in the Caribbean. The voluminous records available reveal that the part played by the bankers in Nicaragua has often been a reluctant one, usually a disappointing one, and more productive of grief than of profits.

The activities of the State Department and of the

bankers in Nicaragua have been intertwined almost from the beginning of American intervention in Nicaraguan affairs. Wall Street went into Nicaragua in 1911 at the solicitation of the State Department, which was concerned because Nicaragua had borrowed from European interests and desired to have this European money replaced by American capital. Improvident Latin American states have from time to time found European warships at their doors in the character of bill collectors—an embarrassment which the United States felt it could not permit in Nicaragua.

But Wall Street not only never has had much money in Nicaragua, at the present moment it has not one dollar invested in any manner in the Republic, although one day it probably will be a creditor again. Thus far, one might say, it has been more sinned against than sinning.

Let us turn, then, to America's political domination of Nicaragua. The writer has purposely stated the facts of this domination as baldly as possible. There is another side to this phase of the problem. The United States, as well as Nicaragua, has felt itself to be under compulsion from the first.

A glance down the past of the Western Hemisphere shows the United States striving, with few lapses, to preserve and observe a principle which it has set for itself in Latin America: the territorial integrity and the political equality of all American states. It has violated that principle in spirit while clinging desperately to the letter of it—never more so than in Nicaragua—but even so it has tried to leave Nicaragua a free agent, and has refused to hold the country under a still stronger hand when Nicaragua itself has asked it. There is a considerable element in Nicaragua, wearied of politics, which would like to see the United States take the country over frankly and run it, as it runs Porto Rico, for the sake of Nicaragua itself, just as there are those who would like to see the United States and all its works utterly driven out.

For in this long association—subjugation, if you will—there has been a certain benevolence, a blundering benevolence, often, and not without hypocrisy, in the heart of the Washington Government. It has really wished to help the "little brown brother" of the tropics.

And so in the years that the United States has controlled Nicaragua it has constantly proclaimed, with a certain truth, that it was endeavoring to regenerate the country, to put it at peace within its own borders and with the rest of the world, and to set it in the paths of justice and prosperity. True enough, but it also is quite true that if Nicaragua were in some remote spot where it would not be immediately involved with America's own interests, the United States would leave its people free to govern themselves as badly as they liked.

The real motives for America's interposition whenever war or revolution has broken out in the Isthmian countries have been far deeper than any matter of protecting weak neighbors from their own vices; of grabbing and safeguarding concessions for America's own people; of placing Wall Street bankers in position to bleed these countries, or even of protecting American lives and property.

They are rooted in the basic strategy of America's national defense, which hinges on the canal, and are bolstered when necessary by America's one principle of foreign policy, the Monroe Doctrine.

However mistaken and blundering and unethical, or however righteous and magnanimous, has been the behavior of the United States in Nicaragua, it can be judged understandingly only in relation to those major considerations which have dictated it.

CHAPTER I

THE RIVALRY FOR THE CANAL

I T has been Nicaragua's fate, often an evil fate like that of a woman too lovely, to be desired by many nations. Geological forces laid out the area which was to be Nicaragua at a point destined to be of enormous strategic importance to the great powers of the world. The existence across the territory of Nicaragua of a favorable route for a trans-Isthmian canal to join the two great seas of the world made Nicaragua a potential Gibraltar of the West which a strong nation inevitably would some day dominate.

The interest of the United States in Nicaragua, reaching far back into the Nineteenth Century, has pivoted on this canal route. Little by little, through administrations Democratic and Republican, the United States has prized that route away from other ambitious countries and made it at last its own.

Even so, the United States was slow to awake to the full significance of the Isthmus to its own future growth. The importance of an Isthmian canal was to some extent understood in North America a century ago, but it was not dreamed then that such a canal would in time become what it now is, the keystone of the military strategy of the United States.

The problem of the military security of the United States is peculiar. The country fronts both oceans, with Europe on one side and Asia on the other; and on both coasts, from the viewpoint of the professional military man, there is always the possibility of future conflict.

The first arm of the American defense is the navy, but with Central and South America presenting a long, unbroken barrier between the Atlantic and the Pacific, it was necessary before the Panama Canal was built for American warships to travel half way around the world to get from one coast to the other. This meant that the United States must divide its naval forces if both coasts were to be guarded, and this necessity carried with it the danger of being unable to assemble the two halves quickly enough to form one strong united fleet in the event of an attack on one coast or the other. The alternative was to mass the fleet on one coast, leaving the other unprotected. Thus from the standpoint of national defense it would be theoretically necessary for the United States to maintain two fleets, each capable of coping with the strongest competitor with whom a clash was conceivable, if the nation was to be completely protected.

The possibility of, in effect, doubling the size of the American fleet if it could be moved through the Isthmus was made graphically apparent by the voyage of the battleship Oregon around the Horn in the Spanish-American War, and stimulated the movement to pierce Central America.

Henry L. Stimson, the man who, as President Coolidge's representative, was to compel the warring parties in Nicaragua to lay down their arms in 1927, described the military importance of a canal across the Isthmus in 1912, when he was Secretary of War, and the question of fortifying the Panama Canal, then nearing completion, was under debate.

". . . it is of vital importance to this country not only that the canal shall be open to *our* fleet in case of war, but that it shall be closed to the fleet of our enemy," said Mr. Stimson.

". . . The Panama Canal, when completed, will shorten the distance between our East and West coasts from 13,000 miles to 5,000 miles," the then Secretary of War wrote. "The long peninsula of South America, stretching down nearly into the Antarctic Ocean, offers an almost insuperable obstacle, not only to the transfer of our own fleet from one coast to another, but to a similar transfer of an enemy's fleet. . . . In case of war it (the canal) enables us to concentrate our entire defense upon the threatened side, and it thereby tends to give us the absolutely necessary time which will be required in order to create and train a citizen army. The three months which would be consumed by a foreign enemy in going around Cape Horn, or through the Straits of Magellan, might make the difference between a successful defense or complete disaster on the part of those communities against which the attack was intended. On the other hand, if in case of war our enemy's fleet were to pass through the Isthmus of Panamá and transfer its activities from coast to coast at will, we should be in a very much more defenseless position than we are today without the canal."

Admiral Alfred T. Mahan fully agreed with Mr. Stimson. The Panama Canal, he said, would have a closer relation to the Pacific than Gibraltar has had to the Mediterranean, where the supremacy of the British has shaped modern history.

But the construction and security of the Panama Canal only half solve the problem—speaking still from the standpoint of the professional military strategist. Not only must the United States be able to move its fleet swiftly and safely from one ocean to the other but, as Secretary Stimson indicated, it must be the only nation able to move a fleet from one side of the Isthmus to the other.

Charles Evans Hughes, when Secretary of State, developed this conception publicly in an address before the American Bar Association on August 30, 1923, when he said:

"By building the Panama Canal we have not only established a new and convenient highway of commerce, but we have created new exigencies and new conditions of strategy and defense. It is for us to protect that highway. It may also be necessary for us at some time to build another canal between the Atlantic and the Pacific Oceans and to protect that."

Mr. Hughes was even more specific on November 30 of the same year in an address before the American

Academy of Political and Social Science at Philadelphia.

"We have established a waterway between the Atlantic and the Pacific Oceans—the Panama Canal," he remarked then. "Apart from obvious commercial considerations, the adequate protection of this canal—its complete immunity from any adverse control—is essential to our peace and security. We intend in all circumstances to safeguard the Panama Canal. We could not afford to take any different position with respect to any other waterway that may be built between the Atlantic and Pacific Oceans. Disturbances in the Caribbean region are therefore of special interest to us, not for the purpose of seeking control over others, but of being assured that our own safety is free from menace."

The Panama Canal became, the day the first ship passed through it, a part of the coast line of the United States and the most vital and vulnerable point in the whole American system of communications. And this costly and indispensable strip of the American coast was separated from the remainder of the country by 2,000 miles of territory, inhabited by people whose governments had been notoriously unstable, toward which foreign powers had often cast scheming glances. The United States, as its Government has always viewed it, could not allow any other powerful country, or any country which might become the tool of another powerful country, to assume a position of dominant influence between the Southern borders of the United States and the Panama Canal. And above all, whether or not the United States intended to use the Nicaraguan route, a shorter route than the one at Panamá and lying within it as well, it could not allow any other country, strong or weak, even to think of using it. It would as soon permit a foreign power to establish a military base in Pittsburgh.

But if the United States was slow to initiate definite efforts to gain the Nicaraguan route, other nations were not. Wars have been waged over it. England gained a foothold early; for three quarters of a century the route was an issue between the United States and Great Britain and brought the two countries uncomfortably close to a break.

From the time when the Spanish *conquistadores* first set eyes on the waters so nearly separating the Northern and Southern continents, and so nearly furnishing ready made the short route to Cathay for which Columbus searched, the enormous potentialities of that route were recognized in Europe.

Early in the Sixteenth Century, when the Spaniards were first finding their way into the jungles and volcanic plains of what is now Nicaragua, Hernando Cortes, commissioned by Emperor Charles V. of Spain, wrote his master that if a strait could be found between the two seas it "would render the King of Spain master of so many kingdoms that he could consider himself Lord of all the World." And in Nicaragua the Spaniards stumbled on a route which the Indians even then were traversing in their crude canoes.

The route in Nicaragua is approximately 180 miles long. Its essentials are the San Juan River and the Great Lake of Nicaragua. The San Juan flows from the lake, which is in the volcanic belt close to the Pacific shore of Nicaragua, to the Caribbean at Greytown, and along a portion of its length it forms the boundary between Nicaragua and Costa Rica, a fact giving rise to a further set of difficulties and ill-feeling which will be related later.

The Lake of Nicaragua, across which shipping would steam in the event the canal was completed, is 100 miles long and 45 miles wide. From the western shore of the lake to the waters of the Pacific is only 13 miles, and this rim of land is also the lowest point in the Continental Divide which runs through the western portion of the three Americas. It would be necessary to dig through this part. It would be necessary also to canalize much of the San Juan River and to build locks to lift ships to and from the shallow lake, 110 feet above the level of the sea.

A dozen surveys of the route have been made; a dozen contracts for its utilization have been signed, and at times it has seemed that the ancient dream was about to be realized. But the route still lies placid and unused through the jungle and in the shadows of the dying volcanoes of the lake, as beautifully primitive as when the first Spaniard came wonderingly upon it.

England, which had harried Spain's possessions in the New World from the days of Sir Francis Drake, began the long battle for the canal before the Eight-

〜 ON THE NICARAGUAN CANAL ROUTE 〜

Castillo Viejo, on the San Juan River, Where Nelson Was Defeated

eenth Century came in. In 1780 an English expedition attacked Nicaragua with its objective the sundering of the Spanish province of Central America and the acquisition of the canal route. The expedition was headed by Horatio Nelson, afterward Lord Nelson of Trafalgar. It was ambushed on the river and malaria nearly completed the disaster. Nelson all but lost his life and only a handful of Englishmen got back to the Atlantic Coast.

After Spain's hold finally was broken early in the Nineteenth Century, the canal route was every man's game. The United States officially displayed no interest in the project, even though in 1825 the then united Central American Republic broached it to the Washington Government. DeWitt Clinton took a concession to build the canal, but lacked sufficient capital. A few years later the Netherlands entered the field, but withdrew. In 1835 the United States Government considered the project, but dropped it. In 1846 Louis Napoleon, inspired, it was said, by the hope of freeing Latin America from the growing influence of Anglo-Saxon countries, determined to form a French dominated state in Central America, and to that end seriously set about planning a canal.

"There exists in the New World," said the Third Napoleon, "a state as admirably situated as Constantinople, and, we must say, up to this time as uselessly occupied. We allude to the State of Nicaragua. As Constantinople is the centre of the ancient world, so is the town of Léon the centre of the new, and if the tongue of land which separates its two lakes from the Pacific Ocean were cut through, she would command by virtue of her central position, the entire coast of North and South America. The State of Nicaragua can become, better than Constantinople, the necessary route of the great commerce of the world, and is destined to attain an extraordinary degree of prosperity and grandeur."

Other problems forced the French to relinquish their Nicaraguan ambitions, but British activities in Central America, treading close to the margin of the Monroe Doctrine if they were not actually transgressing it, stimulated the North American Government to counter efforts. These efforts were welcomed in Nicaragua, where there was much concern over the rapid extension of British influence. Elijah Hise, a State Department agent, negotiated without instructions a treaty giving the United States exclusive right to build a canal through Nicaragua, a treaty which aroused deep suspicion in London but which never was acted upon by the United States. He was followed by E. G. Squier, who, also attempting to secure the canal for his government, got into a serious controversy with Chatfield, a British agent, which prompted the British to seize Tigre Island in the Gulf of Fonseca and created a brief crisis between their governments.

Commodore Cornelius Vanderbilt, doughty and ruthless financial warrior in the period of America's early expansion, appreciated the tremendous possibilities in the canal route after personally inspecting

it, and in 1849 obtained a concession to construct it
and had an elaborate survey made. This project also
died as the rest had done, but the Commodore used the
route nevertheless, employing boats on the river and
the lake and stage coaches the remainder of the way
across the Isthmus, to carry passengers and freight to
and from booming California. A strident, disorderly
settlement of American adventurers came into being
at the Caribbean terminus of the route.

After the Vanderbilt failure, interest in the United
States lapsed until after the Civil War, but throughout this period of American initiative England was
watching the progress of the United States in Central America through none too friendly eyes. The
United States was threatening the position which
England had won when the power of Spain relaxed
and finally was thrown off. In time the United States
was to displace England altogether, although not until within the present century.

It is enough for our purpose to begin the account
of Great Britain's efforts along the Eastern shore of
Nicaragua in 1841 when MacDonald, a British agent
who had been furthering British colonial efforts in
Honduras, saw the importance of obtaining possession of the mouth of the San Juan River for transit
purposes, and developed a plan to use the King of
the Mosquitos, a tribe of Indians inhabiting the eastern littoral of Nicaragua, for his purpose. MacDonald took the Mosquito king with him to the mouth of
the San Juan, raised the Mosquito flag, ordered the

Nicaraguan commandant to leave the port and proclaimed a British protectorate over the kingdom.

This protectorate was not relinquished until 1860 when Great Britain, at the instance of the United States, acknowledged a limited sovereignty of Nicaragua over the Indians, but the ghost of this protectorate showed itself at intervals until 1904 when the British Government reconfirmed its acceptance of American dominance in the canal area.

Following the establishment of the British protectorate, a decade of ill-feeling between the United States and England, caused by their rival ambitions in the Caribbean, came to an apparent end in 1850 in the signing of the Bulwer-Clayton Treaty by Sir Henry Bulwer, British special agent sent to Washington to deal with the misunderstandings between the two countries, and John M. Clayton, American Secretary of State.

By this treaty England surrendered the dominance which it had obtained in Nicaragua. Each government bound itself never to assume exclusive control over the canal, never to maintain any fortifications in the vicinity of the canal, and never to fortify, colonize, or exercise any dominion over Nicaragua, Costa Rica, the Mosquito Coast, or any part of Central America. This treaty restored cordial relations between Great Britain and the United States for a time, but with both nations so vitally interested in the Caribbean, and with the agents of both constantly active in that region, new causes of friction were constantly arising. England continued to exercise its protectorate over the strategically important Mosquito Coast, and the United States kept endeavoring to extend its influence in Nicaragua and Honduras. The activities of American filibusters, carrying on private wars in Latin America at that period, intensified the mutual ill-will.

The two governments worked themselves into the sort of a crisis which produces wars, and war might have been the result except that public opinion in both countries obviously would not have countenanced such an extreme. The cloud blew over.

The Central American issue between the two governments long remained unsettled, but in time, as the United States continued to exploit its foothold in Central America, the British came to feel that they would share in the commercial development of the region if it were kept stable under American influence, and learned to look upon American efforts there with apparent equanimity.

America's canal aspirations rose again immediately after the Civil War. William H. Seward, Lincoln's Secretary of State, believed that the nation's future lay in the Pacific and sent an emissary to Nicaragua with the following instructions, reflecting an attitude which might be found in the State Department today:

"Everybody wishes the Spanish-American States well, and yet everybody loses patience with them for not being wiser, more constant, and more stable.

Such, I imagine, is the temper in which every foreign state finds itself when it proposes to consider its relation to those republics, and especially the republics of Central America. . . .

"Assure the Republic of Nicaragua that the President will deal with that government justly, fairly, and in the most friendly spirit; that he desires only its welfare and prosperity. Cultivate friendly dispositions there towards the United States. See that no partiality arises in behalf of any other foreign state to our prejudice, and favor, in every way you can, the improvement of the transit route, seeking only such facilities for our commerce as Nicaragua can afford profitably to herself."

The result of this mission was the negotiation of another treaty, ratified in 1868, by which the United States was pledged to protect the neutrality of any canal constructed in Nicaragua.

France had not yet given up its ambitions in the Western Hemisphere, and in 1878 a Frenchman, Ferdinand de Lesseps, builder of the Suez Canal, obtained a concession from Colombia to build a canal across Panamá. This event stimulated enormously the already strong opinion in the United States that the Bulwer-Clayton Treaty should be abrogated and that the United States should set about building a canal of its own.

President Hayes voiced this opinion in a special message to Congress on March 8, 1880.

"The policy of this country is a canal under

American control," declared the President. "The United States cannot consent to the surrender of this control to any European power or to any combination of European powers. If existing treaties between the United States and other nations, or if the rights of sovereignty or property of other nations stand in the way of this policy—a contingency which is not apprehended—suitable steps should be taken by just and liberal negotiations to promote and establish the American policy on this subject consistently with the rights of the nations to be affected by it.

"The capital invested by corporations or citizens of other countries in such an enterprise must in a great degree look for protection to one or more of the great powers of the world. No European power can intervene for such protection without adopting measures on this continent which the United States would deem wholly inadmissible. If the protection of the United States is relied upon, the United States must exercise such control as will enable this country to protect its national interests and maintain the rights of those whose private capital is embarked in the work."

Within five weeks steps were under way looking toward the abrogation of the Bulwer-Clayton Treaty and the thwarting of the plans for a French canal at Panamá.

American enterprise did not wait for a new settlement with England to push ahead with elaborate plans. A "Provisional Canal Society" was formed immediately by a group of men in New York including ex-President Grant. The society obtained a concession from the Government of Nicaragua and proposed to build a canal under American control. This project went down in the crash of the Marine Bank, which ruined Grant, and its concession lapsed. Meanwhile President Arthur was secretly negotiating a new treaty with the Nicaraguan Government for the construction of a canal by the United States Government. These negotiations resulted in 1884 in the signing of an agreement by Frederick T. Frelinghuysen, American Secretary of State, and President Joaquin Zavala of Nicaragua by which the United States was to build a canal which would be owned jointly by the two countries. The United States also was to be the perpetual guarantor of Nicaragua's territorial integrity. Nicaragua, as always, ratified the treaty; the United States, as in so many other instances, failed to do so. President Cleveland found it pending in the Senate when he took office and withdrew it on the ground that it violated the historic American policy of avoiding entangling alliances.

Sentiment in the United States that a canal should be built was strong, however, and in 1887 another enterprise, which grew into the Maritime Canal Company of Nicaragua, was launched by private American interests. Concessions were obtained from Nicaragua and Costa Rica, and a charter was granted by the American Government authorizing a capital up to $200,000,000. After three centuries of dreaming, actual work was started at Greytown and in the delta of the San Juan. But again there was insufficient money and in 1893, after $2,000,000 had been expended, the company was obliged to give up the enterprise.

But the canal idea survived this new disappointment. The United States, now a full grown nation, was looking ahead very definitely to the day, not distant, when it would tower over a hemisphere. It was strong and self-confident, with a slight tendency to swagger.

"The construction of the Nicaraguan canal under present auspices," wrote William L. Merry, American Minister to Nicaragua, in 1890, "will secure the domination of the United States over the American continent, politically as well as commercially. The position of Lake Nicaragua is unique: Gibraltar is not a circumstance to it in importance. A naval station on this inland sea, with fortified termini and an efficient fleet, will control the Atlantic eastward to the Windward Islands of the West Indies, and westward to the Hawaiian Islands and Samoa. On its fresh waters ironclads can lie without diminished speed caused by foul bottoms, with fresh water for boilers, in a delightful climate, splendid harbors, surrounded by a territory producing maintenance for the personnel of fleets and armies. The nation that with the Nicaraguan Government on a joint agreement, controls Lake Nicaragua will then control the destiny of the Western Hemisphere; it will be, in fact, a constant assertion of the Monroe Doctrine, securing respect for its requirements by the peaceable possession of power to assert them. The foreign policy of our country will become of greater importance every year. . . . The public demand for a modern navy indicates the will of our countrymen on this momentous question."

Further surveys were made, the last one part of a comprehensive investigation of all possible sites for the canal in Central America by an expert commission appointed by President McKinley.

The Nineteenth Century ended with Great Britain more friendly to the United States than at any previous time in its history. In 1901 England consented to the abrogation of the Bulwer-Clayton agreement by signing the Hay-Pauncefote Treaty, negotiated by John Hay, American Secretary of State, and Sir Julian Pauncefote, British Ambassador at Washington. By its terms the United States was empowered to build a canal, under its own control and its own protection.

It was only a matter of time now until a canal would be built across the Isthmus. As the project grew in the minds of the American people, there developed a rivalry between advocates of the two leading routes, Nicaragua and Panamá.

The French company, headed by de Lesseps, had sunk $265,000,000 in its concession in Panamá, had gone bankrupt, had been reorganized, and, seeing only further ruin ahead, was eager to sell its rights and equipment and the work already done to the United States. Philippe Bunau-Varilla, one-time chief engineer of the Panama Canal Company, strove hard in Washington to swing sentiment toward Panamá. The McKinley commission was unanimously in favor of the Nicaraguan route, and public opinion sided with it. On Nicaragua's part, President Zelaya was eager to reach a definite agreement with the United States for the construction of a canal through his country.

Now the chief objection to the Nicaraguan route was the fear of the volcanoes which stretch through Nicaragua in a straight line close to the Pacific from the Gulf of Fonseca to the Costa Rican border. Two of the most beautiful of these rise side by side from the Lake of Nicaragua on the canal route. They are dying, geologists say, but plumes of steam still rise from them. Nicaraguans are proud of this oddly beautiful feature of their country.

Just when it seemed that the American Congress would vote to build the canal across Nicaragua, there came a report of an eruption of Mount Momotombo, in full sight of the Nicaraguan capital. This alarmed the American government. President Zelaya cabled a denial that there had been such an eruption and the alarm was allayed. Bunau-Varilla searched for a telling argument, and found one in his hands—a Nicaraguan postage stamp portraying this very Momotombo belching smoke. He obtained all the copies of this stamp that he could get, pasted them on sheets of paper, and sent one to each Senator. It was enough to convince them. They agreed to purchase the French interest for $40,000,000. Congress passed the necessary legislation in 1902, and, with the aid of the revolution in Panamá against Colombia, acquired the route and started to build the canal. It was completed in 1914 at a cost of $375,000,000.

Panamá got the canal, but the Nicaraguan route remained as a potential temptation to some other power, some day, unless the United States kept it in its hands. And at that period Nicaragua was ruled by President Zelaya, whom the United States regarded as a trouble-maker and an enemy of American interests. The American Government could not consider the problem effectively out of the way until this alternative route was definitely and completely under its control.

". . . it may be said that the canal question is the principal disturbing issue in Nicaraguan affairs, whether international, interstate, or internal," wrote George T. Weitzel, American Minister to Nicaragua a few years later in the period when America's present Nicaraguan policy was being shaped. "And this is none the less true, even though the Panamá route has long since been chosen as the world's highway of commerce. It still offers to the cupidity of the professional revolutionist a prize as valuable as the possession of the custom houses, and affords as much as ever an opportunity for intrigues among the Central American Republics, and a basis for negotiations with

foreign countries, if not a provocation for their in--
terference in the affairs of Nicaragua."

Mr. Weitzel found definite evidence of the way the
route could be used by an unfriendly Nicaraguan
government in a letter in the archives of that country.
It was written by Zelaya's Foreign Minister to the
Nicaraguan Minister in Paris on April 29, 1908, a
year and a half before the first American intervention
which unseated Zelaya, and it proposed overtures to
the Japanese concerning the canal route.

"You no doubt are aware," the letter said, "of the
turn of the policy of the Republic of Colombia with
relation to Panamá and the United States, chiefly in
regard to the opening of the canal, tending at present
to make closer their relations with Japan and showing
overtly their intentions to enter formally into negotiations having to do with the canal south of the
Panama Canal and to induce Japanese immigration
into their territory, etc.

"We are well acquainted with the desires of aggrandizement of the Japanese Empire and the spirit
of the Government of Colombia, which never will
forget the secession of its important department, in-
fluenced by the United States, and which in its excited desire to win back what it has lost grasps at
any project whatsoever which is offered to it as a
realization of its hopes. In view of this it is not impossible that what is now considered doubtful may later
be consummated if possible obstacles do not interfere.

"Nicaragua cannot remain indifferent before such eventualities. As you know positively, the canal through our country offers at all times various advantages over that of Panamá, and that it was international policy which resolved the selection of this last-mentioned route; also, that the present proposal of the Colombians presents innumerable disadvantages.

"But even withdrawing from this point of view and supposing, as is most likely, that in the end the Panama Canal will be the only canal, yet we have to take into account that the United States fears, and rightly, that another or other powers may render null and void a great part of their tremendous labor. And in this sense it is indubitable that Colombia or Nicaragua may obtain no inconsiderable political advantage from the insecure or be it false position in which the United States finds itself.

"Now, through the instrumentality of a certain English consul to this country who may be well informed in the premises, we have learned that Great Britain and Japan have lately concerted the idea of the canal by way of Nicaragua. . . .

"It is my wish, therefore, that you, in an absolutely personal character and with the greatest possible care and discretion, should talk with the Japanese ambassador in Paris, saying that, although you are not in possession of instructions from your Government to the effect, you would venture if the Government of Japan should send agents to Nicaragua the overtures which they might make in connection with this important matter would be very well received. All this without putting on paper a single word of your conversations.

"You are not to forget that this matter is of the utmost confidence, for you will plainly understand that if the United States were prematurely to get wind of our proceedings, whatever we might do in the matter would cost us dear.

"If success is ours we shall procure at the very least most enviable political advantages, above all greater consideration and respect from the United States, and it may be an enviable position in respect to Central America."

This letter in itself of course did not actuate the American intervention. Its existence was not known to the United States until two years after the United States drove out Zelaya. Nor is there any evidence, as far as the writer can learn, that Japan paid the least attention to Zelaya's proposal. But it gave point to American anxiety over a canal route which still might be the subject of bargaining.

This phase of the Nicaraguan situation was finally settled, if anything in Central America may be regarded as settled, when by a treaty with Nicaragua the United States bought an exclusive option on the route, together with other important concessions, for $3,000,000. That was in 1916, in the midst of the

World War. Just before the ratification of the treaty there was a flurry among the American Senators over a rumor that Germany was scheming to obtain the route.

CHAPTER II

GUARDING THE CARIBBEAN

STEP by step—Cuba, Porto Rico, Panamá, Nicaragua, Haiti, the Virgin Islands—the Caribbean has become an "American Lake."

It was an expansion of great strategic significance, placing sentinels here and there in the region of the canal, yet luck, fate, played quite as important a part in it as calculated design.

Cuba, at the door of the Gulf of Mexico, which the United States often had wished to acquire, fell into its lap as a result of the war with Spain. The United States restored the country and handed it back to its inhabitants. But it did so with a proviso, accepted by the Cubans, which made it a satellite. By means of the Platt Amendment Cuba was bound to surrender no portion of its sovereignty to any foreign power, to assume no financial obligations beyond its means, and to permit American intervention. Cuba also gave the United States a strong naval base in the Caribbean by leasing to it the splendid harbor of Guantanamo Bay on the southern shore of the island.

Porto Rico also was a fruit of the Spanish-American War, and remains an American dependency; the Panama Canal Zone was acquired by purchase, and revolution; Nicaragua and Haiti came under American influence by way of intervention; the Virgin Islands were acquired by purchase. And in the midst of this the United States picked Santo Domingo from the gutter of debt and European interference, dusted it off, put it on its feet, and turned it over to its own people.

Again and again in the course of this extension of American power and influence, the Monroe Doctrine —that unique dictum having the force of international law, which Bismarck once characterized as "a species of arrogance particular to the American and quite inexcusable"—has been cited as justification.

And coincidentally with American expansion the Monroe Doctrine has been interpreted, reinterpreted, and sometimes misinterpreted far beyond what President Monroe meant when he uttered it: in fact sometimes into something the very reverse of what he meant. It has become what Albert Bushnell Hart has called with both truth and wit, the "Monrovoid Doctrine"—whose purpose is "preventing anyone from interfering with the Latin Americans—except ourselves."

Indeed this very development—or distortion—of the Monroe Doctrine from the simple declaration that Europe must encroach no further in the Western Hemisphere, into a law to sanction encroachments of the United States in the countries to the South, has been one of the most potent causes of distrust of the United States in Latin America.

The Monroe Doctrine was contained in the message of President Monroe to Congress on December 2, 1823. It was in two separate parts of the message, referring in one part to ambitions of Russia on the Pacific Coast of North America and in the other to designs of the Holy Alliance, a combination of European monarchies devoted to sustaining their form of government against the rising democratic spirit, to restore the revolted colonies of Spain to their former master.

". . . the American continents, by the free and independent condition which they have assumed and maintain, are henceforth not to be considered as subjects for future colonization by any European powers. . . ." Monroe wrote in relation to the Russian plan.

And of the intentions of the monarchies to restore the Spanish colonies he said:

"We owe it, therefore, to candor, and to the amicable relations existing between the United States and those powers, to declare that we should consider any attempt on their part to extend their system to any portion of this hemisphere as dangerous to our peace and safety. With the existing colonies or dependencies of any European power we have not interfered and shall not interfere. But with the Governments who have declared their independence, and maintained it, and whose independence we have, on

great consideration and on just principles, acknowledged, we could not view any interposition for the
purpose of oppressing them, or controlling in any
other manner their destiny, by any European power,
in any other light than as the manifestation of
an unfriendly disposition towards the United
States. . . .

". . . It is impossible that the allied powers should
extend their political system to any portion of either
continent without endangering our peace and happiness; nor can any one believe that our Southern
brethren, if left to themselves, would adopt it of
their own accord. It is equally impossible, therefore,
that we should behold such interposition, in any form,
with indifference.

"If we look to the comparative strength and resources of Spain and those new Governments, and
their distance from each other, it must be obvious
that she can never subdue them. It is still the true
policy of the United States to leave the parties to
themselves, in the hope that other powers will pursue the same course."

The Monroe Doctrine in its inception was wholly
egoistic. It grew out of the desire of the young and
not too powerful republic of the United States to
work out its destiny free from European interference. And at the same time it was a stroke for the
safety of the Latin Republics which had so recently
rid themselves of their Spanish and Portuguese op-
pressors.

The Latin American states hailed the Doctrine with gratitude. They believed that its enunciation had forestalled the sending against them of armed expeditions from Europe. A call was issued for a Pan-American Congress to be held at Panamá in 1826 with the object of forming a sort of Pan-American League of Nations, with the benevolent United States as its mentor and protector.

But the American Congress had no wish to assume such a rôle. It felt that "there is no proposition concerning which the people of the United States are now and ever have been more unanimous than that which denies not merely the expediency, but the right of intermeddling with the internal affairs of other states." The Pan-American Congress met, with no North American representatives present, and accomplished nothing.

The unwillingness of the United States to construe the right or obligation to assume protectorates into the Monroe Doctrine was exemplified even in so serious a situation as the one confronting Haiti in 1897, when German cruisers threatened to bombard Port au Prince to enforce a demand for an indemnity and an apology as the result of the arrest of a German.

"This Government is not under any obligation to become involved in the constantly recurring quarrels of the republics of this hemisphere," said Secretary of State Sherman. "The Monroe Doctrine . . . is wholly inapplicable to the case, and the relations

and interests of this Government with its neighbors
are not benefited by erroneous conceptions of the
scope of the policy announced by President Monroe
and since strictly followed."

To the American Minister to Haiti the Secretary
of State wrote:

"Protectorates over our neighbors have never been
advocated in our foreign policy, being contrary to
the principles upon which this Government is
founded. A protectorate, however qualified, assumes
a greater or less degree of responsibility on the part
of the protector for the acts of the protected state,
without the ability to shape or control those acts,
unless the relation created be virtually that of a colonial dependency, with paramount intervention of
the protector in the domestic concerns of the protected community."

In justice to the American Government, it has
clung to its determination to avoid protectorates, together with its respect for the territorial integrity of
the Latin American states, even to the present day,
notwithstanding that often events have coerced it into
assuming protectorates in fact while it denied them
in theory.

The first interpretation of the Doctrine away from
its original intent, the first distortion of it into a
tool of expansion, was made by President James K.
Polk in 1845, when the United States began its campaign of annexation in the heyday of Manifest Destiny. Polk cited the Monroe Doctrine as justification

for his seizure of Texas, and intended to employ it also in his plans for the acquisition of Yucatan and Cuba.

Such ruthless use of the Doctrine of course could not survive after the country had come of age and acquired urbanity, but Monroe's sentences did expand into a doctrine of paramount interest and thus became a factor in the upbuilding of American hegemony in the region strategically most vital to it. Secretary of State William M. Evarts made the phrase "paramount interest" famous in 1880, linking the Monroe Doctrine to American aspirations for a canal across the Isthmus, and paved the way for President Hayes's pronouncement that "the policy of this country is a canal under American control."

But in the later development of the Monroe Doctrine there was evident a keen sense of obligation to the Latin American states, viewed, it is true, with resentment by many in Latin America as a paternalistic invitation to the lesser republics to put themselves under the beneficent direction of North America. The United States undertook to protect and did protect its weaker neighbors from aggression or exploitation by European powers, most notably perhaps in its interposition on behalf of Venezuela.

European aggressions most often grew out of loans on which Latin American countries defaulted. The American Government considered that it could not allow a European government to take any measures in attempting to collect a loan which would infringe the independence of a Latin American state. And the necessary corollary to that was that the United States itself must be ready to take adequate action to assure the payment of Latin American debts.

President Roosevelt faced this problem in 1905, when the finances of Santo Domingo were in a hopeless snarl and Europeans had taken over various custom houses to collect their obligations.

"It has for some time been obvious that those who profit by the Monroe Doctrine must accept certain responsibilities along with the rights which it confers, and that the same statement applies to those who uphold the Doctrine," said Roosevelt in a message to the Senate in February. "An aggrieved nation can, without interfering with the Monroe Doctrine, take what action it sees fit in the adjustment of its disputes with American states, provided that action does not take the shape of interference with their form of government or of the despoilment of their territory under any disguise. But short of this, when the question is one of a money claim, the only way which remains, finally, to collect it is a blockade or bombardment or seizure of the custom houses, and this means . . . what is in effect a possession, even though only a temporary possession, of territory. The United States then becomes a party in interest, because under the Monroe Doctrine it cannot see any European power seize and permanently occupy the territory of one of these republics; and yet such seizure of territory, disguised or undisguised, may eventually offer the only way in which the power in question can collect any debts, unless there is interference on the part of the United States."

He pursued the subject still further in his message of December 5, 1905:

"We must make it evident that we do not intend to permit the Monroe Doctrine to be used by any nation on this continent as a shield to protect it from the consequences of its own misdeeds against foreign nations. . . . This country would certainly decline to go to war to prevent a foreign government from collecting a just debt; on the other hand, it is very inadvisable to permit any foreign power to take possession, even temporarily, of the custom houses of an American republic in order to enforce the payment of its obligations; for such temporary occupation might turn into a permanent occupation. The only escape from these alternatives may at any time be that we must ourselves undertake to bring about some arrangement by which so much as possible of a just obligation shall be paid. It is far better that this country should put through such an arrangement, rather than allow any foreign country to undertake it."

This was the foundation of dollar diplomacy, of which Taft and Knox were to be the most famous practitioners. It was in the carrying out of the Roosevelt principle that the United States took over the financial affairs of Santo Domingo, and developed a technique of economic control which later was applied to Nicaragua.

This conception of Roosevelt's was of course only a step from the admission of a protectorate. Woodrow Wilson recognized this and took that step in 1916 when in an address before the Second Pan-American Scientific Congress in Washington he discussed "the use which the United States intended to make of her power on this side of the Atlantic."

"It (the Monroe Doctrine) was a hand held up in warning (to the European governments)," said President Wilson, "but there was no promise in it of what America was going to do with the implied and partial protectorate which she apparently was trying to set up on this side of the water. . . . It has been fears and suspicions on this score which have hitherto prevented the greater intimacy and confidence and trust between the Americas."

Eradicating the distrust of American intentions in Latin America would be accomplished, President Wilson said later in this address, "by the states of America uniting in guaranteeing to each other absolute political independence and territorial integrity."

Thus has the Monroe Doctrine become the watchdog of the canal region, and so proclaimed by the country's statesmen. It is necessary to quote only one of them, Secretary Knox:

"The logic of political geography and of strategy and now our tremendous national interest created by the Panama Canal make the safety, the peace, and the prosperity of Central America and the zone of the Caribbean of paramount interest to the Government of the United States. Thus the malady of revolutions and financial collapse is most acute precisely in the region where it is most dangerous to us. It is here that we seek to apply a remedy. It would not be sane to uphold a great policy like the Monroe Doctrine and to repudiate its necessary corollaries and neglect the sensible measures which reason dictates as its safeguards."

Here was the reason for dollar diplomacy, for pushing out foreign loans wherever possible and replacing them with American money, for endeavoring, in President Taft's phrase, to substitute dollars for bullets, and for suppressing revolutions which might damage foreigners—to remove all cause for any European power ever interfering in the affairs of the countries on the Isthmus and in the regions around it.

CHAPTER III

MAHOMET'S PARADISE

A BRIEF description of Nicaragua itself, of its people and its products, and a glance at the country's early history, will help greatly to an understanding of the more recent period in which the United States has so largely controlled the country.

It must have been a lovely and a happy land before the white man found it. It has known little but torment since then. Blessed by nature with inconceivable riches, Nicaragua has lived in poverty from the day of the first invaders.

Nicaragua is the largest and one of the most backward of the five Central American republics. Its total area is approximately 49,000 square miles, 4,500 of which are covered by Nicaragua's two large lakes, the Great Lake of Nicaragua and the Lake of Managua, in the long volcanic plain near the Pacific Coast. Thus it is about the size of New York State. On its northern border lies Honduras, and on its southern, Costa Rica. The population numbers some 638,000, only about 17 per cent of whom are white. The Indian strain is pronounced. English speaking Negroes, descendants of immigrants from the British

West Indies, predominate on the East Coast. The great bulk of the population is a mixture of any two, or all three, of these strains. These mixtures ascend even into the highest social and political circles of the Republic.

The masses of the population are illiterate, cheerful, charming, and, where civilization has touched them, likely to be dishonest. If they like you they will die for you and feel honored in doing it. If they dislike you, or fear you, they will kill you, mutilate you unspeakably, and consider that they have glorified God in the murder. Hookworm and malaria have made them dull, sluggish, and unambitious.

They are hopelessly poor. Fifty cents a day is probably the average wage for labor throughout the country. Many receive no more than five or six dollars a month. In the cities these people dwell in flimsy unfloored shacks at the edge of town. The costume of the men is a tattered shirt, a pair of ragged breeches, and a straw hat. The women, barefoot as well, are clothed in long cotton dresses. Their naked children play in the filth of the street. Their diet is beans, rice, and plantains. And they are always smiling, except on Sundays, when the men get drunk on their appalling native rum and engage in murderous fights with their *machetes*.

Far out in the jungle fastnesses, reached only afoot or on muleback over trails often indistinguishable to the unskilled eyes of a city dweller, one still finds pure bred Indians, descendants of those who escaped the lances of the conquering Spaniards. They are clean-limbed, handsome, affectionate, and hospitable. To the traveler riding up to one of their rude, grass-thatched huts, the woman of the house extends a carved gourd of cool water and fills his bottle smilingly, though most likely she has carried that water in an earthen jar on her head from the nearest stream miles away.

Yet these same people, when aroused by a clever propagandist, or even when impressed into some army, government or revolutionary, by armed recruiting squads roving the bush for "volunteers," fight with dreadful ferocity and bravery. Revolutions in Nicaragua are often comic opera affairs, but people get killed in them.

The eastern part of the country—the old Mosquito Kingdom—is largely jungle land, with a narrow fringe of inhabited country along the Caribbean Coast. There lie vast banana plantations and forests of precious woods. There also are gold mines, less productive now, it would seem, than when the Indians of Columbus's day dug out their metal for trinkets.

The western part of the country in the neighborhood of the two big lakes contains the principal cities of the country, and half its population. Its soil, decayed volcanic lava, is magically fertile.

Jungles which are passable only slowly and with difficulty separate the two sides of the country so completely that it is only politically that they can be said to be of the same nation. Practically they are almost two separate countries even to this day.

The climate is as varied as are the people and the topography. The breezes of the Caribbean sweep the rainy East Coast and make tolerable its moist heat. In the mountains bordering the smothering western plateau, on whose luscious slopes lie the coffee plantations, it is pleasantly cool. There one can live at the level of the clouds.

It would be hard to find in all the world a territory which has seen as much of blood and suffering as has Nicaragua. In the four centuries since the Spaniards first came upon it until the present there have been few long periods which were free of massacre, war, or revolution. Even today Nicaragua, enjoying at last a peace which it is hoped may be less evanescent than previous ones, is still nursing the wounds of past internal conflicts, and paying for their material damage.

The original inhabitants, of course, were Indians; an admirable and innocent people, by the accounts of early chroniclers. They cherished the remnants of a high culture which Toltec immigrants had brought from Mexico.

When the Spaniards first pushed up from the South with the double object of gathering gold for their King and souls for their church, they looked out upon the purple Lake of Nicaragua, dotted with palm-plumed islands, upon the smoking volcanoes, the blue-grey mountains and the verdant hills, and called it Mahomet's Paradise in their joy at escaping from the pestilential swamps of Panamá. Straightway they turned this Paradise into a hell of carnage, for the *conquistadores* were as frightfully cruel as they were admirably brave.

The first Spaniard to invade Nicaragua (Columbus on his final voyage had sailed past the mouth of the San Juan River, not knowing that there lay a passage to Cathay for which he spent his life searching) was Gil Gonzales Davila. He made his way up from Panamá in 1522 with a small band of fearsome, helmeted adventurers, and was courteously received by the ruler of the lake region, Chief Nicarao, from whom the country was named. The guileless natives sealed their fate by lading the greedy Spaniards with presents of gold. The chief must have been a delightful old fellow. He consented to the baptism of himself and 9,000 of his subjects, but he mildly objected to the condition that the baptized must give up war and "dancing when drunk," for he contended that neither indulgence did one any harm.

Chief Nicarao also was fascinated by the theology which the Spaniards gave him in return for his gold, and catechised them with embarrassing acuteness. Why did so few men covet so much gold? he asked them, and by what method was religious knowledge transmitted to the Spaniards from on high; would another deluge destroy the world; where did the sun and moon get their light; whence came heat, cold, and darkness; how large were the stars and what held

↗ Islands in the Great Lake of Nicaragua ↖
One of Countless Lovely Spots on the Canal Route

them in place; why did not the Christian God make a better world; whither went the soul when it left the body, and did the Pope ever die?

Davila would have pushed on further into this agreeable country, but a neighboring chieftain showed hostility and he withdrew to Panamá, where the stories and evidences of riches which he brought inflamed the cupidity of his brother conquerors.

Others struggled to get at the new store of gold. Francisco Hernandez de Cordoba followed in Davila's footsteps and founded the first Spanish settlement, Granada, on the shore of the lake, where a great Indian city had long existed. Cortes sent an expedition from Mexico. Still others succeeded them. Nicaragua's day of peace had ended.

The Spaniards took the Indians' gold, killed them for amusement, and converted the frightened remnants of the population. Rival Spanish discoverers rested from massacring only to fight one another, and invented ingenious tortures when they wearied of plain murder. Great Indian cities were wiped out. Droves of slaves were carried away. The race was well-nigh exterminated and those who survived were broken in spirit. Native temples were burned, and overturned idols still lie smothered in tropical underbrush on the islands of the Great Lake.

Nicaragua and its sister domains of the Isthmus knew little but oppression until decadence began to weaken the hand of Spain. In 1821 Central America threw off the yoke. Five months later the liberated colonies were annexed by Mexico, under the Emperor Itúrbide. The new states refused to accept this régime and under the leadership of Salvador petitioned to be annexed to the United States. The American Government did not look with favor on this proposal. The next year the states banded into a federation known as the United Provinces of Central America, which endured until 1839 and whose revival is still dreamed of on the Isthmus. With frank admiration for the United States, they drew up constitutions modelled after that of the first republic of the New World and endeavored to live as democracies in a land where only an aristocratic few were able to read and write, and where the overwhelming mass were inured by centuries to serfdom.

In the eighteen-fifties, however, there occurred a series of events which robbed the United States of much of the admiration which Central America had accorded it and engendered a distrust and a fear of the United States which persisted for years.

William Walker, the most famous of American filibusters, who already had made one expedition, unsuccessful, into Mexico, landed in Nicaragua in 1855 with 58 adventurers and for five years thereafter conducted an intermittent war. He was the mad apostle of manifest destiny. America was intoxicated with its rapid growth through the conquest of Texas and California, and its sense of international decorum had not had time to develop. Men of Walker's stamp saw in Central America the next field for encroachment. Walker's adventures were entirely unofficial, but there were indications that he had the tacit good wishes of the American Government in his bloody, illegal enterprise. Indeed, the government which Walker set up in Nicaragua actually was recognized by President Pierce.

Walker crashed on to the Nicaraguan stage at a period of intense warfare between the two parties of Nicaragua, the Liberals centering at León, and the Conservatives at Granada. He allied himself with the Liberals, from whom he had obtained an invitation to come to Nicaragua, and with his hardy Californians and Texans swiftly became master of the country. He made himself president in 1856 and administered his power from the ancient Conservative capital, Granada. The picturesque old convent of San Francisco, where American marines now stand guard, was his military headquarters. In the meantime Walker was receiving aid from both Vanderbilt and the Morgan and Garrison shipping interests, bitter rivals who were manœuvering for control of the traffic across the Isthmus, then very lucrative because of the California gold rush. Vanderbilt sent on his ships recruits garnered in New York, and Morgan and Garrison sent soldiers of fortune from the West.

Nicaragua in time saw the peril which threatened it unless Walker was driven out, and rose against him. Vanderbilt learned that Walker had duped him and set out implacably to ruin him. He spent his money and his influence arousing feeling in Central

America against the adventurer and Walker's little force at last was crushed by an allied Central American army after months of hard fighting.

Before Walker's men retreated from Granada they destroyed much of the old Spanish city and posted on a tree at the waterfront a sign reading "Here Was Granada."

Even this crushing defeat did not extinguish Walker's ambitions in Central America. He finally died before a firing squad in Honduras, where he had made a last attempt at an invasion.

The true motives of the indomitable but blundering Walker remain obscure to this day. The Southern States in North America contributed to him enthusiastically in the understanding that he intended to acquire more territory which could be made into slave states. His own wish probably was for power —to carve out a domain in Central America and the tropical islands to the east of it and rule it as emperor.

He accomplished nothing except death and destruction. By blocking communication he forced Vanderbilt's Accessory Transit Company to suspend operation, and Vanderbilt diverted the flow of travelers and freight to Panamá. With this went all hope for early construction of a canal in Nicaragua.

Walker's memory is still green in Nicaragua. One night not long ago, at a club in Managua, a mixed group of Nicaraguans and Americans fell to discussing the reckless old filibuster.

"Ah, but Walker's men did good for Nicaragua, too," remarked Carmen Diaz, brother of the President, a cynical philosopher with an intense antipathy for politics. "Around Rivas you find many people with fair hair and blue eyes. And that is good for our country."

The fact that Walker was able to get a foothold in Nicaragua was due to a characteristic of Nicaraguan politics which persists today.

Almost from the beginning of Nicaragua's career as a republic two principal parties, the Conservative and the Liberal, have vied for control of the country. These parties are not opposed on issues—it can hardly be said that they have issues or principles—but are based on locality and personal leadership, *localismo* and *personalismo*, the Nicaraguans call them.

The Conservative party grew up around Granada; the Liberal party around León. These two cities have historically carried on a blood feud, and there are persons in Nicaragua who believe that feud had its origins before the Spanish conquest in tribal animosities among the Indians. The rivalry among them now as in the past is bitter enough to carry always the threat of flaring up in civil war.

A North American or a European will have a clearer understanding of Nicaraguan politics if he divests the names Conservative and Liberal of the connotations which they normally have for him. An investigator in Nicaragua must try in vain to obtain any coherent statement of principles from either party. He will receive much rhetoric but no enlightenment.

One vague difference between the parties lies in the fact that the Conservatives have historically been the party of the Catholic Church, membership in which is almost universal in Nicaragua. That, however, is a heritage from the early days and has lost most of its meaning, since Liberal leaders of the present make every profession also of being loyal to the Church.

Perhaps the principal difference is in the composition of the parties' leadership. The direction of the Conservative party is in the hands of the land-owning and prosperous merchant class of the region around Granada. These leaders conduct cattle and coffee ranches and may be described as the Big Business element of the country. They form an aristocracy and maintain a delightful culture. A large proportion of them have been educated in American universities and have traveled in the United States and Europe. They tend to have a world point of view. They lean naturally toward friendliness to the United States, because its restraining hand seems to them to promise peace, which is good for their business. Furthermore they see in a Nicaraguan canal, which would carry a great avenue of travel and commerce past their very doors, the prospect of enormous future prosperity.

The leadership of the Liberals at León is no less pleasant and cultivated. It is drawn from the professional class and has a strong following among the smaller merchants and the artisans. In León, as in Granada, one meets gentlemen, notably physicians, who have studied in the United States and understand the American point of view. The Liberals are inclined to be less practical than the Conservatives and more idealistic.

It was because of the feud between León and Granada, which alternated as capitals of the country according to the party which was in power, and which warred with each other like the cities of ancient Greece, that Managua became the political centre of the Republic. When both parties became tired of the situation they selected the unimportant and far less habitable city lying midway between them as a compromise capital.

Each party has, and always has had, its popular leaders, and it is extraordinary how they are revered and loved by the illiterate lower classes, who have not an iota to gain by the ascendancy of either party, but who follow their chieftains to battle or to the polls with equal devotion.

The bitterness between the two parties can hardly be conceived by an American, used to the good nature of the loser which follows the decision of even the most acrimonious political contest. In Nicaragua, party likes and hatreds are carried over even into the social and business intercourse of the people. A man of circumstance is a Liberal or a Conservative first, a Nicaraguan afterward.

Furthermore the division into Liberals and Conservatives reaches throughout Central America and there are frequently alliances between the Liberals, say, of one country and the Liberals of a neighboring country. The ease with which revolutionary leaders have obtained military aid from men of the same party across the border often has aggravated disturbances in Nicaragua.

In these unbounded hatreds between the faction dominated by Granada and the faction dominated by León and in the entire absence of any conception of fair play which characterizes their contests one finds the basis of many of the phenomena which have brought grief to Nicaragua and to its North American stepfather.

It has been traditional for the party in power to oppress and exploit the members of the party out of power by every means from stealing their horses and expropriating their lands to imprisonment, torture, and death. Victory normally has meant riches for the leaders of the victorious party, ruin for the defeated.

Once in power also, a party has been able to maintain itself in power by its complete control of the election machinery until the forces against it have gathered strength enough to dispossess their enemies by force of arms. That is the reason in a few words for Nicaraguan revolutions.

Nicaragua's wealth is in its soil. It is almost devoid of manufactories. Its greatest source of wealth is coffee, grown in the hills of the western part of the country. Nicaragua's coffee crops have been extremely valuable in the past five years, because of the high prices. In 1926 the country exported eight million dollars worth of this product. This industry is largely under the control of wealthy Nicaraguans, although a number of coffee *fincas* are owned by foreigners. Exports of wood, chiefly mahogany and pine, average a million and a half dollars annually. Banana exports run from a million and a half to two million dollars a year, and this trade, which flourishes only on the East Coast, is controlled entirely by Americans. Exports of sugar average $1,000,000 a year. Exports of gold are now well under $1,000,000 a year. The country also is a large producer of cattle.

A substantial proportion of the wealth-producing industries are owned by foreigners, chiefly Americans, but even so, for all of "dollar diplomacy," American investments are smaller in Nicaragua than in any other Latin American country, with the possible exception of Paraguay. This is because Nicaragua is relatively so little developed industrially.

The largest American interest in Nicaragua is that of the Standard Fruit Company and its subsidiary, the Bragman's Bluff Lumber Company, which have $8,000,000 in timber and fruit production. The Cuyamel Fruit Company also has large banana interests centering at Bluefields and the Rio Grande Bar. The gigantic United Fruit Company, which plays so important a rôle in other Central American countries, has now no interests in Nicaragua except plants of its subsidiary, the Tropical Radio Telegraph Company, and banana lands now abandoned because they have become infected with the so-called "banana disease." The La Luz y Los Angeles Mining Company, headed by J. Gilmore Fletcher, brother of Ambassador Fletcher, reports it has invested $1,000,000 in gold mines which were raided by Sandino in April, 1928. The total American investment in Nicaragua probably does not exceed $12,000,000.

English interests rank next to those of Americans in Nicaragua. Their industrial and commercial investments are in sugar refining, coffee growing, and wholesale and retail stores. An English syndicate, however, is the holder of the only foreign loan to Nicaragua, of which less than $3,297,000 remains unpaid.

CHAPTER IV

THE BEGINNING OF INTERVENTION

NOW let us see how the United States established and maintained its unavowed protectorate over Nicaragua when it came to feel that conditions there threatened the peace and stability of the Isthmus and American interests in the canal route.

President José Santos Zelaya was the unsaintly victim of American paramount interest in this instance. Zelaya, a Liberal in politics and well-educated, widely traveled, handsome, ingratiating and dominating, had been ruler of Nicaragua for 16 years when a revolution encouraged by the United States overwhelmed him and forced him to flee the country in fear for his life.

Zelaya had come into office in 1893, at the end of an unbroken succession of Conservative governments which had maintained a régime still remembered as the "Thirty Years of Peace." A division in the Conservative leadership gave the León Liberals the opportunity for which they long had hungered, and on April 28 the first blow was struck. Managua, which then as now housed a number of Americans, was fired on without warning and on June 1, 1893,

President Roberto Sacasa was forced to abdicate.

Zelaya was the strong man of the revolution, and for a few months the country was ruled by a *junta* which he headed. On September 15 Zelaya was elected President by a constituent assembly and inaugurated on the same day. There were doubts as to the legality of his election, even among members of his own party, but they did not matter, for he had the power and with that went the office.

Zelaya probably was no worse and no better than the run of Latin American dictators. But he was exceptionally clever. At first he made a favorable impression on the Americans. Lewis Baker, then American Minister, commended Zelaya's government in early reports to Washington. Soon, however, friction arose; it grew constantly more aggravated through the years until the American Government at last found occasion to strike.

The first difficulties came when Zelaya, finding the treasury empty as incoming Nicaraguan executives normally do, imposed forced war loans on the inhabitants, including foreigners. American citizens refused to pay and Zelaya's troops resorted to terrorization in some instances to collect them.

Then, too, Zelaya had hardly taken office when there were rumblings of war with Honduras, culminating in a brief conflict. From that early moment until the end of his long dictatorship Zelaya kept the rest of Central America in constant turmoil, fomenting revolutions first in one country and then in another, actuated apparently by an ambition to reëstablish the old Central American Union, with himself at its head.

He was an absolute ruler and a tyrant. He confiscated the property of political enemies, imprisoned Conservative leaders when he felt so inclined, and enriched himself and his favorites by the sale of concessions and by other questionable means.

Zelaya tossed these concessions about on a first come first served basis, and Americans were among the chief beneficiaries, for a price, of his elaborately careless administration of his country's boundless resources. The rights of exclusive navigation of important rivers bordered with banana plantations were sold to an American company; vast tracts of land were conceded to Americans for the cutting of timber and the working of gold deposits; the right to construct a dock at Corinto, the principal port on the West Coast, and to collect port duties for 50 years was disposed of to other foreigners; even the sale of liquors was leased to a Nicaraguan corporation in which Government officials were prominent. Much, and sometimes all, of the sales prices of these concessions went into the pockets of Zelaya and his lieutenants.

"The door seems open to any foreigner or native adventurer who will pay the price for the surrender of any part of the country's resources," wrote Frederick Palmer in 1909. "Practically every staple of existence is a monopoly in Nicaragua. The sole right

of manufacture or sale is granted to a company or
an individual. In return Zelaya either receives a per-
quisite through Joaquin Passos, the President's son-
in-law and go-between, or, if he sees more profit in
that direction, an interest in the investment."

Zelaya also was quite above the law in his manner
of keeping his office in a theoretical democracy. So
long as his chief subordinates and the army were
loyal to him, his continuation in power was a routine
affair. When election time came around he simply
had himself reëlected, by old-fashioned Nicaraguan
methods. They still tell of an election in which the
rural voters were permitted their choice of three candidates, José, Santos, and Zelaya, which election, by
an odd chance, was won by José Santos Zelaya.

Nevertheless this vigorous and covetous president
was not unenlightened. He was a benevolent despot
—to his friends—and a portion of this benevolence
trickled down to the humbler people of the country.
Trade flourished under Zelaya. Government subsidies
were granted to encourage the coffee growers in the
mountains of Western Nicaragua. The country's
communications were improved by extension of railway service and steamship facilities on the lakes.
Schools were opened in all parts of the country, and
a better educational system was maintained then
than the feeble one existing today.

One of Zelaya's earliest efforts was the perfectly
legitimate one of extending his authority over the
Mosquito Coast, where foreign business interests, most

of all American business interests, had large sums invested in banana plantations, in the gold mines, and
in the forests from which they took mahogany,
ebony, and pine. The Mosquito Coast was then even
further separated from the western part of Nicaragua than it is now, and, as at present, more closely
linked to New Orleans than to Managua. The
Americans and other foreign residents enjoyed low
taxation and other privileges and virtually ruled the
Reservation. Zelaya's efforts to extend his authority
over the eastern portion of his country led to a four-
cornered controversy among the Nicaraguan Government, the Mosquito Coast natives, the Americans and
the English, with both the latter two certainly cul-
pable on many points.

By the terms of the old treaty of Managua the
Mosquito Reservation was enjoying local self-
government, under the sovereignty of Nicaragua,
and free of the ancient British protectorate against
which the United States had contended. Because of
the inaccessibility of the region, this had amounted to
independence, and the Coast lived under the easy-
going authority of local chiefs of Jamaican extraction
and British sympathies who still claimed the especial
protection of Great Britain.

In 1894 the Zelaya Government landed troops in
Bluefields, chief city of the Mosquito Coast, because
of rumors that the Hondurans intended to invade
the Reservation. Rioting ensued, the British landed
marines, the American consular agent asked the

United States to send a warship, and meantime called on the British to protect him and his nationals.

The American State Department at once was concerned about the attitude of the British, whose local officials on the face of things appeared to be asserting a right to regulate affairs on the Coast. Washington took up the matter with London and was assured that "no protectorate in substance or form, nor anything in the nature of a protectorate, is desired or intended by the British Government." The British Foreign Office further assured the United States that it had no inclination to interfere in any way with the plans or works of the United States in relation to the projected canal. And that calmed the last serious flurry over British intentions in the canal region.

The British naval forces withdrew when the situation was in hand, receiving as they did so the thanks of the American residents for the protection which they had accorded, and American warships took over the duties of protecting foreigners.

But much friction arose between the American residents and the Nicaraguan authorities as the central government continued its efforts to consolidate the Mosquito Reservation into the Republic. The Nicaraguan officials suspected that American residents were encouraging the Mosquitoes to oppose the efforts of Nicaragua. There were riots and revolts. One American was killed. Two American planters and a dozen English citizens, including the British vice consul at Bluefields, were accused of actions unfriendly to the Republic of Nicaragua and were expelled. Both the British and American governments protested. The British called for a money indemnity and occupied Corinto to enforce its collection. A compromise settlement between England and Nicaragua was made through the good offices of the United States and Corinto was evacuated. The Nicaraguan Government permitted the return of the expelled Americans.

Difficulties such as these occurred at intervals and the Nicaraguan authorities became increasingly impatient with the Americans. Individual Americans appeared often to be at fault. Some of them unquestionably joined in revolutionary enterprises for commercial reasons. The State Department, however, observed a correct attitude. William L. Merry, the American Minister, ordered his nationals to abstain completely from all political meddling, and warned them that they would not have the protection of the American Government unless their "skirts were clean."

Meanwhile the restless Zelaya was stirring up so much trouble among Nicaragua's neighbors that in 1907 a general Central American war threatened. The United States and Mexico, through their presidents, Roosevelt and Porfirio Diaz, coöperated in offering mediation and invited the Central American states to send representatives to Washington to seek a peaceable settlement of their disputes.

The invitation was accepted, by President Zelaya

among others. Old animosities were officially buried with elaborate obsequies and the labors of the conference were crowned with the adoption by the five countries of the Central American Conventions of 1907, looking toward eradication of the causes of war and revolution and the promotion of the common interests of the peoples of the Isthmus. The republics set up a Central American Court of Justice and bound themselves to refer all disputes to it; they recorded their opposition to any changes in their existing form of government and agreed on measures designed to prevent the fostering in one country of revolutions against a neighboring country.

In a supplementary convention the five republics promised not to recognize any government resulting from a *coup d'état* or revolution, not to intervene in any civil war in a neighboring country, and to adopt constitutional provisions prohibiting the reëlection of a president, in order to avoid the common practice of a dictator continuing himself in power until overthrown by a revolution.

The Court of Justice was inaugurated the next year with the utmost pomp and with elaborate expressions of gratitude to the United States for thus making possible a new era in Central American relations. These ceremonies took place in a palace erected for the Court by Andrew Carnegie, at Cartago, Costa Rica. From the start the Court functioned imperfectly, and it early went into a decline. And it was the United States which was instrumental in giving the *coup de grâce* to the Court which it had fathered when, nine years later, that Court decided against what the United States considered to be its interests in the canal route.

But after the Central American Conference had completed its efforts in 1907 it seemed indeed that the countries of the Isthmus could now count on a period of peace. The period proved to be only a breathing spell. The United States still considered Zelaya a trouble-maker, and it had had enough of him.

In 1908, near the end of the Zelaya régime, John Gardner Coolidge, of long diplomatic experience, became Minister to Nicaragua. President Zelaya treated the Minister with great cordiality. Minister Coolidge gradually became convinced, however, as he has expressed it since, that Zelaya was "all to the bad." He felt that "the Chamorro Conservative party was mainly composed of the richer, more responsible, class of men with more to lose, who consequently would be less likely to involve their country in all sorts of wildcat ventures than the Liberals, whose leaders were too often but military adventurers, with nothing to lose, who devoted their energies to bettering themselves, and cared little for the interests of their country or its people, except their own immediate following."

Minister Coolidge believed that Zelaya could never be turned out while he had the apparent sympathy and support of the American Government. He felt furthermore that the United States should cease maintaining cordial relations with Zelaya when it so distrusted and disapproved of him. Accordingly Minister Coolidge resigned after a few months' service.

On his return to Washington Mr. Coolidge recommended that no new minister be sent, and that the American Government's relations with Nicaragua be reduced to the lowest possible point while Zelaya remained in power.

There were several concrete factors in the situation distinctly disquieting to the United States. Zelaya had persisted in his mischievous undertakings in other Central American countries in the face of the Conventions of 1907, and maintained an attitude which Washington interpreted as pointedly anti-American. But in addition to these factors, in addition also to the cancellation of concessions and the consequent protests of the Americans who held them, Zelaya in this period refunded his country's external debt by contracting a loan of 1,250,000 pounds sterling with the Ethelburga syndicate of London, representing investors of several foreign countries. To the United States such an arrangement implied the possibility of interference from Europe if Nicaragua should at any time default, and Nicaragua's debt, by its own official figures, was heavy.

The recommendations of Mr. Coolidge were followed. No minister was sent to take his place. A revolution against Zelaya broke out a few months later. There were bizarre elements in that revolution, destined to have such far-reaching effects. It began at Bluefields, chief centre of the American and other foreign commercial interests in Nicaragua.

Thomas P. Moffat was then the American Consul at Bluefields. He had arrived only a few weeks previously from Venezuela, where he had officiated at the time of the Castro crisis, and, as he testified in 1927 before a Senate committee, he had no inkling of what lay before him. He only knew—"there was something in the air."

General Juan J. Estrada, holding his power under President Zelaya, was Governor of the Mosquito Coast with headquarters at Bluefields and commanded the Government force of some 400 men there.

There, too, was Adolfo Diaz, later to play so important a part in the relations between the United States and Nicaragua. Young Diaz, member of a respectable and moderately well-to-do family of pure Spanish descent, was employed in Bluefields as secretary of the La Luz y Los Angeles Mining Company, operating an American gold mining concession in the East Coast region. The salary of Adolfo Diaz was $150 a month, a handsome salary for a Nicaraguan in those days.

Every night, from early August on, as Mr. Moffat has told the story, there was unwonted, mysterious agitation in the town. General Estrada and Don Adolfo Diaz were to be seen holding discussions and there were crowds in the various American offices—all talking. As he circulated about in the streets of Bluefields he heard intimations that American officials and American naval officers had been asking the people, "Why don't you get up and get rid of Zelaya?"

People told him, he said, that naval officers had remarked that "some of the Americans up home are not satisfied with some of the concessions that are being interfered with, and Zelaya, they think, ought to get out."

Estrada said he asked the officers, according to Mr. Moffat, what the attitude of the American Government would be, and they had told him to "go ahead; you will get the support."

In the first week of October there came a knock at night on a rear door of the consulate, a large frame building on the principal street.

To continue with the Consul's account:

"A man outside said, 'We are going to have a revolution at midnight on the Ninth of October; Estrada is going to take the Bluff.'

"I got up quickly, and I could not find anybody. I went around behind the consulate, in the bushes back of the office, and looked all around, but I could not see anybody, and indeed I have never known until this day."

The "Bluff" is the tip of a semicircular peninsula embracing the harbor of Bluefields and commanding its narrow entrance. There the wharf for ocean going vessels and the custom house are situated. Early on the morning of October 10 it was taken, as Moffat's mysterious visitor had predicted. Emiliano Chamorro, destined to become in his maturity the most striking figure in Central America, had slipped into Bluefields from Costa Rica to take a leading part in the revolution, and thus there were at this sprawling, brawling spot, three future presidents of Nicaragua.

The Conservative revolutionists had won Estrada's much-needed connivance, it was soon revealed, by promising to make him President in the event the revolution succeeded. So he delivered his troops over to the revolution, and with them took the Bluff. Thus in one bloodless stroke the Conservatives made themselves masters of the East Coast, and of one of the country's most remunerative custom houses. The revolution spread swiftly throughout the Mosquito Reservation and Estrada was declared Provisional President, all without the firing of a shot.

The foreign business men were jubilant, Moffat reported to the State Department. Immediate reduction of the tariff which had so annoyed foreign interests on the East Coast was assured, all concessions not owned by foreigners would be annulled, and the entire population expected great prosperity. Consul Moffat characterized the new government as progressive and friendly to American interests. The new President, General Estrada, he added, had "granted him recognition," and had sent him assurances in writing of his friendship for the American Government.

On receipt of this enthusiastic information the State Department evidently feared that Mr. Moffat might be committing the American Government. It counseled the Consul by cable to have no official intercourse with the provisional administration in his representative capacity and added that "if any action of the temporary power should require interposition to protect American interests Mr. Moffat should personally and informally address whatever visible local agency may be in a position to afford de facto relief."

"Mr. Moffat is directed to confine himself strictly within these limits," the Department's warning concluded.

Thus the State Department asserted its neutrality.

While the revolutionary leaders were declaring their intention to cut the Mosquito Coast off from the rest of Nicaragua, make it an independent republic and march on Managua to seize control there, Zelaya got his forces hastily under way to the East Coast to attempt to wrest back the sovereignty.

By steaming down rivers and marching through the jungles, the Zelaya army, of two to four thousand men, approached within a few miles of Bluefields, with its American, English, French, German, and Chinese interests and its $2,000,000 worth of tempting supplies.

Estrada realized that with his small army he could not hope to protect the town and the foreigners.

"I cannot, with my forces, lead those people (the foreigners) out," he told Moffat. "Zelaya's soldiers have been given instructions through their generals to loot the town if they get in, for they feel that the Americans have started this revolution, and it will be a grave loss to many Americans."

Moffat agreed with Estrada that foreign life and property must be protected, but said that that must be the limit of outside interference. He cabled a report of the threatening situation to the State Department and 400 marines were disembarked at Bluefields under the command of Major, now Brigadier General, Smedley D. Butler.

Major Butler ordered that there be no fighting in the town.

"If you want to fight, you must leave the city to fight," Moffat reported the marine officer as declaring. "Whoever wins in the fight can come in, if they want to, if they lay down their arms, and take the city."

General Estrada led his little force on a forlorn hope to the swampy battleground up the river from the town. He was decisively defeated and fled with his remnants back within the sheltering arms of the marines guarding Bluefields. His wounded were cared for by Consul Moffat with funds of the American Government.

This might have been considered the untimely end

of a revolution which had started auspiciously. But the rebels still had Bluefields and were safe in the town because the marines would not permit any fighting there which might jeopardize foreign lives and property. The crisis over, Consul Moffat was hurried to Managua to take charge of the Legation in the absence of an American minister.

But the forced march of the Government troops to engage the rebels had been attended by an incident, a small incident in itself as the affairs of nations go, the capture and subsequent execution of two American soldiers of fortune, Lee Roy Cannon and Leonard Groce.

Before relating in detail the story of these two men, however, it is well to recur to the beginning of the revolution and view certain facts and assertions which have seemed significant to many critics of the American policy in Nicaragua.

Liberals have repeatedly asserted that Adolfo Diaz lent the revolution $200,000 in American gold three weeks after the outbreak of the revolution and later gave a note for $400,000 more. These assertions apparently have never been disputed. Liberals have pointed out that it was inconceivable that Diaz, a salaried employee of the American mining company, could have had that amount himself. Inquiry about this in Managua by the writer elicited hypothetical explanations that these funds may well have been contributed by wealthy Conservatives who wished their identities kept secret for fear of reprisals by

Zelaya if the revolution failed. This explanation is credible. But there is little doubt that foreigners contributed to the revolution whose early success they greeted so rapturously. Indeed, Estrada himself asserted three years afterward, in an interview in New York, that American commercial interests on the East Coast had contributed about $1,000,000 to the revolution.

But, whatever the means by which the revolution was financed, the American Government could not be expected to regret an uprising against a President whom it so thoroughly disapproved. The deaths of Cannon and Groce gave it an opportunity to say what it thought of Zelaya and provided the immediate occasion for intervention.

These two Americans had joined the revolution at its beginning and had been commissioned as officers. Both were reported to have suffered from persecution by Zelaya and at least one of them, according to the Liberals, had been imprisoned in Honduras for taking part in a military movement there against Nicaragua. One was a civil engineer and the other a miner.

Together with another foreigner, a French citizen, the two Americans had the task of defending the San Juan river route, over which the Government was about to ship troops to the East Coast. They made dynamite mines and set them off in the river. According to one of several conflicting versions, a mine exploded a few feet in front of an oncoming

troop transport and several men were washed over-
board and drowned.

The three men tried to escape through the woods
but became lost and gave themselves up to the Government troops as prisoners of war under the promise, it is related, that their lives should be spared. They
were taken to an isolated inland village, put on trial
within an hour and convicted of "rebellion." The
Frenchman was sentenced to a year in prison; the
Americans to death.

The American consul at Managua heard of their
peril and tried hard to save their lives. The Nicaraguan general whose men had captured the three
dynamiters recommended clemency. Zelaya assured
the American consul that he knew nothing of the
matter but would investigate. Two hours before he
gave this assurance, it was disclosed afterward, he
had telegraphed an order for the immediate execution
of the Americans. They died before a firing squad.

The news caused much popular indignation in the
United States. The American Government regarded
the affair as insult, treachery, and murder. It was
adding the last straw to an already heavy burden of
vexation and of danger to American interests. On
December 1, 1909, Secretary Knox presented to the
Nicaraguan chargé d'affaires at Washington one of
the most denunciatory notes in diplomatic annals,
breaking off relations between the two countries.

"Since the Washington Conventions of 1907,"
Knox wrote, "it is notorious that President Zelaya has

almost continuously kept Central America in tension or turmoil; that he has repeatedly and flagrantly violated the provisions of the Conventions, and, by a baleful influence upon Honduras, whose neutrality the Conventions were to assure, has sought to discredit those sacred international obligations. . . .

"It is equally a matter of common knowledge that under the régime of President Zelaya republican institutions have ceased in Nicaragua to exist except in name, that public opinion and the press have been throttled, and that prison has been the reward of any tendency to real patriotism. My consideration for you personally impels me to abstain from unnecessary discussion of the painful details of a régime which, unfortunately, has been a blot upon the history of Nicaragua and a discouragement to a group of republics whose aspirations need only the opportunity of free and honest government.

". . . Two Americans who, this Government is now convinced, were officers connected with the revolutionary forces, and therefore entitled to be dealt with according to the enlightened practice of civilized nations, have been killed by direct order of President Zelaya. Their execution is said to have been preceded by barbarous cruelties. The consulate at Managua is now officially reported to have been menaced. There is thus a sinister culmination of an administration also characterized by a cruelty to its own citizens which has, until the recent outrage, found vent in the case of this country in a series of petty annoyances and indignities which many months ago made it impossible to ask an American minister longer to reside at Managua. From every point of view it has evidently become difficult for the United States further to delay more active response to the appeals so long made, to its duty to its citizens, to its dignity, to Central America, and to civilization.

"The Government of the United States is convinced that the revolution represents the ideals and the will of a majority of the Nicaraguan people more faithfully than does the Government of President Zelaya, and that its peaceable control is well-nigh as extensive as that hitherto so sternly attempted by the government at Managua. . . ."

The revolution was dying, even with the marines at Bluefields, but now it took new life. Secretary Knox's tempestuous action was cheered in the United States, where Zelaya was excoriated as a highwayman, a tyrant, a usurper, and an assassin, and where demands were voiced for his apprehension by whatever means necessary, in order to bring him to book for his crimes.

It was the end for Zelaya. He knew that he could not continue with the United States openly against him. So 15 days later, "to avoid the shedding of blood" as he said in a manifesto to the National Legislative Assembly, "and to contribute efficiently to the pacification of the country" he deposited his power with Dr. José Madriz and resigned his office.

His final message as President was to protest

against "the hostile attitude of a powerful nation which, against all right, has intervened in our political affairs and publicly furnished the rebels with the aid which they have asked for."

Shortly thereafter he left the country on a Mexican warship.

Even then Zelaya's entanglements with the United States were not finished. He slipped into New York under an assumed name in 1913, to raise money on bonds in his possession. He was arrested by federal detectives and locked in the Tombs for eight days awaiting extradition to face murder charges in Nicaragua based on executions which he had authorized. Political malice was evident in the proceedings.

Eventually the charges were dropped and Zelaya was permitted to go to Spain. He returned three years later, however, and lived in an apartment in New York until his death in 1919. In Managua it is said that he died in poverty. He had invested the money he had wrung from Nicaragua in Belgian bonds, people who once knew him say, and his fortune was wiped out in the course of the war.

The huge and lordly house which once was his palace in Managua is a weather beaten ruin, its gaudy cornices sagging and its smashed windows boarded. Rubbish and wrecks of wagons clutter what once was its lawn. It is directly across the street from the National Bank of Nicaragua, established by Zelaya's political enemies and American financiers.

CHAPTER V

CHOOSING A PRESIDENT TO SUIT

D R. MADRIZ undertook to lead the disrupted country with a fighting chance of success. He was a lawyer of León, of high character and unusual attainments. American officials who knew him in the nervous days when he took up his residence in the Campo de Marte in Managua have spoken of him admiringly, even affectionately.

Dr. Madriz's designation as President was unanimously approved by Zelaya's Congress which hoped thereby to placate the United States, and he took office on December 21, 1909. Nevertheless he did not have the whole-hearted support of all the Liberals, only that of a few close personal friends, and of the usual horde of self-seekers.

Dr. Madriz and the revolutionary leaders both put out feelers looking toward mediation, the Conservatives proposing terms including the selection by the United States of some other man than Madriz or Estrada as President. The United States looked on these attempts cordially, but while they were still in an amorphous state hostilities were resumed on the East Coast and nothing came of them.

Madriz hoped for recognition by the United

States, so essential to the life of a Central American administration. The United States failed to extend it. Secretary Knox had acted, it was explained, not only against Zelaya, but against the whole system which Zelaya represented, and was not willing to grant the sanction of American recognition to any one who had been identified with the Zelaya régime —notwithstanding that Madriz once had characterized the dictator as a traitor and usurper, as "a dishonest public official who had trampled upon the laws of the republic." The United States also withheld recognition of Estrada for the time being, and officially regarded both Madriz and Estrada as de facto leaders of separate regions.

Forced to fight out the issue on the battlefield, the Madriz forces were at first successful. They captured Cape Gracias, far to the north on the Mosquito Coast, and in fact every other place of importance except Rama, on the Escondido River, 60 miles west of Bluefields, Bluefields itself, and the Bluff.

Meanwhile the Madriz government was supplementing its successful land operations with activity on the sea. It had purchased and fitted out the steamship Venus, of British registry, at New Orleans. The ship cleared from New Orleans as a merchant vessel with a crew largely composed of American seamen. Arrived in Nicaraguan waters, however, it broke out the Nicaraguan colors and was transformed into a "man of war."

On May 16, 1910, Dr. Julian Irias, commanding

the Madriz forces in the East, transmitted from aboard the Venus an ultimatum calling on the revolutionists to evacuate Bluefields and the Bluff by eight o'clock next evening, failing which he would bombard the town and the Bluff.

Two American cruisers, the Paducah and the Dubuque, were then lying off Bluefields. Commander Gilmer of the Paducah issued proclamations to the commanding generals of the forces of Madriz and Estrada ordering:

"First, that there be no armed conflict in Bluefields.

"Second, that until a stable government is established only such armed force, not to exceed 100 men, will be allowed in Bluefields as is necessary to preserve peace and order.

"Third, there being no armed men of revolutionary forces in Bluefields, no bombardment of the city will be permitted, as it could result only in destruction of lives and property of American and other foreign citizens."

Estrada replied to Irias with a refusal to surrender the town, and a declaration of his intentions to oust from the Coast, and from all Nicaragua, "the usurpers of the public rights and powers."

Nevertheless the Madriz forces stormed the Bluff eleven days later,. gained possession of the one custom house in the entire region, and put their guns in position to block the narrow entrance to Bluefields harbor. Their intention was to proceed from that base to the capture of the town itself.

Commander Gilmer forbade the movement against Bluefields and informed Irias that if he attempted it the American forces would oppose him. Marines were landed in Bluefields to back up this warning. Thus, as the Liberal leaders complained to the American Government, the Conservatives were secure in their little capital and from that as a base were able to fare forth and inflict defeats on the Government troops.

The Madriz forces, however, used their position on the Bluff to blockade the port, through which came munitions and supplies for the Conservatives, and the Venus lying outside reinforced this blockade. The American authorities regarded this as an interference with American commerce. They ruled that the Estrada government, inasmuch as it remained in control of Bluefields, was entitled to collect duties on cargoes coming into the port. Accordingly a new custom house was established in the harbor.

According to American officials, as related in messages of the period, the Madriz forces stopped American ships, and this inspired further determined action by the commander of the Paducah. Dr. Madriz, in a protest to President Taft recounting these incidents, contended that these ships were in the service of the revolution and said that the commanding officers of the Paducah and the Dubuque had threatened to "enforce respect for American commerce with the firing of their guns, even though such commerce should consist of arms and ammunition for the revolution, and that one shot fired at the said boats would mean a declaration of war to the United States."

The American cruisers refused to permit the Venus to interfere with shipping on the ground that it had violated the neutrality laws by clearing from New Orleans under false pretenses. The protection was extended to ships of Norwegian registry leased by the Bluefields Steamship Company, an American concern. Commander Gilmer placed sailors and marines on all ships carrying American cargoes past the Bluff into Bluefields and warned Irias that the American ships would fire on Nicaraguan vessels attempting to hinder their passage.

The crippling effect of this policy on the efforts of the Liberals to stamp out the revolution has been testified to volubly by Liberals. How it appeared to the Americans was shown by a statement of Commander Witherspoon, of the Prairie, in an interview in New Orleans just after he had returned from Nicaraguan waters.

"Bluefields is almost an American city and the protection of American interests in that place is only right and proper no matter whom it affects," said the Commander. "Unless intervention comes the struggle will go on indefinitely, for Madriz cannot take the East Coast, and Estrada cannot take the West Coast."

The official American explanation of this decisive intervention against the Liberals was that it was necessary to protect American lives and property. It cannot be disputed that if the Madriz troops had been permitted to bombard the town, or attack the Conservatives in it, a great amount of American and other foreign property might have been destroyed and the lives of any persons who remained would have been imperilled. At the same time that the United States was wrecking the attempts of Dr. Irias to blockade Bluefields, it should be noted that Estrada had established a blockade at Greytown, at the mouth of the San Juan River which affords access to the Lake of Nicaragua and the great western plain of Managua and León. There were British interests there, and the British naval commander forbade hostilities in the town, thereby hampering the revolutionists, in the same manner and for the same reasons that the American had forbidden hostilities at Bluefields.

A Conservative army operating in the interior had suffered a fearful defeat, but with American naval forces blocking every move of the Madriz troops and confining them to the swamps in the Bluefields region in the rear of the town, the Conservatives were able to turn inland with their heavy force in that region and so began a triumphal march on the capital.

In his extremity Dr. Madriz secretly proposed to the British Minister in Guatemala, according to

Weitzel, that England should intervene, in recompense for which Nicaragua would cede Great Corn Island in the Caribbean, off the mouth of the canal route, for a coaling station. This proposal was ignored by the English.

Disaster followed disaster for Madriz through that Summer until, with the remnants of his defeated army falling back into Granada, some into Managua itself, he gave up the fight, deposited his power with Deputy José Dolores Estrada, brother of Juan, and with his family fled the country to Mexico where a few years later he died. Irias and other Liberal chieftains also took refuge in exile.

Turmoil reigned in Managua as the Liberal government finally collapsed. Partisans of the defeated Liberal leader shouted "Death to the Yankees!" in the streets. A heavy guard was posted at the American Legation. And on the night of August 20, 1910, when Madriz departed for Corinto, Conservative partisans celebrated his downfall with fireworks and the ringing of bells.

On the next day the vanguard of the Conservative army entered the capital without disorder and José Estrada announced on behalf of his brother, the Provisional President, that free elections for the choice of the Republic's executives would be held in accordance with the constitution.

On that day began the American rule of Nicaragua, political and economic.

The first official act of the Provisional President,

even before he reached the capital to assume office, was to telegraph to the Secretary of State assuring the American people of "the warm regard entertained for them by the victorious party of the revolution." He also assured the State Department of his eagerness to make "proper restitution for the unfortunate killing of your citizens Cannon and Groce and for other atrocities committed by my predecessors."

General Estrada and General Emiliano Chamorro entered the capital on the evening of August 28. Within two weeks the Estrada Government formally applied to the State Department for recognition and made the following promises:

1. That a general election will be held within one year, the date to be fixed by a constitutional convention convoked for that purpose.

2. That the Provisional Government will endeavor to improve and rehabilitate the national finances, to which end the aid of the Department of State will be asked in procuring a loan in the United States.

3. That such loan will be secured by a percentage of the custom revenues, to be collected in a manner agreed upon between the two countries.

4. That those responsible for the death of Cannon and Groce will be prosecuted and punished and a suitable indemnity paid to the families of the deceased.

5. That, in order to facilitate compliance with the foregoing and in the event there exists necessity for formal agreement, the Department of State is re-

quested to send to Nicaragua a commission for that purpose.

This was exactly what the State Department wished. It replied in cordial fashion on September 14 and prepared to send the commission. Actual recognition, however, was delayed until the new government had stabilized itself several months later and had begun the reorganization of the country under the guidance of the United States.

The war-torn country was now in a pitiable condition. The small amount of money which Dr. Madriz had left in the treasury was quickly exhausted, much of it in paying claims of Conservatives for losses and troubles under the Liberal administration. Heavy obligations for damages suffered by members of both parties and by foreigners in the revolution confronted the weakened, impoverished country. A mass of depreciated paper money was afloat and was being augmented by the issuance of more depreciated currency by the needy government. The country already had defaulted in payments on the European loan.

In keeping with its long-standing philosophy that the security of the United States demands tranquillity and stability, political and financial, in the region of the Caribbean, the United States set about immediately to assist in the reorganization of Nicaragua and dispatched Thomas C. Dawson, Minister to Panamá, to Managua for that purpose.

Mr. Dawson promptly set to work with the leaders

of the revolution, President Estrada, Foreign Minister Diaz, and Generals Chamorro and Luis Mena. There issued from their conferences a compact, signed by the revolutionary leaders and known since as the Dawson agreements, which was the basis for the course the United States was to pursue in Nicaragua. It provided for the following procedure:

The people were to elect a constituent assembly which would choose the president and the vice president for the ensuing two years and adopt a constitution abolishing monopolies and guaranteeing the rights of foreigners. The leaders of the revolution bound themselves to support Estrada for President and Adolfo Diaz for Vice President.

All unsettlted claims growing out of the Zelaya régime and the revolution were to be passed upon by a mixed commission appointed by the Nicaraguan Government "in harmony with" the Government of the United States.

The new government would solicit the good offices of the United States toward obtaining a loan which would be guaranteed by customs receipts.

Estrada would not be permitted to succeed himself after the end of the two year term. The Zelayist element was to have no part in the new government.

His work finished, Mr. Dawson left Nicaragua and the provisional government proceeded to the explicit carrying out of the promises it had made. The constituent—or more accurately constitutional—assembly was elected according to schedule. It was overwhelmingly Conservative, and Consul Moffat reported to the State Department that hundreds of León Liberals had supported Conservative candidates, a fact which would imply ingenious work at the polls. The Assembly duly chose Estrada for President and Diaz for Vice President, to take office on the coming January 1 for the provisional term of two years. On January 1 the new government was recognized by the United States and President Taft sent felicitations to President Estrada.

Estrada entered office on a platform promising religious freedom, freedom of the press "within proper limits," independence of the judiciary, noninterference in Central American political affairs, gratitude to the United States, a modern school system, gradual decrease of the army to minimum police status, agricultural development, construction of a railroad to the Atlantic Coast, reduction of import duties, negotiation of a loan through the good offices of the United States, currency reform, and strict economy in government administration.

Despite the backing of the United States, however—to some extent because of that very backing—the new government was in difficulty from the start. Estrada had tried to construct a cabinet which, while having no taint of Zelayism, would represent the whole nation. The result was to bring together an ill-assorted group of jealous rivals in a combination as unstable as nitroglycerin.

Interestingly enough, one member of this discordant cabinet was José Maria Moncada, school-master and journalist, an anti-Zelaya Liberal of pro-American sympathies, destined one day to lead a revolution in his own right against Adolfo Diaz, and eventually to rise to the Presidency. Moncada soon was being accused of trying to stir up trouble among his Conservative colleagues. Another member of the cabinet was General Mena, who had overshadowed all other military leaders of the revolution and to whom was intrusted the portfolio of war, a danger-ous plaything to give an ambitious man in Central America. Mena and Moncada cherished for each other a beautiful hatred.

Chamorro had wished to be President. He was dis-appointed when this office went to Estrada and again when the Ministry of War fell to his rival, Mena, but with Chamorro's shrewdness he contrived to pack the new Assembly with his own partisans. So while the Zelayist die-hards were stirring up riots through-out the Republic, Chamorro was causing Estrada abundant grief within the Government. According to the State Department view, Chamorro was pre-venting President Estrada "carrying through im-portant and desirable reconstructive legislation." According to partisans of Chamorro he was seeking to prevent Estrada giving away the liberties of his country. The Mixed Commission stipulated in the Dawson agreements was authorized by the Assembly only with much delay and difficulty. Estrada finally dissolved his recalcitrant Assembly because he could

not control it and virtually expelled Chamorro from
the country.

Violence was directed against the new government
from within and without Nicaragua's boundaries.
Estrada had just begun his term when the magazines
at the Campo de Marte, near the Presidential Palace, were blown up in what was reputed to be a plot
of Zelayist Liberals to capture Managua and León
as the first blows of a counter revolution. Martial
law was declared throughout the country. President
Estrada learned also of threats of revolution against
him, fomented by Liberal leaders in neighboring
countries, and in his harassment appealed to the
United States for help.

All Central America meanwhile was watching the
events in Nicaragua through hostile and suspicious
eyes. The new American Minister, Elliott Northcott,
who had arrived early in the year, reported to his
Government that the new régime was being strongly
attacked in the press of the neighboring republics.

"In addition to this," said Minister Northcott,
"the natural sentiment of an overwhelming majority
of the Nicaraguans is antagonistic to the United
States, and even with some members of Estrada's
cabinet I find a decided suspicion, if not distrust, of
our motives."

President Estrada had decided, said the new Minister, that the only hope for Nicaragua was close
alliance with the United States.

"Estrada," he reported, "believes he can force

through his policies until such a time as they will justify themselves in the face of all difficulties, provided he can move without delay and can count on the earnest support of the United States. Whether or not he can succeed is, I must confess, in my opinion somewhat problematical, but it is at least worth a trial. Not again for a long time may come another such opportunity to prove our good faith in Central America."

Mr. Northcott expressed the opinion in conclusion that the loan should not be long delayed. Huntington Wilson, acting Secretary of State, informed him in reply that it was hoped that the loan and the settlement of claims would go far toward bringing peace and prosperity to Nicaragua. The State Department had sent Ernest H. Wands as financial expert. He had made a study of Nicaragua's deplorable financial situation and plans for financial relief were being formulated.

As if his troubles were not enough, Estrada began to have reason to fear the intentions of General Mena, who, with Chamorro safely away in Honduras, was unquestionably the most formidable figure in Nicaragua. And Mena had control of the army.

Estrada was none too strong or clever at best. Of the artisan class of Managua, he had been placed in command of the East Coast by Zelaya, and had won his leadership in the new Government by playing turn-coat to his own partisans. A better man, involved in such difficulties as enmeshed Estrada, might have taken to drink. Estrada did. With alcoholic daring he seized the bull 'by the horns.

On the night of May 8 President Estrada, showing the effects of liquor, called upon Minister Northcott with Vice President Diaz and informed the Minister that he had caused Mena's arrest on the ground of "contemplated treason." Northcott was convinced that Estrada's wild stroke had been inspired by Moncada.

The day following his escapade Estrada resigned and immediately left the country. Diaz took charge, and his first act was to release Mena and thus relax the tension of one of those situations of which revolutions are born.

Northcott cabled to the Department of State that the Diaz Government was "especially anxious to go on with the program as arranged" and that he had been assured that the Assembly would confirm Diaz in the Presidency according to any one of three plans which the Department might indicate. These were, to recognize Diaz without further action; to declare the presidency vacant and elect Diaz, or to declare the presidency vacant because of Estrada's action and allow Diaz to succeed by virtue of being Vice President. A war vessel, he said, was necessary, for the moral effect.

Washington replied suggesting that the first or third formula be used and asked the American Minister to make suitable expression of the American Government's satisfaction with the Diaz Govern-

➤ Adolfo Diaz ➤
Ex-President of Nicaragua

ment's assurance of its desire to carry out the agreed policy.

Thus on May 9, 1911, Don Adolfo Diaz became for the first time President of Nicaragua. Inasmuch as he was to play so important a part in the working out of the American policy, it may be well to record something of his career, and of his character as one sees him today.

Adolfo Diaz was born July 15, 1875, in Costa Rica, the son of a Nicaraguan father and a Costa Rican mother, both of pure Spanish ancestry. He is of unusually agreeable personality; a quiet, kindly gentleman. He is of less than average height, but carries himself with dignity and is always scrupulously groomed. He is unassuming, with a manner almost shy.

He has a good education, with a fair knowledge of English, although he speaks it hesitatingly, and has made himself, by virtue of his responsibilities no doubt, well versed in government and finance. His contacts in early manhood as an employee of the Fletcher mining interests were American and his closest friends to this day are Americans. He believes, and with complete sincerity in the opinion of the writer, based on many private conversations with him, that the welfare of Nicaragua is dependent on his country's maintaining close and harmonious relations with the United States. He understands fully the significance of the Nicaraguan canal route to the American scheme of things and, like most Nicaraguans of his class, he looks forward to the day when the canal actually will be built.

President Diaz is disdainful of politics in which he has spent his life. He is known to have little confidence in the financial ability of his own people and desires the continuance of American oversight of Nicaragua's finances. He has frequently asked both the United States Government and the American bankers to take more radical measures than they were willing to take because of the reaction which could be expected both in Latin America and in the United States if the American control of the country were more extensive and obvious.

With all his ingratiating qualities, President Diaz has not the sort of personality which commands a big following in a Latin state. It is doubtful that he could have retained the Presidency long, if indeed he could have obtained it at all, without the support of the United States.

Throughout his long tenure he has been a reluctant and unhappy President. Several times he has been on the point of resigning and has been persuaded to stay in office only by the urgent representations of the State Department.

In the many predicaments in which the United States has found itself in Nicaragua, President Diaz has done everything the State Department has suggested, even to adopting courses which seemed certain to wreck his own fortunes and those of his party. At the same time he has not hesitated to send indignant messages to Washington when he felt that his rights were being infringed, or his motives impugned.

Don Adolfo Diaz is now a man of moderate wealth, whose fortune is mostly in cattle and coffee ranches. His most conspicuous trait is a detestation of militarism and of the squabbles that politics engenders. He seems almost to shrink from conflict, yet he is personally courageous and has stayed at his post in the face of attempts at assassination which narrowly escaped being successful.

Fate has played odd tricks on this peace-loving man. Hating war, he has had to put down two revolutions, and, always amiable, he has had to struggle with bitter animosities. He came into power intent on the peaceful regeneration of his country. Yet hardly had he been installed in office when the fortress of La Loma, on the rim of a long-dead, water-filled volcano crater overlooking Managua, blew up with the death of some three score of the garrison. That roar was the tragic keynote of his administration.

CHAPTER VI

A REVOLUTION—AND THE MARINES

IN Don Adolfo Diaz, the United States, after
long years of difficulty and uncertainty in Nicaragua, at last could deal with a chief executive who saw eye to eye with it in all essential
matters and who had given his pledge to coöperate
in carrying the American policy through to success.
The success sought was the double one of peace,
stability, and prosperity to Nicaragua, and security
in the canal region for the United States.

But from the moment he took office, President
Diaz had to cope with intense opposition from the
Liberals, jealousy and treachery within his own government, and eventually with a formidable revolution which would have brought about his downfall
except for the marines.

The Liberals were determined to regain power by
no matter what means. They were equally bitter at
the United States, which had made possible their
ejection from control of the country, and at the
Conservative government, which they charged was
merely the tool by which the United States was to
enslave the republic.

Invasions led by Zelayist refugees were reported to

be in preparation in neighboring countries; rumors of filibusters and gun-running ships poured into Managua. Mena, the Minister of War, and the most successful general of the recent revolution, was conspiring brazenly with certain Liberals against the Diaz government and Diaz must have known it. With his instinct for seeking always an amicable solution of difficulties, however, the President refused to admit that a crisis was coming, tried at all costs to remain on friendly terms with Mena, signed with him a written compact of mutual coöperation, and even defended Mena as a "good fellow" in conversation with the American Minister. Probably Diaz felt that he had no other choice, for Mena, controlling the army and dominating a powerful faction in the Constitutional Assembly, was a far stronger man than Diaz himself. All this was humiliating to Don Adolfo, who found himself only a figurehead, ignored by Mena's followers and with no voice in decisions on any executive act.

In this situation, so distressing to a man of Diaz's unwarlike temperament, the President's most ardent wish from the beginning was to resign. This of course would have caused great confusion to the American program in its inception. The State Department through Minister Northcott, reminded Diaz that he had promised the United States to remain in office, and renewed its pledge to support him. Diaz reluctantly agreed to remain, but the Legation was not optimistic about the prospects.

"The matter resolves itself," Minister Northcott wrote the Department, "into a question of how long the present status, supported as it is by Mena's strength, Diaz having in himself no following or strength, can be maintained. If the loan contracts were submitted now they would at once be approved. That trouble will come, and continue to come until the loan question is settled, I am convinced."

Mena's ambitions for the Presidency grew apace, and he tentatively planned to have the Constitutional Assembly elect him for the four year term succeeding Diaz's emergency period. This of course would have violated the Dawson agreement under which the succeeding President was to be chosen by a "free election," but President Diaz, far from opposing this scheme of his Minister of War, gave it his hearty approval and asked Franklin Mott Gunther, then in charge of the Legation, to submit it to the Department. The country, Diaz argued with justice, would not be ready for free elections for a long period. He even threatened to resign and deposit the executive power with Mena.

The State Department declined to be drawn into an imbroglio over Nicaraguan party politics and Mena, finding no definite check against him anywhere, was emboldened to push ahead. He caused the pliant Assembly to elect him President for the term beginning January 1. At this juncture, the late fall of 1911, the strong-willed Emiliano Chamorro, displeased as ever with Mena's preëminence, returned from the United States and the fragile balance in Nicaragua's affairs was further disturbed by rumors that Chamorro was planning a *coup d'état* with the help of the President of Guatemala.

Still the United States held aloof from any declaration of purpose or policy. Its only action was to cause Diaz to prolong the life of the Constitutional Assembly, which had finished its work, until the arrival of the financial experts and the collector general of customs, in the expectation that further legislation would then be needed to put the projected financial reforms in operation.

Diaz knew, however, that everything was pointing to disaster and at length in December, 1911, he desperately proposed the only course which he felt could save the situation. He called upon the United States virtually to take over the country.

In a dejected, almost pathetic, letter to Gunther he sketched the difficulties in the way of every attempt to "effect a truly reconstructive program"—the friction with other Central American nations, where there was acute disapproval of the relations of Nicaragua to the United States, and the bitterness between the parties and the conspiracies of opponents in his own country.

"Lasting and stable peace, order, economy, moderation, and liberty cannot come through our own means," the President disconsolately admitted. "The grave evils affecting us can be destroyed only by means of more direct and efficient assistance from the United States, like that which resulted so well in Cuba."

"It is therefore my intention," President Diaz concluded, "by means of a treaty with the American Government, so to amend or add to the constitution as to assure that assistance, permitting the United States to intervene in our internal affairs in order to maintain peace and the existence of a lawful government, thus giving the people a guaranty of proper administration."

It was the first of a series of similar proposals which Adolfo Diaz was to make to the United States in the course of his long career in the Presidency. The State Department tactfully rejected it, as it has rejected the succeeding ones. Secretary Knox briefly instructed the chargé d'affaires at Managua to express to President Diaz "the Department's intense gratification upon noting the spirit of confidence in the good faith of the United States which he displayed in his proposal, which implicates recognition by President Diaz of this Government's benevolent and sympathetic attitude toward Nicaragua and the other Central American republics," but went no further.

Each day brought renewed justification of Diaz's nervousness. Before the end of the year Mena was in full opposition to the American program, and the majority in the Assembly were enthusiastically in accord with him.

President Diaz and Diego Manuel Chamorro,

uncle of Emiliano Chamorro, and Minister of Foreign Affairs, were trying, as they had promised the Legation they would do; to prevent the promulgation of the new constitution until the arrival of the new Minister, Mr. Weitzel, but the Assembly was determined to force the United States to recognize Mena's election. The Mena deputies even counseled their leader to overthrow President Diaz. They obviously believed that the United States would yield on the Mena issue in order to save the financial plan.

The Assembly inserted a provision in the Constitution designed to make the election of Mena constitutional, and then adopted a decree referring sarcastically to the interference of the American chargé in the matter of the constitution and calling his interposition "an insult to the national autonomy and the honor of the Assembly."

It put a capstone on its defiance on January 12, 1912, by obtaining by stealth a copy of the constitution bearing Diaz's signature, and promulgating it after an outburst of anti-American speeches in the dingy old halls of the National Palace.

Washington at last was stung to decisive action. Secretary Knox cabled this order to the chargé:

"Summon Mena to the Legation and inform him that this Government regards the Dawson agreements—which he signed with the others—as still effective; that in pursuance thereof Diaz must complete his term of office; that the Government of the United States expects Mena, as a patriotic Nicaraguan, strictly to abide by and support those agreements."

When Mr. Weitzel arrived late in January he determined to ignore the whole controversy, reporting to Secretary Knox that he doubted whether the objectionable clauses in the constitution were important enough to warrant trying to influence the Assembly to rescind its action and that the Assembly's election of Mena appeared to be in violation of another section of the constitution.

"It is possible that if matters are allowed to take their regular course the unfriendly factions will soon exhaust themselves and thereafter become more receptive to reason," he remarked.

This proved to be wise counsel. The tension, so far as the Assembly was concerned, did relax after the Mena delegates had had their fling of defiance. Furthermore the arrival of Emiliano Chamorro in the late Autumn of 1911 had not produced the difficulties which had been predicted. In his long and forceful career in Nicaragua Chamorro has been accused of plotting more than one war which never happened, although heaven knows he has been the author of enough confusion and his clashes with the State Department have furnished some of the most exciting chapters in Caribbean history.

Chamorro demanded just one thing on his return. That was that the Dawson agreements be carried out. This meant that the successor to President Diaz must be chosen in a free election, not, as Mena had been, by a vote of the Assembly. Gunther asked him point-blank whether he intended to start a revolution.

"If a free election is not provided I most certainly will," said Chamorro.

All through the Winter of 1911–1912 there were murmurs of a coming conflict; Julian Irias was reported to be marshalling forces in Guatemala and Costa Rica to throw against the Conservative régime in Nicaragua.

In the Spring—luckily it proved to be a respite in the Nicaraguan crisis—Secretary Knox made a good-will trip to Latin America, as Elihu Root had done before him, and as Lindbergh, the aviator, and Herbert Hoover, the President-elect, were to do after him. He was less fortunate than any of these "ambassadors." Indeed he did rather well to escape with his life.

Colombia refused to invite him, as a rebuke to the United States for its manner of acquiring the Panamá canal route. Cuba received him coolly. In Nicaragua there were plots to kill him.

Knox arrived in Managua on March 5, 1912. On the eve of his arrival there were reports that a conspiracy to blow up the train bearing him from Corinto had been discovered. There were anti-American demonstrations in the streets and 100 persons were thrown into jail and kept there until after the Secretary's departure. The editorial staffs of two Liberal newspapers in the capital were imprisoned and a rigid censorship was applied to other newspapers.

Mr. Knox probably did not know of these extreme precautions at the time, for he received a most gratifying ovation. Nicaraguans, always loving a festival, celebrated the extra holiday in their best attire.

President Diaz accorded the Secretary and his party elaborate official courtesies and entertained them at the Presidential Palace.

There were of course the usual formal speeches of felicitation. President Diaz expressed the thanks of the Nicaraguan people for the friendly aid of the United States.

"The name of your worthy President, William H. Taft, and your own name are pronounced by all Nicaraguans, from the statesman to the humblest countryman, as though they were the names of personages of our fatherland," Don Adolfo told him.

Secretary Knox graciously responded. "In the zone of the Caribbean," he said, "the responsibilities of the United States are becoming increasingly great as the opening of the great waterway which is to change the trade routes of the world draws nearer and the desire of the United States to see order and prosperity becomes even more intensified. We are especially interested in the prosperity of all the people of Nicaragua. Their prosperity means contentment, and contentment means repose."

International amenities demanded that Mr. Knox visit the Constitutional Assembly which under Mena's dominance had been enthusiastically defying the Knox measures and making faces at the United

States. It fell necessarily to Dr. Ignacio Suarez, President of the Assembly, and Mena's right hand man, to deliver the address of welcome. It was a remarkable production. Suarez contrived to voice the hostility of his partisans to American interference and at the same time to extend proper Latin American courtesy to the distinguished visitor. He held a sort of debate with himself.

"It cannot be denied," he said, "that your visit, which the peoples of America, and ourselves especially, have been awaiting with suspense, has awakened fears and misgivings in timid minds, who see in it a peril to our autonomy."

Immediately Dr. Suarez rebutted this with: "Undoubtedly it is because they are unaware of the many proofs which on divers and solemn occasions North American statesmen have given officially, which eliminate all tendency to expansion or to interference in foreign dominions which might compromise the latter's sovereignty and independence."

"It must be recognized also," Dr. Suarez went on, "that a propaganda nearly continental in proportion denouncing expansionism has been initiated. This propaganda first took form in the famous Monroe Doctrine, so opportunely formulated, now amplifying and restricting its terms, or diluting it in a strong solution of unbiased criticism in order to arrive at the exact conception of its true meaning. Those unfounded fears of which I have just made mention arise from this. To dissipate them it is enough for me to recall some of those proofs, unimpeachable through having been confirmed in the international practice of the United States." And then the Nicaraguan official recited a list of occasions in which the United States had rejected opportunities for territorial aggrandizement. Secretary Knox assured Dr. Suarez in reply that the United States did not covet "an inch of territory south of the Rio Grande."

After Mr. Knox had departed the enemies of Diaz and American intervention renewed hostilities.

Mena had gradually concentrated munitions in strategic places under his control. He became complete master of Granada and Masaya. He attempted to make his final disposition of forces by bringing 150 recruits from his home town, Nandaime, to garrison the capital. Managua, situated on a flat plain alongside the large Lake of Managua, is commanded on its northern side by the citadel of La Loma on the dead volcano's rim. There is a saying in that country that "he who holds La Loma rules Nicaragua." The Loma more than once has played a dramatic part in the turbulent history of Nicaragua since the United States entered the country. At the present moment United States marines are holding it.

Managua was to be taken July 29, 1912. President Diaz heard of the plot on the day it was to be executed. Trying even at this last hour to avert a complete rupture with Mena, he allowed him to remain as Minister of War, but himself took over command of the Loma, where the majority of the troops were loyal to him.

Mena nevertheless adhered to his plan. That same afternoon he sent his men against the Loma. His forces were met with a heavy fire, however, and fled down the hill to the barracks of the President's guard of honor while Mena escaped to the barracks through a secret passage from his official residence at one side of the parade ground. General Chamorro, hearing the firing, hurried to the scene and took command of the government troops. Mena and his forces found themselves in a trap.

President Diaz called at the American Legation in the late afternoon, and on his request Minister Weitzel drove through a tropical rainstorm to the scene of hostilities. In a lull in the firing he entered Mena's headquarters and obtained his compliance with the President's peace terms, which were that Mena should resign as Minister of War and be succeeded by a civilian. The American Minister also visited General Chamorro and got his promise to turn over his command to the person whom the President should designate.

The first act had ended disastrously, but Mena, his life saved in all likelihood by the interposition of President Diaz, continued with his revolution. He had the electric light cables in Managua cut and under cover of darkness he departed with his followers for Masaya, midway between Managua and

Granada. There he rallied his partisans and soon had a war in full progress.

Immediately he was in conflict with American interests. One of his first manœuvres was to seize steamships on the Lake of Nicaragua and turn them into gunboats to shell towns on the shore. These boats, part of the railroad system, were technically under the authority of the American bankers and they of course protested. The National Bank of Nicaragua, also under American control, asked that the money in its vaults be protected and the Mixed Claims Commission and the customs officials wished their records safeguarded.

Weitzel called on the Nicaraguan government for assurances that it could protect the lives and the property of American citizens, and of course the Nicaraguan government could not give them. It could spare no forces from their employment of putting down the rebellion. The Nicaraguan Foreign Office admitted this in a note which closed by saying that "my government desires that the Government of the United States guarantee with its forces security for the property of American citizens in Nicaragua and that it extend its protection to all the inhabitants of the Republic."

The American Minister sent word of the crisis to the cruiser Annapolis, then steaming along the West Coast. In response 90 bluejackets were sent to Managua and quartered at the Legation. Washington ordered the battalion of marines stationed at Panamá to proceed to Nicaragua immediately and the United States soon found itself engaged in serious military operations.

While these steps were being taken letters were intercepted which showed that Mena was conspiring with the Zelayists. Foreign residents of many nationalities were greatly alarmed, the more so as word came in of the rapid spread of the rebellion, with uprisings in León and Chinandega, which not only menaced substantial foreign interests but which also, occurring along the railway route, threatened the one avenue of escape from the capital.

President Diaz prepared peace conditions and the diplomatic representatives of Costa Rica and Salvador, after consultation with the American Minister, carried them to Mena at Masaya. The terms were that the rebels surrender all their arms, in return for which the Government would grant them amnesty and pay the cost of the conflict. The diplomats arranged a 48 hour armistice with Mena, to end on August 12.

While the armistice was still in force, one of Mena's chief aides, General Benjamin F. Zelédon, sent a note to Minister Weitzel, as dean of the diplomatic corps, informing him of his intention to bombard Managua within twelve hours.

The diplomatic and consular officers protested, but early on the morning of August 11 the artillery fire began. Three-inch shells fell into the city all day. At night the rebels attacked but were repulsed with heavy losses. Prisoners captured by the government troops said that they had been promised four days looting in the city if they captured it.

The shelling continued with short intermissions for three days. One shell struck in the street directly in front of the Legation and dozens came uncomfortably close. Three shells, aimed there purposely, Weitzel believed, fell in the Hotel Lupone, the chief hotel of Managua, where many foreigners had taken refuge. Thousands of persons fled into the country. The Salvadorean Minister and the British Vice Consul departed for Corinto. Other families built places of shelter in their courtyards and the bluejackets, who could do little but remain barricaded in the Legation, constructed a bombproof in the house of the British Consul General.

The rebels, unable to take the city, retired toward Masaya after a final burst of artillery fire at daybreak on August 14. A checking up of casualties revealed that 132 women and children in the city had been killed or wounded. No Americans were killed, but one was injured, and considerable damage was done to foreign-owned property.

Two hours after the attack had been abandoned, Major Smedley D. Butler arrived in Managua with 360 marines from the Canal Zone and, Minister Weitzel related, was greeted warmly by Nicaraguans and foreigners alike.

Throughout this period stories of lawlessness and outrages poured in from the vicinity of Granada,

Masaya, and Jinotepe, where the rebels were operating in force. Italian, British, and Austrian consular officers received reports of unlawful seizure of property belonging to their nationals. Both foreigners and Nicaraguans were subjected to personal abuse and to forced levies of money and merchandise. The British Consul General, under instructions from his Government, called at the American Legation to ask what protection the United States proposed to afford to foreigners in Nicaragua and what naval vessels were available. He inquired about the advisability of having a British man-of-war sent to Nicaraguan waters. Minister Weitzel replied that such action would be inopportune and unnecessary.

Calm was restored to the capital after more than a week of anxiety by Minister Weitzel's insistence, in notes to General Mena, that Managua was a place of refuge and that bombardment or attack would not be tolerated.

Disorders continued, however, in other centres. There was a serious anti-American uprising in León, in which two Americans, Harvey Dodd and Philip Craven, were killed. The Salvadorean Minister intervened to restore order. In other localities two British subjects and a German were assassinated. Captain Terhune of the American navy went from Managua to León with 40 sailors and ten marines on their way to the Annapolis at Corinto. At León a mob stopped them and took away their train, and they were compelled to go back to Managua afoot.

The revolt had spread far up into the mountain country around Matagalpa, where Americans and other foreigners operated coffee plantations and where, in 1928, Sandino and his allied bands again were causing alarm. Residents feared a massacre and appealed for marine protection, but the American officials could not give it for fear of new attacks on Managua. Major Butler restored order along the railroad from Managua to Corinto and reopened that line of escape.

Meanwhile the disembarking of marines in Nicaragua provoked protests in other Central American countries, most of all in Salvador, where demonstrations against the "invasion" were held. At the beginning of September President Araujo of Salvador telegraphed to President Taft a suggestion for mediation of the dispute in Nicaragua. He expressed concern lest the presence of American troops in Nicaraguan territory cause serious complications.

President Taft sent President Araujo a flat refusal, tinged with sarcasm, referring to the rumors that the rebellion in Nicaragua was receiving help from Salvadorean territory and reminding him of the promise of Salvador to keep the peace under the Washington Conventions of 1907.

"The Government of the United States has no thought of leaving its legation and the lives and safety of its citizens and their property and its important interests in Nicaragua at the mercy of a rebellion based on no principle," Mr. Taft wrote, "and carried on with motives and methods vividly recalling the times of Zelaya and doing the most flagrant violence to all the principles of honor, of humanity, of order and of civilization."

President Araujo intimated in reply that the American forces were exceeding their proclaimed mission of protecting American lives and property and were in fact engaged in "warlike activities against the revolutionists who occupy Granada."

Nicaraguan Liberals in exile helped to keep the storm blowing. A group in Costa Rica addressed an appeal to the American Minister there in which they hinted that the ghost of William Walker was directing the State Department.

"Adolfo Diaz does not represent public opinion in Nicaragua, not even the unpopular and discredited authority of a government sustained by sheer violence," they maintained. "The present National Congress has disowned Diaz as a ruler and declared him to be a traitor to the Republic for having requested, in order to support himself in the Presidency, the coöperation of American soldiers."

The State Department was enough impressed by the agitation to prepare an official statement of the American policy which it had communicated to the rebels in Nicaragua and made public throughout Central America. It stated that the United States intended to maintain an adequate legation guard in Managua, keep communications open, and protect American life and property. It restated its hostility

to Zelayism and its intention to lend its moral support to legally constituted good government, recited
the damage and danger to Americans in a rebellion
which was characterized as selfish, inexcusable, and
barbarous, and pointed out that the Nicaraguan government had confessed its inability to protect foreigners.

"In this situation," said the statement, "the policy
of the Government of the United States will be to
protect the life and property of its citizens in the
manner indicated and, meanwhile, to contribute its
influence in all appropriate ways to the restoration
of lawful and orderly government in order that Nicaragua may resume its program of reforms unham-
pered by the vicious elements who would restore the
methods of Zelaya."

Reinforced by the additional warships under command of Rear Admiral W. H. H. Southerland and a
regiment of marines under Colonel J. H. Pendleton,
the American naval forces extended their occupation
to the large towns along the railroad from the sea-
coast to the capital, although it took a battle in which
three marines were killed to master León, the Liberal centre. Granada, however, was still under the
control of Mena's forces and disturbing reports came
from there. Americans were being insulted and
robbed. Young girls of the aristocracy attending a
boarding school were treated outrageously by the
rampant rabble of Mena's army. The civil population were in a state bordering on famine.

The Americans determined to push a force through to Granada to protect foreigners and take Red Cross relief to the hungry populace. Major Butler's battalion and 100 bluejackets started on this mission, traveling cautiously on a train bearing a white flag and the American colors. Near Masaya the train was fired on by artillery under Zelédon's command, and the Americans believed that a trap had been set to ambush them. The marines attacked the hills of Barranca and Coyotepe and in a brisk battle captured them. Four marines were killed and six wounded. The losses of the rebels were reported by the marines as 56 killed outright and 70 wounded, of whom 12 died.

With the rebels driven from these strategically important hills by the Americans, the government troops, with Emiliano Chamorro in command, took the town of Masaya. Zelédon was killed as he fled.

Another Mena force was trying to open a line of retreat into Costa Rica; it was routed at the same time and forced back on Granada. When Butler arrived at the old Conservative capital Mena was a beaten man, ill and in despair in the Convent of San Francisco where William Walker before him had had to confess defeat.

Mena surrendered to the Americans and was exiled with his son to Panamá where he was soon put at liberty on orders of Secretary Knox, who believed that he was no longer dangerous.

The rebellion crushed, the marines distributed relief supplies given by the Red Cross and the American colony in Managua, and even shared their rations with the needy. A group of women of Granada sent flowers to Admiral Southerland, accompanied by a long letter expressing their thanksgiving to their deliverers and concluding:

"Already we have enjoyed for these few days real peace and tranquillity with the stay of the American forces in our midst. It is for us to express the desire that our elder sister, the great Republic of the United States, so wise, so powerful, will bring to us permanently the benefits which all her sons enjoy throughout all her vast and peaceful domain."

That was in Conservative Granada. In León, capital of the Liberals, a poet wrote of "the blond pigs of Pennsylvania advancing on our gardens of beauty," and of the tremblings of the Latin soul at "the pawing of Nietzsche's blond beast."

Another crisis was over, but Nicaragua had lost 1,000 men and millions of dollars more had been added to its debts.

Minister Weitzel commended the energy and discretion shown by the naval and marine commanders, and Secretary Knox commended Mr. Weitzel for the course he had pursued.

In November the so-called free elections stipulated in the Dawson agreements were held. There was a strong movement in the Conservative party to nominate General Chamorro, but eventually it was decided that a civilian, not a military leader, should be

chosen. Chamorro appealed to the American Legation to further his candidacy, but Mr. Weitzel refused and urged him, in the interest of patriotism, to
decline to be a candidate for either President or Vice
President. Chamorro acceded to the Legation's wishes.
Adolfo Diaz was nominated and, with the Conservatives controlling the machinery, was reëlected President for the four year term. Chamorro was rewarded
with the post of Minister to Washington.

As soon as could be done without risking further
disorders, the American forces were withdrawn, except for a legation guard of 100 men in Managua and
a war vessel at Corinto.

Before he sailed away, Admiral Southerland entertained President Diaz and his cabinet aboard the
battleship California, flagship of the Pacific Fleet.
Full presidential honors were rendered and speeches
of great cordiality and friendliness were exchanged.

CHAPTER VII

BUYING THE CANAL RIGHTS

WHEN a split in the Republican party brought the Democrats into power in 1913, with Woodrow Wilson as President, the new administration inherited a first class Latin American problem. Affairs in Mexico were shaping toward a crisis, with elements in that country fearful that the United States was moving toward annexation. In Nicaragua the chronically impecunious government was in the most desperate financial difficulties in its history.

There was every indication that President Wilson, the idealist, intended to bring about a new era in the relations of Washington with the republics of the South.

Early in his administration, in an address at Mobile on October 27, 1913, President Wilson endeavored to reassure suspicious Latin American neighbors with the following utterance:

"They (the Latin American states) have had harder bargains driven with them in the matter of loans than any other peoples in the world. Interest has been exacted of them that was not exacted of anybody else, because the risk was said to be greater, and then securities were taken that destroyed the risks.

"I rejoice in nothing so much as in the prospect that they will now be emancipated from these conditions, and we ought to be the first to take part in assisting that emancipation. . . . We must prove ourselves their friends and champions upon terms of equality and honor."

The United States, he pledged, "will never again seek one additional foot of territory by conquest."

But, whatever the wishes of the new President and of William Jennings Bryan, his pacifist, anti-imperialist Secretary of State, the problem itself shaped and dictated the handling of it. Ironically enough, with all their good intentions, they discovered that they could only go on with the established policy in Nicaragua. Their administration was attacked at home with more vehemence than any other has been, unless it was that of Mr. Coolidge, on the very grounds of imperialism and of subservience to the bankers of Wall Street.

The Nicaraguan Government was in acute need of ready money and the State Department and the American bankers were anxious to remedy the situation. The Nicaraguan canal route offered an opportunity, which both the State Department and the Nicaraguan Government were glad to seize, to move ahead along the lines of North America's strategy in the Caribbean and to rescue Nicaragua from its most pressing money troubles.

The advantages of this to Nicaragua, as conceived

by the State Department and expounded by Minister Weitzel, were, besides the much needed payment of $3,000,000 for the canal option, the guaranty of the peace and independence of the Republic, the development of its great resources through capital attracted by the definite settlement of the question, the prospect of eventual construction of the canal, and the definite elimination of a constant incentive to revolution. The advantages to the United States were, in Weitzel's opinion, the preparation for further growth of its coastwise commerce, elimination of foreign political influence, the service of a caveat against any more canal concessions or territorial privileges such as had been attempted with European and Asiatic powers, an additional important defense of the Panama Canal, and an effective means of guaranteeing the Washington Conventions.

To this end, less than a month before the Taft administration expired, Minister Weitzel negotiated with the government in Managua a treaty providing for the sale to the United States of the option to build the canal and also of the right to construct naval stations in the Gulf of Fonseca and on one of the Corn Islands. It was submitted to the United States Senate, but was not acted upon for three years, during which it was the focal point of a bitter controversy in the United States and in Central America over the whole Caribbean policy.

Shortly after Secretary Bryan had taken over Mr. Knox's portfolio the Latin American Division of the

State Department prepared for him a memorandum on the Nicaraguan situation.

"What Nicaragua needs and wants is peace," the memorandum emphasized. "It seems doubtful whether she can secure it without some support and coöperation on the part of the United States. She can certainly not secure it unless she can obtain the funds necessary to pay the awards of the Claims Commission, to refund all of her old foreign and internal debts, to pay the salaries of government employes which are now in arrears, and to undertake much needed work in developing the resources of the country.

"Perhaps the most marked instance of the so-called dollar diplomacy of the past administration was to secure these results to Nicaragua by means of the loan convention (the uncompleted arrangements for the financing of Nicaragua). The time has now arrived for the present administration to define its attitude toward that loan convention and toward the Nicaraguan questions in general."

Nicaragua's obligations were listed at this time by the Nicaraguan legation in Washington as totalling $11,450,000, of which the greater part, $6,200,000, was owing to the Ethelburga Syndicate of London. The Republic also owed $750,000 to New York bankers. The most urgent obligation was $1,500,000 owing to miscellaneous creditors for unpaid salaries, supplies, and the like. Besides there was approximately $3,000,000 in claims arising from the revolutions; a considerable portion of this was due to poor natives who had been ruined in the wars.

The Wilson administration took up the canal problem where the Republicans had left it. Immediately the administration was confronted with protests from Costa Rica and Salvador charging that the proposed treaty violated their rights. Costa Rica pointed to a boundary treaty executed between that country and Nicaragua in 1858. This treaty had been interpreted by President Cleveland, in making an arbitral award, as binding Nicaragua not to make any grants for canal purposes across her territory without first asking the opinion of the Republic of Costa Rica, and as securing to Costa Rica free navigation of the San Juan River which forms part of the boundary between the two republics. Costa Rica also said that the proposed treaty violated the Washington Conventions of 1907 by which rights of free navigation were guaranteed.

Salvador protested vigorously that the provision in the proposed canal treaty for the construction of a naval base in the Gulf of Fonseca, even though the base itself was in Nicaraguan waters, would jeopardize Salvadorean territory, which also abutted on the bay.

"In any armed conflict that might arise between the United States and one or more military powers," the Salvadorean Government asserted, "the territories bounded by the Gulf of Fonseca would be converted, to an extent incalculable in view of the offensive power and range of modern armaments, into belligerent camps wherein would be decided the fate of the proposed naval establishments—a decision that would inevitably involve the sacrifice of the independence and the sovereignty of the weaker Central American States."

Salvador also revived the dormant issue of the old Central American Union. The Fonseca grant, Salvador said, infringed the interests of Central America in general. Furthermore, the Republic argued, the grant violated its proprietary rights in the Gulf inherited from the joint ownership exercised by Salvador, Honduras, and Nicaragua after the sundering of the Federation. The Salvadorean Government sought to call a conference of Central American states to protest, but no result was achieved beyond drawing a regretful note from Secretary Bryan.

The public in Salvador, always quick to resent what appeared to it to be encroachments by the Government of the North, again held demonstrations, and the newspapers were filled with inflammatory articles.

While the ill-feeling in Central America was at its height, there occurred another incident which aggravated their fear of American aggrandizement.

On February 4, 1914, President Diaz approached President Wilson by cablegram with the second proposal he had made for the establishment of an out and out protectorate over his country. He besought the United States to ratify the canal treaty in order to provide funds for his bankrupt government, and at the same time proposed that the substance of the Platt Amendment be incorporated in the canal convention, since its application to Cuba had produced such satisfactory results.

The Platt Amendment, if applied to Nicaragua, would have forbidden that country to enter into any treaty or compact with any foreign power or powers which might impair Nicaragua's independence, or permit any power to obtain lodgment or control over any part of its territory for colonization or military purposes. It would have forbidden Nicaragua to contract any debt for whose payment the ordinary revenues would be inadequate and would have obligated it to consent to the right of the United States to intervene for the preservation of Nicaragua's independence and its maintenance of a government adequate for the protection of life, property, liberty, and the discharge of the Republic's treaty obligations, and to sell or lease to the United States the lands necessary for coaling or naval stations.

"I believe that revolutions will cease if your government can see its way clear to grant the addition of the Amendment as requested," President Diaz cabled to President Wilson.

"The present government has adopted, frankly and decisively," the minister of Nicaragua advised the Secretary of State, "a policy of rapprochement towards the United States, seeking through that friendship the assurance of peace in Nicaragua, the development of its natural resources, and a means of improving its finances; and in the pursuance of this policy it has moved steadily forward without regard to the protests and opposition of certain Latin countries. I believe, therefore, that in accordance with this spirit of amity the time has arrived for the Government of the United States to lend some aid to Nicaragua."

Secretary Bryan agreed, and a provision embodying the suggestions of President Diaz was added to the treaty. News that this proposal was before the American Government stirred up a new series of protests, for Central America foresaw in such a proceeding an eventual American protectorate over the entire Isthmus.

"My Government believes any weakening of the autonomy of the Republic of Nicaragua would seriously affect the autonomy of the Republic of Costa Rica, considering the special nature of the relations between the states of Central America since the beginning of their existence," said J. B. Calvo, Minister of Costa Rica, in a protesting note.

The Platt Amendment never got beyond the stage of "consideration and discussion." The Senate opposed it and it eventually was dropped, but the very suggestion of it was enough to inflame Yankeephobes in Central America.

In the course of the long controversy within and without the United States over the canal treaty itself, it became apparent that lack of tact on the part of the United States was perhaps as potent a factor in the opposition to American proposals as were the proposals themselves.

President Gonzalez of Costa Rica so explained the feeling in his country to E. J. Hale, the American Minister, in the Summer of 1914. Costa Rica's national pride had been touched, the President said, by the failure of the United States to consult it about the canal before entering into a treaty. Costa Rica did not ask for money, but asked only that its interest in the canal be recognized.

A few months later President Meléndez of Salvador spoke in a similar vein in a confidential conversation with the American Minister Long. He went further and suggested that the United States inaugurate in his country some phases of the very policy which it had pursued in Nicaragua in the face of so much criticism.

Salvador did not wish a money payment for the right to place a naval station in the waters over which the Republic claimed jurisdiction, Meléndez intimated. Instead it would prefer, as compensation, that the United States put Salvador on a gold basis, that it have an American bank of large capital established there, that it create a school teaching agricultural, economic, and business courses, and the English language, and that it assist in the development of ship and wireless communications. He suggested furthermore an offensive and defensive alliance between the United States and the Central American republics.

Meanwhile Nicaragua was standing stoutly on the position taken by the United States in regard to the canal treaty and was pressing Washington to act on it so that it could apply the $3,000,000 to the alleviation of its financial embarrassments. Secretary Bryan was compelled to put Nicaragua off. The Senate was busy with other matters.

A new draft of the treaty, omitting the protectorate feature, was signed in August, 1914, but it was a year and a half before it was ratified by the United States. Like its predecessor, it was subjected to determined attacks, partisan and otherwise, in the Senate. Borah denounced it as a product of "deception, misrepresentation, fraud, tyranny, and corruption" and charged that the United States was making a treaty with itself. Elihu Root, one-time Secretary of State, expressed doubt about the ethics of the treaty in a letter to Senator Borah while the treaty was still pending.

"I am troubled," he wrote, "about the question whether the Nicaraguan government which has made the treaty is really representative of the people of Nicaragua, and whether it will be regarded in Nicaragua and in Central America as having been a free agent in making the treaty. I have been looking over the report of the commanding officer of our marines in Nicaragua, and I find there the following:

" 'The present government is not in power by the will of the people; the elections of the House of Congress were most fraudulent.'

"And a further statement that the Liberals, that is to say the opposition, 'constitute three-fourths of the country.' It is apparent from this report and from other information which has in a casual way come to me from various sources that the present government with which we are making this treaty is really maintained in office by the presence of United States marines in Nicaragua."

The treaty affair dragged along until February 1916, when the Senate at last approved it, with the addition of a stipulation that nothing in the treaty was intended to affect any existing right of Costa Rica, Salvador, or Honduras, as a sop to these protesting republics.

The principal provisions of the treaty were as follows:

"Article I. The Government of Nicaragua grants in perpetuity to the Government of the United States, forever free from all taxation or other public charge, the exclusive proprietary rights necessary and convenient for the construction, operation and maintenance of an interoceanic canal by way of the San Juan River and the great Lake of Nicaragua or by way of any route over Nicaraguan territory, the details of the terms upon which such canal shall be constructed, operated and maintained to be agreed to by the two governments whenever the Government of the United States shall notify the Government of Nicaragua of its desire or intention to construct such canal.

"Article II. To enable the Government of the United States to protect the Panama Canal and the proprietary rights granted to the Government of the United States by the foregoing article, and also to enable the Government of the United States to take any measure necessary to the ends contemplated herein, the Government of Nicaragua hereby leases for a term of ninety-nine years to the Government of the United States the islands in the Caribbean Sea known as Great Corn Island and Little Corn Island; and the Government of Nicaragua further grants to the Government of the United States for a like period of ninety-nine years the right to establish, operate and maintain a naval base at such place on the territory of Nicaragua bordering upon the Gulf of Fonseca as the Government of the United States may select. The Government of the United States shall have the option of renewing for a further term of ninety-nine years the above leases and grants upon the expiration of their respective terms. . . .

"Article III. In consideration of the foregoing stipulations and for the purposes contemplated by this Convention and for the purpose of reducing the present indebtedness of Nicaragua, the Government of the United States shall, upon the date of the exchange of ratification of this Convention, pay for the benefit of the Republic of Nicaragua the sum of three million dollars . . . to be deposited to the order of the Government of Nicaragua in such bank or banks . . . as the Government of the United

States may determine, to be applied by Nicaragua upon its indebtedness or other public purposes for the advancement of the welfare of Nicaragua in a manner to be determined by the two High Contracting Parties, all such disbursements to be made by orders drawn by the Minister of Finance of the Republic of Nicaragua and approved by the Secretary of State of the United States or by such person as he may designate."

After the Nicaraguan Congress had been reassured by Secretary of State Lansing that the treaty gave the United States only an option, leaving for future settlement the terms on which the canal actually would be constructed, it approved the treaty by large majorities in both houses.

Even then the objections in the American Congress were not silenced, for the whole affair came up once more in debates over the $3,000,000 appropriation and there were sarcastic comments on Mr. Bryan's embracing of the dollar diplomacy which he had so lately condemned.

Nor did Costa Rica and Salvador cease their opposition when the treaty became an accomplished fact. To their voices was added that of Honduras, whose shores also were washed by the Gulf of Fonseca, and even Colombia protested, reviving an ancient claim to the Mosquito Coast and the Corn Islands. In Nicaragua an election was approaching and critics of the government denounced Adolfo Diaz and what they called the rule by guns of the American marines.

There was some apprehension in Washington. Two American warships hovered near, one in the Gulf of Fonseca and the other at Corinto.

In March Costa Rica and Honduras brought suit against Nicaragua over the treaty in the Central American Court of Justice at Cartago.

The Central American Court decided against Nicaragua in the dispute, on September 30, 1916, in the case brought by Costa Rica, and on March 2, 1917 in the case brought by Salvador. The Court held that Nicaragua had violated the rights of both countries in making the treaty, but it did not attack the validity of the treaty since it had no jurisdiction over the United States.

The decisions were ignored by both the Nicaraguan and American Governments. This occasioned further protests in North America. The American Peace Society, for example, contended that the United States, by tacitly consenting to the flouting of the decision of the Central American Court of Justice by Nicaragua and going through with the program of acquiring rights to the canal and to a naval base in the Gulf of Fonseca, was endangering the peace of Central America. It appealed in vain for the submission of the question by the United States to the Central American Court.

The attitude of the United States in this has often been criticized by students of Latin American affairs. It may be technically unassailable in international law, but it served as the death blow to the

Court which the United States had fathered with high hopes of providing the machinery for peaceable settlement of Central American disputes.

But at any rate, the United States had put the rights to the canal safely away where no one else could aspire to them.

Theodore Roosevelt had spoken with pride of his acquisition of the Panamá route:

"I took the Canal Zone and let Congress debate."

President Wilson bought the Nicaraguan route and let Central America argue.

There the matter has rested until recent months when again there has been agitation for the early construction of the canal to relieve the congestion at Panamá. News of this was received with satisfaction by leaders of both Conservative and Liberal parties in Nicaragua in the Spring of 1928.

CHAPTER VIII

WALL STREET'S RÔLE IN NICARAGUA

IT will be well now, before proceeding further with the narrative of Nicaragua, to return to the early days of Conservative administration and trace out the rôle which Wall Street was playing in the Republic.

It will be remembered that the refinancing of the country, the settling of the cloud of debts and claims which hung over it, and the establishing of a sound and stable monetary system had constituted the task immediately facing Don Adolfo Diaz when he first assumed the presidency in 1911. No man in the Republic, probably, was better fitted for that task.

The plan for the financial reorganization of Nicaragua worked out by the State Department with the experience in Santo Domingo as its model was only less necessary to the fulfilment of American purposes than was the definite acquisition of the canal route, for it involved the replacement of European loans by American loans. And no chapter in the history of America's relations with Nicaragua illustrates more clearly the duality of motive of the United States: its insistence on keeping the country in its own hands in order to safeguard what it considered to be American strategic interests, and its sincere effort at the same time to benefit Nicaragua.

Doggedly Don Adolfo slogged away at Nicaragua's financial difficulties in the face of revolution and partisan hostility within his country and threats of war from without; of grasshopper plagues and ruined crops, economic paralysis and famine; of fear of the American protectorate in all Central America and denunciation of it in the United States as well, where a portion of the population, including prominent members of the United States Senate, conceived that Nicaragua was being exploited for the benefit of Wall Street.

Diaz and the State Department and the bankers carried through their reorganization of the finances successfully, and honorably, too, it would appear, now that we can look back on the whole procession of events.

When Adolfo Diaz first became President the country had a paper indebtedness of $32,200,000, according to regrettably vague statistics. Of this sum nearly $14,000,000 was composed of claims for damages to Nicaraguans and to foreigners growing out of the Zelaya régime and the revolution which unhorsed him, claims which later were reduced, under American administration, to less than $2,000,000. The Mena rebellion saddled another three million dollars of debt on the country. But the most serious item of all, from the point of view of American interest, was a debt to European bondholders of 1,250,000 pounds sterling—the old Zelaya loan—on which the Republic had defaulted in the expensive confusion accompanying the driving out of Zelaya and Madriz.

Nicaragua's financial difficulties were further complicated by a depreciated currency, which was continually being still further depreciated by additional issues of fiat money.

President Diaz set about to remedy these conditions with the sentiment of much of the population, the Liberals, that is, violently opposing anything suggested by the Conservatives and by the United States, which had made the ascendency of the Conservatives possible. But this unrest only made speedy action the more essential, in the view of the State Department and the Nicaraguan Government. A few days after Diaz succeeded Estrada in 1911 Minister Northcott urged that a warship be stationed at Corinto, "at least until the loan is put through."

On June 6, 1911, just after Diaz became president, a convention for an American loan intended primarily to fund the Nicaraguan debt was signed by Secretary of State Knox and Dr. Salvador Castrillo, Nicaraguan Minister to Washington. The loan was to be secured by the customs receipts, which in turn were to be administered by a collector general appointed by the Government of Nicaragua from a list of names presented to that government by the American bankers and approved by the President of the United States. The convention also included the usual clause in such arrangements pledging Nicaragua not to alter import or export duties during the life of the loan without the agreement of the United States. The United States, on its side, promised to afford such protection as might be necessary. The understanding was that the loan was not to exceed $20,000,000; the sum in mind was $15,000,000.

President Taft presented the convention to the Senate on June 8, 1911, with strong recommendations that it be ratified, since he considered it of the utmost importance to the peace and prosperity of Nicaragua. Furthermore, he said, there was the Monroe Doctrine to consider.

"Much of the debt of Nicaragua is external and held in Europe," said President Taft, "and, while it may not be claimed that by the Monroe Doctrine we may be called upon to protect an American Republic from the payment of its just foreign claims, still complications might result from the attempted enforced collection of such claims, from the involutions of which this Government might not escape.

"Hence it should be the policy of this Government, especially with respect to countries in geographical proximity to the Canal Zone, to give to them when requested all proper assistance, within the scope of our limitations, in the promotion of peace, in the development of their resources, and in a sound reorganization of their fiscal systems, thus, by contributing to the removal of conditions of turbulence and instability, enabling them by better established governments to take their rightful places among the law-abiding and progressive countries of the world."

The convention had to be ratified by both the Nicaraguan Assembly and the American Senate. Its submission was the signal for attack in each. In Managua the smarting Liberals and a disaffected group among the Conservatives tested the resources of their ornate language for invective. They accused the administration of selling the country's liberty for "thirty pieces of silver" and shuddered oratorically at the shadow of the American eagle.

"By the shades of your ancestors, what becomes of the national autonomy under this ignominy which snatches the future from our children and stains the honor of our forebears?" shouted Deputy Edouard Doña. "Let us try to die as free men, not as slaves with chains riveted upon us forever! Some deputies think that the Republic is an untamed savage beast that needs to be mastered by the bridle and spurs of the conquerors. No, gentlemen, the Republic is a virgin, not to be brutally violated, but to be guarded in the sacred urn of our hearts."

"The bankers of New York have attempted to dazzle us with their gold and buy our consciences," declaimed another. "They treat us as if we were an imbecile people who knew not how to govern themselves."

There was much more like this, and when everybody had had his say, the Nicaraguan Assembly ratified the convention, within a few days of the signing.

The United States Senate was less oratorical but less tractable. It refused to ratify the convention and indeed the convention has not been ratified to this day, although its provisions have been the basis of the financial operations in Nicaragua for the past seventeen years.

Before the Nicaraguan Assembly had acted on the convention, New York bankers became interested in Nicaraguan financing. They were Brown Brothers & Co. and J. & W. Seligman & Co. Brown Brothers were interested because they had purchased the Emery Claim, whose settlement has occasioned much criticism of the bankers and which will be discussed further on. The Seligmans had for some time been prominent in Latin American finance.

The two firms, working in conjunction, therefore notified the State Department that they wished to handle the loan. The Nicaraguan Government meanwhile had appointed Ernest H. Wands financial adviser and Wands, after making a survey in Nicaragua, went to New York, where the Browns and the Seligmans conferred with him on the projected $15,-000,000 loan.

The bankers' project was to buy $12,000,000 of a proposed Nicaraguan bond issue for $10,860,000, that is at ninety and one half. The bonds were to bear five per cent interest. After five years the bankers were to purchase the remaining $3,000,000 on the same terms. By this arrangement the Republic would have paid a shade less than six per cent for the use of the money. No commission was to be charged. The money was to be used for the reform of the currency, the refunding of the internal and external debts, and the construction of railroads, including one across the country to unite the Eastern and Western sections of the Republic.

This loan was never made because of the failure of the loan convention in the United States Senate. Nicaragua's finances, largely as a result of the revolution against Zelaya, were in so deplorable a condition, however, that the country could not wait for the hoped-for ratification of the convention. The bankers therefore agreed with the Nicaraguan Government on September 1, 1911, to lend $1,500,000 on treasury bills bearing six per cent interest. No commission was charged. This loan was intended only as a temporary tiding over while the bankers and the Republic awaited the ratification of the Knox-Castrillo convention under which they would lend the remainder of the $15,000,000. The bankers had then no idea that instead of paving the way for a loan of profitable proportions they were entering upon a decade and a half of small, short-term loans which they must extend and renew and refund time and time again in an aggravating procession of petty financing.

The terms of the Knox-Castrillo convention, whose most essential point was that the customs be under American control, were written into the contract for the $1,500,000 loan, and the Nicaraguan

Government agreed that the State Department should be the arbiter of any dispute concerning the contract. The contract also included an option to the bankers for the purchase of the Nicaraguan bond issue when the expected $15,000,000 loan should be authorized.

The first problem attacked under American financial guidance was that of reforming the currency. The paper money outstanding had grown in volume to more than 12,000,000 pesos under Zelaya. After his fall first Madriz and then Estrada issued treasury notes as fast as the presses could run in order to meet their extraordinary military expenses. At the end of 1910 the circulation had increased to nearly 30,000,-000 pesos and in the next few months it was inflated still further—some 10,000,000 of it clandestinely, the Liberals assert—to about 45,000,000 pesos, much of it counterfeit. Eventually 49,000,000 pesos turned up.

Just before Zelaya's fall the paper peso was worth 9.75 to the dollar. Under his first two successors it declined to 20 pesos to the dollar. A large quantity of this new money, genuine and counterfeit, unquestionably went into the pockets of the Conservative leaders whom the Liberals had kept away from the political trough for seventeen years.

The currency reform was instituted by means of the creation of the National Bank of Nicaragua, the sole depository of government funds and the sole bank of issue of the Republic. The bank was incorporated in Connecticut, with an initial capital of $100,000, later increased to $300,000, which was sub-

scribed by the government on money lent by the
New York bankers. Under the loan contract the
bankers sent two currency experts, F. C. Harrison
and Charles A. Conant, to Managua to work out details of the reform. The bankers had made their
original plans on the supposition that there were 32,-
000,000 paper pesos in circulation. The extra 17,-
000,000 pesos which had to be retired called for more
money. On March 26, 1912, the bankers extended
$500,000 for this purpose and an additional sum of
$255,000 to be doled out monthly for urgent gov-
ernmental expenses. These loans, like most of the
subsequent advances to Nicaragua, were at 6 per cent
with one per cent commission.

The new unit of currency was the cordoba,
equivalent to the American gold dollar, and named
after de Cordoba, Spanish founder of Granada and
León. The conversion was accomplished slowly, so
that the paper money could be bought in as cheaply
as possible, and the rate was not announced until a
large amount of the currency had been called in at
the rate of 16 pesos to the cordoba. As the purchases
continued throughout 1912, the rate decreased to its
final level of twelve and one half to the cordoba.

The conversion was carried out with exceptional
care, but not without scandal. It is highly probable
that members of the Nicaraguan Government who
by their official position knew the details of the
conversion program, and their influential friends,
profited by purchasing pesos at a low rate—if they

had not indeed obtained them at no cost whatever—
and selling them at the top price under the conversion.

While the currency reform was in progress the
bankers turned to the matter in which the State Department was most deeply interested, the refunding
of the 1,250,000 pound Ethelburga loan. This was
an obligation bearing six per cent interest which
President Zelaya had sold to the European syndicate
in 1909 at 75 per cent of the face value of the bonds.
It had been contracted to pay off a previous British
loan of 245,000 pounds sterling, made in 1886, and
a loan of New Orleans capital made in 1904, and to
provide $2,000,000 for that perennially proposed
and still unrealized project of a railroad from the East
to the West Coast. Most of the proceeds of the Ethelburga Loan had vanished—it does not matter much
where now—and the Republic had received little as
a result except the obligation to repay it.

The American bankers undertook the office of
fiscal agents for this loan, without charge to the Nicaraguan Government. In May, 1912, they induced
the holders of the Ethelburga paper to reduce the
interest rate to five per cent in consideration of the
better security which was now afforded them. This
security was the making of the interest and amortization charges a first lien on the Nicaraguan customs
receipts, and the agreement that the collection of
these receipts should be under the control of an American collector general. The bankers also obtained the

release of 371,000 pounds sterling of the proceeds of the Ethelburga bond sale which the European syndicate had withheld after the Nicaraguan Government defaulted. The entire arrangement was distinctly advantageous to Nicaragua.

Colonel Clifford D. Ham, then surveyor of the port of Manila, was jointly nominated by the bankers and the State Department and took office as Collector General of Customs in December, 1911. Technically he was an official of the Nicaraguan Government, but he considered himself less an employe of Nicaragua than, to use his own words, a "trustee, with obligations to four parties—the Republic of Nicaragua, the Secretary of State of the United States, certain citizens of the United States and certain citizens of England." He therefore declined to recognize the authority over him of the Tribunal of Accounts or any other governmental agencies. He held office continuously until the Summer of 1928, when, well along in years, he retired and returned to the United States.   He was succeeded by Irving A. Lindberg, long his first assistant, whose promotion was cordially greeted by the Nicaraguan press, both Liberal and Conservative, and who may be counted upon to continue the efficient administration carried on by his predecessor.

Often in the early years of his long tenure Colonel Ham was subject to criticism, partly because of jealousy over the considerable number of Americans drawing what to a Nicaraguan were very large sal-

aries from the government treasury, partly because
of his independence of attitude and partly because
of his stamping out of time-honored graft in the
customs service.

In the first two years under Colonel Ham the customs receipts doubled. In his last year, 1927, they
were $3,118,091, double the highest total under the
Zelaya régime, which was $1,595,200 in 1906, and re-
flecting both the increased trade of the country since
the critical years of the World War which cut off its
markets, and the saving to the government resulting
from the elimination of favoritism and corruption
in the collection of taxes. And of this sum collected
by the American customs administrators, $1,724,-
568 remained for the ordinary purposes of the government after payments had been made on the debt
services.

The customs, it is worth recording, are relatively
a light burden on the general public of Nicaragua,
notwithstanding that the rates on imported goods
average 20 to 25 per cent ad valorem. Prices on such
goods are high, but it is the wealthy classes which
pay them. The great majority of Nicaraguans live at
an extremely primitive level and, except for an occasional bit of cloth for a shirt or a shawl, have few
wants which are not supplied by native products.

Under this régime, with an American collecting
the money at the source and turning it over to the
American bankers, to be paid by them to the European bondholders, Nicaragua has been steadily pay-

ing off the interest and principal of the Ethelburga Loan. There now (as of January 31, 1928) remains to be paid $3,297,000, a little more than half the original sum.

The third large undertaking in the Nicaraguan program conceived by the State Department was to attack the onerous burden of claims against the Republic, many of them for concessions cancelled under Zelaya, others for damages suffered or alleged to have been suffered in the civil wars. This task fell to the Mixed Claims Commission, as provided for under the Dawson agreements. The Commission was under American control, with Judge Otto Schoenrich as President.

The Commission labored for three years, and by the end of 1914 had passed on the merits of 7,911 claims, totalling $13,808,161. The heaviest claims were filed by Americans, chiefly those interested in industries on the East Coast, who demanded $7,576,-564. Many of these American claims were for the cancellation of concessions illegally obtained and for expected profits from such concessions. The Commission ruthlessly eliminated the padding. The American claims were cut to $538,749, and the total of all claims was reduced to $1,840,432. Of this total two thirds was composed of small claims presented by natives for such damages as the loss of their crops and herds in the revolutions of 1909 and 1912.

Because of the failure of the loan treaty it was impossible to pay these claims as soon as they were adjudicated, as had been intended, but the government provided $158,548 from the customs receipts which was paid to 4,618 of the neediest claimants.

So outstandingly enlightened was the work of this Commission that it has been praised enthusiastically by even the most uncompromising critics of the American-tutored Conservative administration under which it was conducted. Long afterward, President Diego Manuel Chamorro spoke with warmth of the service of the Commission and its cutting down of American claims, in an address to the Nicaraguan Congress in December, 1922.

". . . if the United States had been inspired by a sordid interest," he said, "it would not have helped us to establish the Mixed Commission nor obliged its citizens to submit themselves to the decisions of that tribunal. Its conduct under those circumstances, altruistic and just, with a weak nation like Nicaragua, is worthy of our gratitude and general applause."

Twice afterward there was need for a similar straightening out of war claims against the Nicaraguan Government, and in each case the task was performed under American control. After the Mena revolution claims mounted to $13,578,314. They were adjudged by a Commission on Public Credit established afterward by the Nicaraguan Government. Its membership consisted of Abram F. Lindberg, brother of the present Collector General of Customs and one of the framers of the Nicaraguan fiscal system, Dr. Jeremiah W. Jenks of New York University, and the Nicaraguan Minister of Finance. This Commission worked in conjunction with the American Minister of that period, Dr. Benjamin L. Jefferson, deflating exaggerated claims. Final awards totalled $5,304,386, a sum which included the claims previously allowed by the Mixed Claims Commission. A great part of these awards was made up of the losses of individual Nicaraguans. Actual payment was begun in 1918. A million and a half dollars of claims were paid in cash, some of which came from the funds received from the United States Government for the canal route and some from customs revenues. The remainder was paid from the proceeds of $3,744,-150 in bonds, guaranteed by a second lien on the customs revenues, and largely held by Nicaraguan citizens.

The third task of this nature fell to the High Commission, also American controlled, which came into being as a part of the Financial Plan of 1917. Its American member was Roscoe R. Hill. Dr. Jenks was arbitrator. Both these Americans were appointed by the Secretary of State. Nicaragua was represented by its Minister of Finance. The duty of this body was to see that the Republic fulfilled its obligations, and thus in a measure it acted as financial advisor. Commissioner Hill also received the claims resulting from the revolutions of 1926 and 1927 and the activities of Sandino and other guerrilla chieftains. The list of these claims is not now complete, but it is expected to be in the neighborhood of $16,000,000.

CHAPTER IX

WHAT THE BANKERS HAVE MADE

I T would be difficult to impart by words an adequate conception of the humiliating poverty under which the sovereign state of Nicaragua labored through the first critical years of reorganization. It was a stern regimen under which the country was living. Heavy debts and war claims had to be met before the government could touch the customs funds; such sums as were available from the customs, together with the internal revenues, wastefully gathered under the Nicaraguan administration, were inadequate to the needs of a government which, however poor, could not learn to be thrifty and which besides was ridden by civil wars.

Public works, even when they were undertaken, had to be abandoned for lack of funds; government salaries were unpaid for many months at a time; the school system collapsed, for the teachers were paid last of all, when they were paid. More than once President Diaz reached into his own pocket and lent the government money to tide it over apparently hopeless crises, or to equip soldiers against rumors of war brewing in neighboring countries.

It would be hard to find a country which has suf-

fered more ill luck than Nicaragua. Whenever it
seemed about to emerge from its poverty, disaster
struck it, usually in the form of a revolution, and
loaded a new burden of debt on the staggering country. It is poor even today, with two more years of
costly fighting just behind it. Wherever the traveler
goes he sees naked beams and rafters of ambitious
buildings left uncompleted, and the explanation,
apologetically given, is always "the money ran
out."

Through the first decade of American direction,
the Republic was constantly and importunately bor-
rowing, hoping first for the ratification by the United
States of the Knox-Castrillo loan convention, and
then, when expectation of that was abandoned, for
the ratification of the canal treaty by which the
country would receive $3,000,000. The American
bankers reluctantly advanced small sums, which seldom were paid when due, and which had to be extended and renewed.

Through it all the bankers insisted on ample security for their money, including control of the Republic's two great tangible assets, the Bank and the
railroad, and this sometimes occasioned protests from
Nicaragua when it was particularly anxious for
money which the bankers were reluctant to lend.

For it must not be supposed that President Diaz,
as his enemies have so often charged, was a "tool of the
Wall Street bankers," notwithstanding his willing-
ness to coöperate with them. Often he wanted money

desperately for the Republic, and although by his own avowal he "appreciated the fair dealing" of the New York financiers, he was tempted, when he found them unwilling to make further advances, to accept loan offers from others who approached him. There were several of these, including one from English sources and another from New Orleans. Diaz was cautioned by the State Department when he flirted with such proposals.

"In view of the interest, repeatedly evidenced, of this Government in the welfare of Nicaragua," the State Department cabled the American Minister in Managua on one such occasion, in January, 1913, "and of the close relationship of the two countries —which would become even closer upon the conclusion of the proposed canal treaty—this Government could not favor any alteration in the present financial system of Nicaragua—a system that promises in a reasonable time to place the country in a stable financial condition hitherto unknown—unless this Government had examined and approved such alteration."

And when in 1917 President Diaz's successor, Emiliano Chamorro, fretting at the delay of the United States in paying for the canal route which it had finally purchased more than a year before, proposed to seize the custom houses to get urgently needed funds, the bankers threatened to withdraw entirely from the financing of Nicaragua, and the State Department delivered a sharp rebuke.

The occasional dissatisfaction of Nicaraguan executives with the New York bankers was because of what Diaz called their "ultra-conservative" policy—their unwillingness to lend more than they thought the country could repay and on any but rock-ribbed security. The interest which the bankers charged was not excessive. All the many loans they made, with one exception, were at six per cent, with an additional one per cent commission on most of them. This exception was a loan of $1,450,000 in 1920, on which nine per cent was charged. This was in the period, however, when all the world was soliciting American money and even stable and normally prosperous countries were paying the same rate exacted of Nicaragua.

The frequent charges of exploitation levelled at the bankers warrant the publication here of the amounts which the New York bankers have loaned to Nicaragua, and the amounts which they have collected from Nicaragua in interest and commissions. They are as follows:

$1,500,000 issue of treasury bills of 1911
 loaned at 6% without commission:
 Total interest paid .... $ 93,600
$500,000 credit of March, 1912
 loaned at 6% with 1% commission:
 Total interest paid .... $ 11,803
 Commission .... $ 5,000
$255,000 credit of March, 1912
 loaned at 6% with 1% commission:

Total interest paid .... $ 5,975
Commission .... $ 2,550
$1,000,000 issue of treasury bills of 1913
loaned at 6%
Total interest paid $238,086
$1,450,000 issue of treasury bills of 1920
loaned at 9%
Total interest paid $349,586
Renewal commissions .... $ 67,330
$1,000,000 credit of March, 1927
loaned at 6% with 1% commission:
Total interest paid .... $ 34,104
Commission .... $ 10,000

Thus the entire sum loaned to Nicaragua by the
American bankers from the beginning of their financing there to the present time was $5,705,000. The en-
tire amount of interest and commissions which they
have gained was $818,034. A considerable proportion
of this latter figure was due to the frequent defaults
and renewals which set odd sums to earning com-
pound interest. At the same time part of the financing was in the form of credits, the unused portions of
which remained in the custody of the bankers and
earned items of interest for Nicaragua which are not
recorded in the above table.

In the midst of the financial complexities there
was a change in the personnel of the American bankers. In 1915 the Mercantile Bank of the Americas
was organized by the two banks then engaged in Nicaragua, Brown Brothers and the Seligmans, and the

Guaranty Trust Company of New York. It took over a host of interests and industries throughout Latin America and developed into a $100,000,000 corporation participated in by banks throughout the United States. Among the interests it acquired were those in Nicaragua then held by the Browns and the Seligmans. The Mercantile Bank was caught in the crash of the sugar market and collapsed in 1924. Brown Brothers had taken advantage of the opportunity which the organization of this bank offered to withdraw from Nicaragua. Their operations there had caused them annoyance and trouble all out of proportion to their magnitude and had brought them so little profit and so much criticism, according to their associates, that they were sick of it. After the breaking up of the Mercantile Bank, the Guaranty Trust Company took Brown Brothers' place in Nicaraguan finance. This change in personnel was the only way in which the crash touched Nicaragua.

Closely involved in the financial operations in Nicaragua were the Republic's nationally owned railway system, the Ferrocarril del Pacifico de Nicaragua, and the National Bank of Nicaragua. The dealings involving the railroad and the Bank have been violently assailed. Let us review the affairs of the railroad first.

When the bankers made their supplementary loans aggregating $755,000 in 1912 they took as security a lien on the railroad and acquired under their contract an option to buy 51 per cent of the stock of the road for $1,000,000. When the Nicaraguan Government tried soon afterward to borrow $2,000,000 the bankers proposed that the Republic raise $1,000,000 of this sum by selling the controlling interest in the railroad. The Nicaraguan Government considered this price too low and Secretary of State Bryan was inclined to agree. In response to an inquiry from him the American Minister, Dr. Jefferson, reported that the road was worth fully $3,000,000. The loan went through, however, on the terms asked by the bankers and Nicaragua sold them 51 per cent of the railway stock and 51 per cent of the Bank stock. At the same time the bankers granted the Republic an option, which they several times renewed, to buy back the controlling interest in the railroad for the same price at which it had sold it, but the option was not exercised and eventually lapsed.

The bankers proceeded to the improvement of the railroad. It was by all accounts "a streak of rust" when they took it over and running at a loss. The bankers called in the J. G. White Management Corporation of New York to operate it for an annual fee which has varied from $12,500 to $15,000 a year, according to the state of prosperity of the road. A separate concern, the J. G. White Engineering Corporation, sold the railroad its equipment and supplies on a two per cent commission basis. Under this management the railroad has consistently earned fair profits. From 1913 to 1927 the railroad paid dividends of $2,817,-774, of which $2,115,122 went to Nicaragua and $702,652 to the bankers.

In October, 1920, when Nicaragua had passed its most critical period, the government bought back the bankers' 51 per cent of the stock for $1,750,000 and since then the government, as sole owner, has received all the dividends. Recently the road has been paying no dividends, however, but has devoted its earnings to building up a surplus of about $2,000,000 for improvements which it plans to install beginning next year. The White Company has continued to operate the railroad since the government recaptured it. The road's manager is Adolfo Cardenas, a Nicaraguan.

It will be seen that the bankers, besides receiving some 10 per cent a year on their investment in the railroad, made a profit of $750,000 when they resold their interest. In return, it can be said for them, they built up a paying industry out of a losing one and surrendered it at the height of its prosperity. Both the bankers and Nicaragua profited.

The story of the National Bank is similar to that of the railroad. Like the railroad, it is incorporated in the United States. The price paid by the bankers for 51 per cent of the stock of the Bank, purchased at the same time that they bought control of the railroad, on October 8, 1913, was $153,000, its par value. They increased the capitalization to $300,000. In 1924 the government bought back the bankers' 51 per cent of the stock for its book value, $300,000. In the intervening years the Bank had been built into a sound, strong structure, profitable financially to Nicaragua, and performing many valuable functions besides the primary ones for which it was established, the reforming and safeguarding of the currency and the providing of a depository for government funds.

The Bank paid no dividends until 1918, devoting its earnings in the early years to building up its surplus. From 1918 to 1926 inclusive it paid dividends of $260,010, of which the Republic received $152,910. The Republic's share of the dividends was $14,700 a year until 1926, when $50,010 was paid. Dividends have been suspended since then because of the financial difficulties caused by revolution.

The Bank engages in a general banking business. It receives ordinary deposits, and encourages savings accounts. It lends chiefly to coffee growers at ten and twelve per cent. Before it entered this field money lending in Nicaragua was to a great extent in the hands of private capitalists who charged 18 or 20 per cent, or even more. The Bank, when it loans to a coffee grower, requires a mortgage on both the crop and the plantation itself. The loan is repayable either in cash or in coffee. This has put the Bank into the coffee exporting business on a large scale, and it handles the purchase, shipment and sale of coffee through a profitable subsidiary, the Compania Mercantile del Ultramar. The Bank has become strong enough to participate in the financing of the government and has several times made loans to it.

The National Bank of Nicaragua has still another means of earning profits, a means which also makes profits for the New York bankers. It now keeps on deposit with the Seligmans and the Guaranty Trust Company about $200,000 in general accounts and a reserve averaging $2,000,000 or more to guarantee the Nicaraguan currency. As security for this gold reserve the American bankers keep on an average $2,-700,000 of Liberty bonds on deposit with the Federal Reserve Bank in New York. About one third of the exchange fund is kept in what is known as the current account, and the Nicaraguan Bank receives three per cent interest on that portion. The remaining two thirds are in a 31-day time account and pay the Nicaraguan Bank four per cent interest. These rates recently were increased voluntarily by the New York bankers from two and one half per cent and three and a half per cent respectively because of the advance in call money rates in Wall Street. Thus both Nicaragua and the American bankers are earning sums of varying and indefinite magnitude on these funds, the American banks profiting by the margin between the interest they pay the Nicaraguan Bank and the interest at which they rent out the money. The manager of the Bank is L. S. Rosenthall, an American, formerly of the Guaranty Trust Company.

The Bank and the railroad are now and have been for several years the sole property of the Republic of Nicaragua. During these years, however, the American bankers have from time to time exercised theoretical control over them by requiring the Republic to pledge the stock of both the Bank and the railroad as security for loans. During such periods all the dividends have gone to the Republic, but the American bankers have maintained a majority on the directorates of both corporations. The most recent use of the Bank and railroad in this manner was incidental to the loan of $1,000,000 in 1927 which paid off the government and revolutionary troops at the close of the Liberal revolution. When this loan was liquidated on April 25,1928, the entire control of the Bank and the railroad reverted to the Republic. Nicaragua then could have thrown out the American management, inflated the currency, or done anything it liked with them. President Diaz, however, did not even change the directorates, allowing the Americans to remain in the majority. In his fearfulness of what might happen if the Nicaraguans took over the management he actually proposed informally, and on his own initiative, to sell the Bank to the New York financiers. This project was discouraged by the State Department, which probably feared the way in which such a transaction would have been interpreted in the United States as well as elsewhere, and the bankers also declined to entertain it.

From 1913 to 1917, through four years of virtual insolvency, the eyes of the Republic of Nicaragua were centred hopefully on the $3,000,000 which it would receive from the United States in return for the option on the canal route. The long delay in ratification by the critical American Senate was trying to the Nicaraguan officials. There was rejoicing when

finally in 1916 the treaty was approved and proclaimed, but even then Nicaragua had to wait more
than a year while American Congressmen debated
and State Department officials weighed technicalities
before it received the money. And to make matters
worse, from the viewpoint of the average Nicaraguan
to whom all things financial are quite mysterious,
when the $3,000,000 at last was paid, less than a
third of it actually came into the country, and that
was immediately absorbed by claims, back salaries and
the like. The remainder was applied to previous debts
of the country.

One still hears criticism of that fact in Nicaragua.
The canal treaty itself had stipulated, however, that
the money was "to be applied by Nicaragua upon
its indebtedness or other public purposes for the advancement of the welfare of Nicaragua in a manner
to be determined by the two High Contracting Parties, all such disbursements to be . . . approved by
the Secretary of State of the United States." The
State Department held up all payments from the canal
fund, except insignificant sums doled out for back
salaries and similar pressing needs, for which the Nicaraguan Government had to beg repeatedly, until
after the approval by the Nicaraguan Congress of a
new financial plan and loan contract in November,
1917.

The money finally was paid in November and December, 1917. The following table shows the distribution of the $3,000,000:

Bonds of 1909, interest to Jan. 1, 1917, and 6% interest thereon	$622,779.77
Bonds of 1909, sinking fund to Jan. 1, 1917	138,906.31
Bonds of 1909, 25% of interest due July 1, 1917	36,773.09
Treasury Bills of 1913, one-half of principal	530,000.00
Treasury Bills of 1913, interest to November 1, 1917	211,181.14
Emery Claim	485,000.00
National Bank of Nicaragua, loans and interest	111,404.83
Internal and floating debts and claims	334,840.83
Expenses, fees, commissions, etc.	26,512.66
Government of Nicaragua, back salaries and expenses	500,000.00
Expense of exchange, etc.	2,601.37

This manner of using Nicaragua's funds was probably the most beneficial to the Republic that could have been devised, for it wiped out old debts which were drawing interest and whose interest was drawing more interest, and placed the country in the soundest position it had been in for many years, but there were and still are persons in Nicaragua who could not understand the transaction and thought that the country had been robbed.

One item in the canal fund settlement was the payment to Brown Brothers of $485,000 in final settlement of the Emery Claim, so often discussed in criticisms of the American bankers. This claim grew out of the annulment by the Zelaya Government of a concession of timber rights held by the George D. Emery Company, a large lumber concern of Boston. The American Government took up the claim diplomatically and in September, 1909, a month before the outbreak of the revolution, the two governments agreed on the payment to the Emery Company of $600,000 in installments to be completed in five years. The obligation thus became in effect an obligation to the United States. Fifty thousand dollars had been paid when Zelaya fell. In 1910 Brown Brothers, before their entry into Nicaraguan financing, took an option on the business and property of the Emery Company both in the United States and in Nicaragua and obtained in this way a four-fifths interest in the $550,000 claim against Nicaragua. They soon sold the lumber business, but the claim remained unrealized until its payment, with interest, from the canal proceeds.

A new arrangement, known as the Financial Plan of 1917, was worked out in that year with the object, as described by Secretary of State Lansing in a telegram of information to President Emiliano Chamorro, of gradually liquidating Nicaragua's foreign indebtedness and at the same time leaving it enough money for its own needs and the payment of other debts. It followed the lines of the original loan contract but established a High Commission under American control to advise the government, and to supervise the expenditure of a portion of its revenues.

The plan extended American authority in theory

by providing that if the internal revenues fell below
a total of $180,000 for any three consecutive months,
except because of unforeseen events, the collection of
such revenues should be taken over by the Collector
General of Customs. There has not thus far been any
occasion to take such action. In 1920 the State Department approved a new plan, whose principal
changes from the plan of 1917 were provisions looking to a loan of $9,000,000 for refunding the debt
and building a railroad from the East to the West
Coasts. The railroad project, however, once more was
dropped, and the loan was not made.

Under these plans, of course, the customs revenues
have been the chief source of the monies used for
reducing the national debt. The customs revenues
have been used in this order: first, for the payment
of amortization and interest of the Ethelburga Loan;
second, for payments on the customs guaranteed
bonds which were used to pay claims resulting from
revolution; third, for payments of sums owing to the
New York bankers; fourth for the ordinary purposes of the government. Under the financial plan
of 1917 a surcharge of twelve and one half per cent
was levied on imports to supply funds for the gradual retirement of the customs guaranteed bonds, and
the same means were resorted to for the payment of
the loan of 1927. The ordinary internal revenues
of the country, constituting half its income, have remained under native administration and their pro-

ceeds have gone to the normal uses of the Government.

Under the financial supervision instituted by the State Department and the bankers Nicaragua has been paying off its debts steadily, so that of the funded debt only $5,669,000 remained unpaid on January 31, 1928. This total consisted of $3,297,000 of the original $6,083,000 of the Ethelburga Loan, and $2,372,000 of the original $3,744,150 of the customs guaranteed bonds. The damage claims growing out of the Liberal revolution are expected to add another $2,000,000 to the country's debt. Other obligations of the country will hardly exceed $500,000. So the Republic's entire debt is now little in excess of $8,000,000.

The Republic recently has undertaken a limited program of road building and is paving the dusty streets of the capital, through the agency of an American engineering company, out of its current revenues.

Wall Street has ceased to be a creditor and its only connection with the Republic now is as fiscal agent for the Ethelburga Loan, from which the bankers derive no profit.

There was much discussion in Managua in the closing months of the Diaz administration of another loan by American financiers to fund the entire debt of the Republic and provide money for the construction of an East and West railroad. Among Nicaraguan officials it was felt that $20,000,000 should be borrowed. An economist sent by the State Department, Dr. W. W. Cumberland, reported after a survey of the country that the railroad was too heavy a project for the Republic to undertake and recommended that not more than $12,000,000 should be borrowed. Out of this sum he would have had $3,-000,000 applied to the construction of highways, in lieu of the railroad. Furthermore, as an accompaniment to such a loan, for the sake of economy, security, and a resulting lower interest rate, he would have had established an even greater control by Americans over the country's finances than is now exercised.

This plan has not been acted upon. The bankers themselves were unwilling to make a large loan to Nicaragua unless both Conservatives and Liberals favored it, and there has thus far been no official indication of the attitude of the Liberals since Moncada became President.

Here we can leave the financial aspects of American intervention and return to the narrative.

➤ GENERAL EMILIANO CHAMORRO ➤
Leader of the Conservatives

CHAPTER X

THE STRONG MAN OF NICARAGUA

THERE had been changes of administration in Nicaragua as well as in the United States in the midst of the financial reorganization, and there had come into the Presidency of the little republic to the South a man of compelling personality. It even has been said of him that "the history of Nicaragua is the biography of Emiliano Chamorro."

Certainly he was the strongest individual figure in the Republic and he is that today. Enormously ambitious, he had had to swallow disappointments during the first years of American guardianship over his country. He had been the chief driving force of the revolution of 1909; he had played a prominent part, in collaboration with the marines, in crushing the Mena revolt in 1912; but he had had to stand aside while others more acceptable to the American Government filled the office he coveted. Now at last, in 1917, he would be denied no longer and came into his own.

In most of his personal qualities General Chamorro is the direct opposite of his friend Adolfo Diaz. Diaz has little appeal for the masses of the people; Chamorro is enormously popular. Diaz seeks always to avoid controversies, to circle around obstacles; Chamorro fights his way through. Diaz dislikes holding office and would rather live quietly on his coffee *finca* than do anything else in the world; Chamorro loves politics and retires to his cattle ranch only to devise his next clever scheme. Diaz is a man of peace; Chamorro is so identified with war that although Nicaragua is crowded with generals, if you mention "the General" it means only one man, Chamorro.

Yet with all his military prowess and his love of authority, Chamorro is anything but a swashbuckler. He is quiet, dignified, soft-spoken, smiling even when he is fighting hardest, and has an odd quality of boyish naïveté which his chuckling laugh accentuates. Behind the naïveté there is tremendous, even ruthless ambition.

He is the idol of the *mozos*. Whenever he goes about the country little knots of barefoot men, women, and children gather about him and discuss their hero in reverent whispers. And at the same time he is greatly liked personally in the American colony in Managua, a cultured little group whose leaders include the American Minister and his aides from the Legation, the manager of the Bank, the Collector General of Customs, the Director of the Rockefeller Institute, a few marine officers, and others prominent in the life of the country.

Chamorro is half Indian. On his father's side he is sprung from one of the great Spanish families of Nicaragua. His mother was a servant girl in his father's house. Chamorro loved her devotedly, and when he became President he often drove about Managua with her in his carriage to show her the sights of the capital over which he ruled. This duality of Chamorro's ancestry accounts partly for his unusual character. He has inherited the will to rule of the old *conquistadores*, and the fortitude, the devious shrewdness, and the shy charm of the Indians.

He apparently lacks the instinct of physical fear, and Nicaragua is full of legends of his courage on the battlefield. He acquired his hatred of the Zelayists legitimately, for he grew up in the period of the Liberal dictatorship. Zelaya had imprisoned and tortured his father. Chamorro himself, as a young man and politically active, was exiled from the cities throughout the Zelaya régime. In those days he liked to disguise himself as a barefoot *mozo* and ride into the forbidden capital on an oxcart; once in the city he would attend to the political errand which had brought him, post a taunting letter to Zelaya complaining about the stupidity of the Chief of Police, and disappear again into the bush.

The manner in which Chamorro became President is interesting and significant.

Adolfo Diaz, throughout his troubled term of office, had well fulfilled the trust which the United States had placed in him. But at the end of 1916 he was compelled by the constitutional provision forbidding a President to succeed himself to lay down his task half finished. The North American Government of course desired that someone be found who would proceed with the carrying out of Nicaragua's part of the financial reorganization.

The end of President Diaz's term came at an awkward time, for the Republic's finances still were in a dreadful condition. If at this delicate moment a Liberal—and the Zelayist element was still strong in the Liberal party—had succeeded to power, the result probably would have been disastrous to Nicaragua's economic regeneration and seriously embarrassing to Washington's Caribbean policy.

Under the constitution which the United States had helped frame, the new national officials of Nicaragua were to be chosen by the people in a free and fair election.

The Conservatives had two principal candidates from whom to choose, Dr. Carlos Cuadra Pasos, a Granada Conservative of great ability, and Emiliano Chamorro, who then was Nicaraguan Minister at Washington. They at last united on Chamorro and it was arranged that Cuadra Pasos should be Minister to the United States in the expected event of Chamorro's election.

Two main groups struggled for ascendency in the Liberal party. One was the militarist group of diehards who still cherished the tradition of Zelaya and were bitterly anti-American. Dr. Irias was still the leader of this group, though he had been in exile since the fall of Madriz. The other was a more moderate

group headed by such intellectuals of León as Dr.
Juan B. Sacasa and Dr. Leonardo Argüello.

At this juncture Irias himself returned to Nicaragua to contest for the Presidency. A delegation of
Liberal leaders met him at Corinto. As the train bearing Irias to León was leaving Chinandega, a dozen
men fired point blank into the coach, wounded some
of the Irias party, and killed a woman. The country
was thrown into excitement, and the shallowly buried
blood enmities of León and Granada seemed about to
burst to the surface. Dr. Irias went on to Managua,
where President Diaz extended to him every courtesy and protection. The American Minister, Dr.
Jefferson, used his good offices to preserve peace between the parties and even succeeded in getting the
hostile leaders to break bread together at a banquet
in the Legation.

A day or two after the banquet Dr. Irias called at
the Legation and in the presence of Admiral Caper-
ton he and the Minister discussed the political situation. The Minister made it plain that the United
States would have something to say about the "free
and fair election." According to his own remem-
brance of that conversation, Dr. Jefferson "recounted
to Dr. Irias the full history of the post—and what the
Government at Washington and the people of Nicaragua fully expected in the future—and unless the
candidate or candidates could conform to the conditions as outlined by me—it would not be possible

for either Washington or the people of Nicaragua to take a chance on having a return of the old order of conditions."

The finances of the Nicaraguan Government, the Minister continued, must be arranged in a way satisfactory to all concerned.

Dr. Irias was very agreeable, according to Dr. Jefferson, and conceded that because he had been Zelaya's chief minister, even though he had not been accountable for what Zelaya had done, he could not qualify as a candidate. He left the country once more and visited the United States.

With Irias departed the Liberals were headless. They could agree on no other candidate. The "free elections" promised jointly by the United States and the Nicaraguan Government were duly held with marine observers in attendance, but few except Conservatives voted. The word had gone out that President Wilson wished Chamorro to win, and the Liberals remained away from the polls, partly as a protest, partly, as they alleged, for fear that American observation of the balloting was intended to control the election and that they would be subjecting themselves to danger if they attempted to vote. General Chamorro was elected.

A month after the election Dr. Irias made public in the United States an indignant account of his elimination from the contest, asserting that the American Minister had laid down conditions for the prospective

candidates which practically closed the lists to all except Chamorro and that he had not been permitted to
carry on a pre-election campaign. The conditions, said
Irias, were as follows:

"No candidate will ever be President of Nicaragua
unless he can fully demonstrate and prove to the
State Department the following:

"First, That he accepts without any modification
the convention agreed upon by the present government of Nicaragua (the Bryan-Chamorro canal
treaty).

"Second, That in all he may do regarding the economic system of Nicaragua, he will proceed in complete accordance with the State Department.

"Third, That he will accept an American police
force for the maintenance of order and peace in the
Republic. The State Department may maintain such
forces or withdraw them from Nicaragua as it may
deem convenient, or bring them in again in case they
have been retired.

"Fourth, The candidate will have to prove that he
has in no way participated in General Zelaya's administration.

"Fifth, The candidate must also prove to the State
Department that he has in no way, either directly or
indirectly, participated in revolutions against the government of Nicaragua since the fall of Zelaya."

If these actually were the conditions, as there is
little doubt they were in substance, they certainly

ruled Irias out, for it was notorious that he had inspired rebellious outbreaks in Nicaragua from neighboring countries.

Compared with the administration of Diaz, the
pacificator, the administration of Chamorro, the soldier, was peaceful. The most serious military alarm
came in the summer of 1919 when an army composed
of Costa Ricans and Nicaraguan Liberals, including
General Irias, was reported to be massing across the
Costa Rican border in preparation for an invasion.
Nicaragua appealed to the United States to land
troops, asserting that "in accordance with the plan
by which the United States gives us friendly advice,
we think that the United States should give us, in this
emergency, the moral and material protection of a
sufficient guard on our frontier to prevent an invasion."

The United States refrained from acting, and the
crisis blew over of itself.

General Chamorro's administration was occupied
almost entirely with intricate financial and economic
problems, with conducting the country through a
period of extreme poverty which was aggravated by
the long delay of the United States in paying for the
canal rights.

It was a period of squabbles between the Nicaraguan Government and the State Department and
the American bankers. Chamorro was too self-willed,
impatient, and determined a man to get along well
with them. Often he fought against details in the

terms of financing which were presented to him—
sometimes with success, as when he blocked the establishment of a supernumerary financial adviser on
the Republic's payroll. Yet essentially he was in sympathy with the fundamentals of the American policy
in his country. As he himself expressed it in his first
message to Congress:

"I am firmly convinced of the advantage which
there is for Nicaragua in maintaining the closest political relations with the great republic of North
America. It is to the interest of our own system of
government, to our own security, to stimulate those
relations, in order that they may grow into an increasing and perfect friendship between both governments and peoples."

Chamorro displayed lively interest in the internal
development of his country and under his administration a definite start was made toward the construction of Nicaragua's most needed improvement,
highways.

When General Chamorro's term neared its end in
1920 he was loth to yield his power, and made plans
to have himself succeeded by his old and feeble uncle,
Diego Manuel Chamorro.

The Liberals, mindful of the one-sided election of
1916, endeavored by various artifices to discover
whether the United States intended this time to put
meaning into the phrase "free elections" or whether
it intended again to determine the result. To quiet
the many conflicting rumors, the State Department

declared in July that it would not intervene in the election—that intervention would be both unnecessary and impertinent. It also suggested to Chamorro that the electoral laws should be revised in the interest of impartiality. Chamorro declined, and the State Department laid the issue aside.

The elections were held in the Fall. Chamorro's admirable political machine functioned perfectly. His uncle was victorious with 58,000 votes against the Liberals' 32,000.

Then, with his successor safely chosen from his own family, Emiliano Chamorro declared for a revision of the electoral laws. After Don Diego had taken office, the retiring President returned to his old post of Minister at Washington. Thus he was complete master in both capitals from which the affairs of Nicaragua were directed.

The new administration, if it could be called a new administration, was as amenable to the American policy as those preceding it had been. There still were outbursts of criticism by the Liberals of the activities of the State Department and the American bankers, to which the new President Chamorro replied spiritedly and in detail in a long message to Congress defending the entire arrangement and recounting the substantial progress made by the country up the long road to financial soundness. The President denied that the United States infringed the independence of the country, although he admitted that the principle of territorial integrity "has had to give way necessarily each time that an attempt has been made to negotiate a canal agreement," and foresaw in the eventual building of the canal a benefit to Nicaragua greater even than the benefit to the United States.

Meanwhile, ever since the suppression of the Mena rebellion, the United States had been watching over its interests in Nicaragua with as little a show of military force as possible. The "rule of guns," against which Liberal orators and journalists occasionally thundered, had been maintained only by a force of marines averaging one hundred whose status was that of Legation guard. The marines lived at the Campo de Marte, hard by the Presidential Palace, and in easy rifle shot of the fortress of La Loma overlooking the Palace.

Cruisers and more marines were never far away, of course, but these hundred men, by their moral effect, had been all that was necessary.

But Managua is a difficult and uncomfortable post. There is little of the amusement to which troops are accustomed. There is almost no agreeable contact with the outside world. Men from the North too often brood in the smothering heat of that dusty capital. As they themselves speak of it, they "go tropical." Perhaps that is as kind and at the same time as true an explanation as any of three outbreaks by Americans which provoked deep resentment in Managua and caused regret and anxiety in Washington.

The first one occurred in the second month of the administration of Diego Manuel Chamorro. A group of about 30 marines raided the offices of La Tribuna, a Liberal newspaper in Managua which was hostile to the Conservative administration and the American supervision and which had referred to the marines in terms which they considered insulting. The marines destroyed the presses and wrecked the offices. Secretary of the Navy Daniels ordered a court martial as a result of which 21 members of the Legation guard were dishonorably discharged and sentenced to two years imprisonment.

Within the year the marines engaged in another brawl in which three policemen were killed and two marines wounded. Three marines were sentenced to ten years imprisonment each.

But again, on January 24, 1922, there was a third such episode. A marine sergeant and three corporals had been reported as deserters. Members of the native police force found them and tried to arrest them. The marines resisted. A fight ensued in which the sergeant was killed and four policemen were wounded.

Nicaragua was accustomed to violence but resentful of violence by outsiders. A resolution calling for the withdrawal of the marines was introduced in the Nicaraguan Congress but was defeated. American military authorities again dealt sternly with the men involved and this allayed the ill-feeling. The Navy Department had the entire. guard relieved by a detachment from Haiti, arranged to provide shorter tours of duty in Managua, and provided places of amusement to keep the men out of the vicious drinking establishments of the town. Eventually the American Government paid indemnities of $11,700 to the families of the native victims.

President Chamorro had difficulty with his own people as well. A series of revolts along the northern border, in which Honduran Liberals participated, created alarms for several months until in the Winter of 1921 the United States sent 10,000 rifles, many machine guns and several million rounds of ammunition to the Nicaraguan Government. By one of those ironies so frequent in the story of American activities in Nicaragua, some of those very guns, long hidden in the mountains of the border, eventually came into the hands of the Sandinistas who inflicted so many casualties on American marines in 1927 and 1928. The munitions were entrusted to the generals for distribution to their men. Many of the officers, ready to turn an honest penny, sold them to whoever would buy, and they have circulated among the outlaw gentry ever since.

The plots of the elements hostile to the Government smoldered on, and in April, 1922, 34 members of the Liberal party were arrested, charged with a conspiracy to overthrow the Chamorro Government, and martial law was proclaimed again for 30 days. On May 21 a party of men suddenly seized the Loma in a fight in which two men were killed.

With this fortress in their hands—a fortress whose possession traditionally carries with it control of all Nicaragua—the rebels attempted to win over the Nicaraguan troops at the bottom of the hill near the Presidential Palace. President Chamorro unexpectedly appeared on the scene without a guard, put a machine gun in the charge of a trusted man and then personally directed his soldiers while they drove the rebels back up the hill to the Loma.

At this point the American Minister, John E. Ramer, arrived and sent a note to the revolutionists warning them that if they fired on the city, or on the Campo de Marte, the marines would return the fire.

This threat was sufficient. After eight hours, the conquerors of the Loma marched down again and after a night conference at the Legation the leaders were set at liberty, to the surprise of the populace, which had expected that they would die before a firing squad. By their presence alone, 100 marines had stopped what might well have been a successful revolution. In the weeks which followed there were other dangerous attempts in the northern part of the country but all were quickly put down.

So threatening, however, was the revolutionary and outlaw activity along the wild borders of Nicaragua, Honduras, and Salvador, that representatives of the three governments met, in response to a proposal by President Chamorro, on the United States Cruiser Tacoma in the Gulf of Fonseca and drew up plans for coping with disorder. The American Ministers of the three countries represented also attended. The fruit of this meeting was an agreement by which each republic bound itself to prevent political immigrants from any other country fomenting invasions and to use armed force against persons who in spite of precautions launched expeditions against any of the other republics.

There had begun while Emiliano Chamorro was still President, and there continued into the Presidency of his uncle, an effort by other Central American nations to revive the old Central American Union, a dream which in a century has never faded from the consciousness of a large and worthy element on the Isthmus. The United States regarded the effort with inactive benevolence.

A union of the five republics actually was achieved, on paper, late in 1920, but it was short-lived. Nicaragua feared that in joining the confederation it might be jeopardizing the treaty by which it had given the United States an option on the canal route and insisted that the proposed treaty of confederation expressly recognize the validity of the Bryan-Chamorro treaty and also be phrased so as to dispose of the judgments against Nicaragua obtained by Salvador and Costa Rica in the Central American Court of Justice. Costa Rica and Salvador could not agree to this.

Nicaragua maintained its opposition, and, situated as it was midway of the Isthmus, separating other countries of the proposed Union, its opposition was fatal. The Confederation collapsed amid outbursts of Yankeephobia from some quarters and from others expressions of desire for the coöperation of the United States.

An atmosphere of distrust now prevailed on the Isthmus and another new deal was urgently needed. The American Government therefore invited the five republics to attend a conference in Washington with the object of strengthening the pacificatory ties forged at the Washington Conference of 1907.

The conference opened on December 4, 1922, with articulate elements in Central America skeptical of its value. Secretary Hughes, in opening it, expressed a hope that the Isthmian countries might set an example to the rest of the continent by devising peaceable means of settling disputes. The purpose of the meeting, as he perceived it, was to find some means of arbitrating controversies to take the place vacated by the defunct Central American Court of Justice; to limit armaments in Central America, and to devise means to end the wasting of the funds of the Central American powers in unnecessary and unproductive outlays.

"In all that you may endeavor to this end you have the assurance of the interest and coöperation of the United States Government," Mr. Hughes assured them.

After the loss of considerable time in bootless debates on irrelevant subjects, the conference adopted a program on February 7, 1923, intended to insure neutrality, stability, peace, and prosperity.

There were agreements for the creation of a new Central American tribunal, for the limitation of armament, for free trade, for better communications and for the development of agricultural resources. Most important of these Conventions of 1923 however, was a general treaty of peace and amity embodying the non-recognition policy so famously promulgated by President Wilson in his controversy over Huerta in Mexico. The second article of this convention read in part as follows:

" . . . the Governments of the Contracting Parties will not recognize any other Government which may come into power in any of the five Republics through a *coup d'état* or a revolution against a recognized Government, so long as the freely elected representatives of the people thereof have not constitutionally reorganized the country. And even in such a case they obligate themselves not to acknowledge the recognition if any of the persons elected as President, Vice-President, or Chief of State designate should fall under any of the following heads:

"(1) If he should be the leader or one of the leaders of a *coup d'état* or revolution, or through blood relationship or marriage, be an ascendent or descendent or brother of such leader or leaders.

"(2) If he should have been a Secretary of State or should have held some high military command during the accomplishment of the *coup d'état*, the revolution, or while the election was being carried on, or if he should have held this office or command within the six months preceding the *coup d'état,* revolution, or election.

"Furthermore, in no case shall recognition be accorded to a government which arises from election to power of a citizen expressly and unquestionably disqualified by the Constitution of his country as eligible to election as President, Vice-President, or Chief of State designate."

This article, strengthening the anti-revolutionary avowals of 1907, was to serve as the foundation of the policy of the American State Department toward the recognition of Central American governments; sooner than anybody in that conference at Washington dreamed, it was to figure in another dizzy twist in Nicaraguan history.

Emiliano Chamorro, as head of the Nicaraguan delegation to the conference, put his signature to this repudiation of revolutions as a feature of party politics on the Isthmus. The compact was to be used against him for his undoing.

CHAPTER XI

THE UNITED STATES TRIES TO GET OUT

IF President Diego Manuel Chamorro had lived it is quite possible that Nicaragua would have gone on in orderly fashion to the peaceful development which the United States was trying to foster. For indeed, with revolutions suppressed within and jealousies under control without, the prospect for Nicaragua looked bright late in 1923. The country's entire debt had now been reduced to nine million and a quarter dollars and the Republic was planning definitely to build that strategic railroad across the plains, the mountains and the jungles which would bind the diverse halves of the country together.

Emiliano Chamorro was on his way from Washington to Managua to discuss a proposed loan of $9,000,-000 by New York bankers for the construction of this railroad when his uncle, the President, died on October 19, 1923.

Bartolomé Martinez, the Vice President, succeeded to the Presidency and in the beginning there was no outward cause to fear that under the new executive, a Conservative like his predecessors, there would be any check to the orderly fulfilment of an

American policy that at last seemed to be justifying the protestations of its benevolence.

In that year the Monroe Doctrine was 100 years old. Secretary of State Hughes, in a centennial address at Philadelphia on November 30, 1923, spoke with pride of the manner in which the United States had interpreted and applied the Doctrine and reiterated as a cardinal principle of the policy of the United States toward Latin America the equality of all nations, great and weak alike.

"We have not sought by opposing the intervention of non-American powers to establish a protectorate or overlordship of our own with respect to these republics," said the Secretary. "Such a pretension not only is not found in the Monroe Doctrine, but would be in opposition to our fundamental affirmative policy."

Secretary Hughes was sincere—disastrously sincere.

He was eager to vindicate the oft-expressed declaration of the United States that it had no wish to interfere with the liberties of the sister republics to the south.

A step toward restoring self-government to Nicaragua already had been taken with the dispatch to that country of Harold W. Dodds, Professor of Government at Princeton University, to frame an electoral law for Nicaragua, at the request of the Republic in agreement with the State Department. Professor Dodds was fitted practically for his task, not only by reason of his standing as an authority on such

problems, but because he had served as observer at
the two preceding national elections in Nicaragua.
By October, 1922, Professor Dodds had completed his
draft of a law designed to reduce so far as possible the
opportunities for chicanery and violence which previously had made Nicaraguan elections only a pretense by which the party in power perpetuated its
control under a fiction of constitutionality.

The very fact that the Dodds system would have
reformed the elections to an appreciable degree made
it unacceptable in its original form to the Conservative
majority in Congress. The Conservatives proposed
modifications which would have so completely defeated its purpose that the State Department cautioned the Nicaraguan government against making
changes in the Dodds draft which affected the safeguards to voters. The law was passed on March 16,
1923, in a form which the State Department accepted as satisfactory, but political exigencies still prevented it being more than a partial advance from the
open coercion of the past. It created a bi-partisan
National Board of Elections and bi-partisan local
boards, but the chairmen of these boards were appointed by the party in power and hence the Ins still
could largely control the polls.

The United States also felt that Nicaragua was
firmly enough established in a life of tranquillity that
the slender force of marines which had been maintained there since the crushing of the Mena rebellion
in 1912 could now safely be withdrawn. Indeed there

had come to be a feeling in the Department that this American force, too small to carry on a large action, might actually pique the curiosity of some daring Nicaraguan general to find out experimentally just what it would do.

Accordingly, on November 14, 1923, the American Legation under instructions from Washington informed the Nicaraguan Government of its desire to withdraw the Legation guard as soon as practicable and to assist in organizing and training a constabulary to maintain order after the marines had left.

The organization of a constabulary already had been prepared for at the Central American Conference of 1923 when Nicaragua and the other republics had agreed to the formation of non-political armed forces to take the place gradually of the old-fashioned armies which normally were the tools of political leaders.

The American Government considered it desirable that the marines remain in Managua through the election period and until the new administration was installed, and also recommended that Professor Dodds and a corps of assistants be invited to Nicaragua to assist in the installation of the new election procedure.

Both these proposals were most welcome to the Liberals. Since 1912 the Liberals had regarded the presence of the marines with mixed sentiments. On the one hand the marines acted as a brake on the instinct of the party in power to exercise the measures of violence and exploitation against Liberals which were the historic privilege of the Ins against the Outs in most Central American countries. But on the other hand the presence of the marines was a tacit threat of action by the United States against any who might start a revolution, as had been well demonstrated in the shortlived revolt against Diego Manuel Chamorro. Some of the more outspoken of the Liberals quoted Thomas Jefferson in support of the necessity of revolution, and argued that since the United States had deprived them of the hope of overturning the Conservative régime by the usual Central American method of force, it was bound to assure them a fair election as the only alternative.

The Martinez government accepted the suggestion of the State Department that the marines remain until after the new government was installed in January, 1925, and accepted the principle of the constabulary, but hedged on American supervision of the elections. President Martinez invited Professor Dodds and his assistants to visit Nicaragua in the spring of 1924, when the registration for the coming election would be held, but neglected to ask for supervision of the election itself. The State Department did not press the point.

As 1924 wore on the reason for the lukewarmness of President Martinez became manifest. He nourished an ambition to succeed himself as President, notwithstanding the plain provision in the constitution forbidding such succession.

President Martinez sounded out Washington on the subject of his prospective candidacy and on June 13 the Legation at Managua informed him that while the Government of the United States had no desire to intervene in the internal affairs of Nicaragua and had no preference as between parties or candidates, it "would be precluded, by the policy which it has already publicly announced with regard to the recognition of new governments in Central America, from recognizing a government arising from the election to the Presidency of a citizen expressly and unquestionably disqualified by the Constitution of the country." Because the United States Government wished "to be in a position to extend the fullest and most sympathetic coöperation to the new government," the warning went on, "it hoped that there should be no question in January, 1925, of the eligibility of the person who shall have been chosen as President of Nicaragua."

Meanwhile Emiliano Chamorro had returned from his post in Washington to conduct his own campaign for the Presidency. The result was a rupture between the Chamorro faction of the party and the anti-Chamorro faction now headed by the President. Riots, with resultant deaths, occurred in the streets of Managua and in Granada. President Martinez saw that continuation in the Presidency was not for him, but he found a way to prevent the Chamorrists getting in.

The regular Conservative party nominated Emiliano Chamorro for President. The intellectual group in the Liberal party succeeded in nominating Dr. Sacasa.

President Martinez contrived to effect a coalition between his faction of the Conservative party and the León Liberals. It resulted in the formation of a party calling itself Conservative-Republican and the nomination of a ticket headed by Carlos Solorzano, an agreeable gentleman, a retired capitalist of the Conservative faith, and with Dr. Sacasa for Vice President. Sacasa was a practicing physician in León concerning whom one hears only complimentary references in Nicaragua. He was educated at Columbia University in New York and is a man of character, culture and intelligence.

With the eagerness for Washington's stamp of approval which has been displayed so consistently in Nicaragua in recent years, President Martinez approached the State Department for an expression as to whether it would look with favor on that alliance between Conservatives and Liberals.

It took the State Department only a few hours to inform the Nicaraguans that it had no preference whatever regarding presidential candidates in Nicaragua; that it neither supported nor opposed any candidate there; that it desired only that free and fair elections should be held; and that it felt that "the transference of the centre of political activity of Nicaragua to Washington would be detrimental to that Government's interests and this Government therefore cannot express its views regarding any ticket." An assurance was added that any person freely and fairly elected in accordance with the electoral law and the constitution of Nicaragua would be recognized by the Government of the United States, which would gladly "lend him its advice and counsel."

Chamorro, who had opposed supervision in the past and was to oppose it stubbornly in the future, knew that the cards were stacked against him and pleaded this time to have Americans watch over the polls. But Martinez was obdurate against it. The election was held in October, with the Martinez administration in full charge of the election machinery. The whole department of Chontales, which Chamorro ruled politically, was placed under martial law and its vote was thrown out.

Eighty-four thousand votes were recorded out of a total registration of 115,000. The results as proclaimed were 48,072 for Solorzano and Sacasa, and 28,760 for Chamorro. The rest of the votes were scattered among minor candidates, among them Dr. Luis Corea, one time Minister to the United States.

Chamorro protested that he had been cheated out of the election and the State Department has since asserted that there were patent frauds. Professor Dodds said that the election was "tainted by some of the old fashioned practices," but that it was distinctly cleaner than previous elections had been. The Chamorristas further charged that the Martinez faction had used force to deprive Conservative deputies of their seats in order to have a friendly Congress to canvass the election returns. Indeed it was asserted that President Martinez had welcomed open outrage in the hope that whoever won would fail, because of the frauds, to obtain recognition and that therefore he would continue in the Presidency.

Whether or not this was so, the State Department had determined on a hands off policy. It preferred to ignore the irregularities of the election and recognized the new President a week after he was sworn in.

President Solorzano inaugurated his administration with an address declaring his intention to maintain constant contact with the Government of the United States in recognition of the fact that the friendly assistance of the United States had been "in the rôle of obtaining the most solid and satisfactory economic situation for Nicaragua." He pledged absolute freedom in the elections of 1928—he previously had promised the United States that he would not permit the mutilation of the Dodds Law—and the creation of a constabulary under the instruction of American officers.

He would not need accomplices in his administration, but collaborators, he announced, and in harmony with this he made up a cabinet composed of members of both parties.

The result was such as normally follows compromises. Instead of having the backing of both parties in this coalition of the two traditionally inimical groups, he had the ill will of both, for each wished to be in the ascendency. He was helpless from the start. Even within his family he could not rule unchallenged, for his wife had two determined brothers, General Alfredo Rivas and Colonel Luis Rivas. To Alfredo President Solorzano entrusted the command of the Loma, and to Luis he gave command of the troops in the Campo de Marte in the shadow of the key-fortress of the Republic. We shall hear more about the Rivas's later.

The well-intentioned new President was a tyro in politics—that was why Martinez had engineered his election—but he well knew that Chamorro, smouldering with fury at the injustice which he believed had been done to him in the election, was only awaiting an opportunity to pounce on him, and that the marines were the only security he had. He dreaded what would happen if the United States withdrew them. So one of his first official acts, on January 7, 1925, was to request the American Government, "in behalf of the peace, order and well-being of Nicaragua," to permit the Legation guard of marines to remain "until there shall have been established under the guidance of American instructors an efficient service of the National Guard, which would be difficult, if not impossible, to effect in the absence of the Legation guard."

The United States replied in a long academic utterance, the gist of which was that it felt that it would be entirely justified in withdrawing the marines, in accordance with the wish it had expressed more than a year earlier, but that if unfortunate results followed the withdrawal the responsibility would rest upon the Nicaraguan Government.

It consented now to the retention of the Legation guard until September of that year at the latest on condition that Nicaragua immediately take up the organization and training of a constabulary. The Nicaraguan Congress passed a law providing for a "Guardia Nacional" of 400 men and in June Major Calvin B. Carter, formerly an officer in the Philippine constabulary, arrived to begin training the new Nicaraguan force.

Solorzano discovered early that his attempts to please all parties in reality were pleasing none. The Liberals and the Conservatives in the government were continuously at odds. The President changed his cabinet repeatedly in an effort to bring about harmony, but with little effect. His Congress also was causing Solorzano grief. Dr. Jeremiah W. Jenks of New York University, long concerned in Nicaraguan affairs as State Department member of the directorates of the Nicaraguan bank and railroad and as member of the High Commission, had come to Nicaragua with Ralph N. Elliott and after investigating Nicaragua's economic structure had proposed a plan for a thorough-going reform of the country's accounting system, for an extension of its banking machinery, and for the actual commencement, by the United

States, of work on the Nicaraguan canal as a means
of bringing money into the country. The Congress,
consistently sniping at Solorzano at every opportunity, refused to adopt the plan and the Senate demanded an investigation of the salaries and expenses
of the Jenks mission. Another flareup of ill-feeling
occurred over a proposed loan of $500,000 from the
New York bankers, which the Nicaraguan Senate refused to authorize.

The Government of Nicaragua had meanwhile
bought the National Bank from the American bankers and almost immediately after the arrival of the
new manager, Mr. Rosenthall, there were unfounded
rumors that he and the directors would resign because of the disagreement over the proposed $500,000
loan. This resulted in a run on the bank, which was
stopped by President Solorzano's announcement that
if the Americans resigned the American Collector of
Customs, Colonel Ham, would be appointed manager
of the bank. This reassured the depositors and the
run ended.

The State Department was well aware of the disturbing factors in the situation and indeed, even before Solorzano's inauguration there had been hints
that Chamorro was contemplating radical measures
to remedy his political situation. The American Government went so far even as to inform Chamorro
that it would discountenance any revolutionary
movement.

But Nicaragua was now at peace with the world,

it had not had a serious revolution for twelve years, and it was directed by a government representing both historic parties. Furthermore the country was steadily paying off its debts, and now owned both the bank and the railroad. More and more it was managing its own affairs. A considerable section of public opinion in Central America had resented the long residence of the marines in Nicaragua as constituting a standing threat of similar interference in other countries of the Isthmus. The United States determined to make the gesture that would show the people of Latin America that it cherished freedom among them.

On August 3, 1925, the withdrawal was made. With colors flying and with a band blaring, the little force marched at attention down the long main street of the capital, past the low Spanish houses of grey masonry from whose doors men, women and girls, white, brown and black, watched them with curious smiles, and boarded the train for Corinto where a transport awaited them. At the station there was a crowd to see them off. Newsreel motion picture cameras were aimed at the rear of the train, and as it pulled away with its brownclad youths cheering and waving from the windows, Martinez stepped out on the rail in front of the cameras and waved a large Nicaraguan flag to signal to the world that Nicaragua now was its own master. The constabulary filed into the barracks just vacated.

Seldom if ever has a nation, having full knowledge

of the danger, taken deliberately a step whose disastrous results were more thoroughly a mathematical certainty than the United States took in ordering this withdrawal.

Some of the Managua newspapers remarked that night that the marines had gone as friends who had come at Nicaragua's request and had never committed acts prejudicial to Nicaragua's sovereignty. Others hailed the departure as the redemption of their country.

But the United States at last had made good its professions of respect for the integrity of the Isthmian nations.

Emiliano Chamorro was probably chuckling to himself.

CHAPTER XII

CHAMPAGNE AND A REVOLUTION

PEACE reigned in Nicaragua for three weeks, four days and thirteen hours after the marines departed.

On the night of August 28, 1925, a reception was being held at the International Club in honor of Dr. Leonardo Argüello, Minister of Public Instruction. The International Club stands at the centre of the city, across a narrow street from the chief hotel and two short blocks from the National Palace. Its membership is predominantly Liberal but includes also the prominent Americans and other foreigners in the city. This was one of those gala affairs attended by the whole social group of the capital, literally and arithmetically the Four Hundred.

At the reception that night President Solorzano and Señora Solorzano were present, as were many of the members of the cabinet, and the leading figures in the Liberal party. The American Minister, Charles C. Eberhardt, attended, with others of the diplomatic corps. Irving A. Lindberg, then deputy collector general of customs, Roscoe R. Hill, High Commissioner, and in fact the entire American colony, were among the group filling the broad halls of the clubhouse. Within a great inner room an orchestra played and the younger merry makers, Nicaraguan and American, were dancing. Champagne bubbled at the tables.

In a main reception hall Dr. Argüello, Dr. Roman y Reyes, Minister of Finance, General Moncada, then a Senator, Senator Andrea Larga Espada, and Juan Ramon Aviles, editors of Liberal newspapers, and other conspicuous members of the party were seated at a long table toasting each other in champagne with the generosity which is a charming feature of Nicaraguan social affairs. Everyone of course was in evening dress. For all the smallness of the city and the shabbiness of the country of which it was the capital, the reception matched in color and gayety the functions of any North American city.

President Solorzano and his wife departed early, but the party danced on.

At its height there swaggered into the ballroom a threatening coatless figure in boots, spurs and military breeches, with a broad brimmed hat pulled well down over his face, flourishing a revolver in each hand. It was Gabry Rivas, Conservative political leader, lurching and flushed in the face. Behind him trooped a rabble of men and boys, all armed. Guests near the door who could glance out saw a dilapidated but dangerous line of straw-hatted soldiers with rifles strung along the street.

Rivas roared at the top of his voice as he strode across the ballroom that he had come as the emissary of General Alfredo Rivas, Governor of Managua, commander of La Loma, to liberate President Solorzano from the domination of the Liberal element in his government. As he advanced toward the table where by now Moncada, Roman y Reyes and the others had risen, he fired a succession of bullets into the ceiling.

Minister Eberhardt was standing in the doorway of the billiard room surveying the gathering when the riot started. At the shots and the shouts women screamed and fainted or clung to the American Minister, imploring him to save them and their husbands.

The Minister asked Rivas as he stamped by why he was terrorizing the women when he and his followers easily could carry off the men they wanted.

"Down with the Liberals," bellowed Rivas in reply.

A few fist fights started among the younger men, but the wiser ones kept quiet, fearing that opposition would provoke the excited and apparently drunken raiders to a massacre. For an hour Rivas and his group charged about in the crowded club, hunting the men he wished to arrest, overpowering those who showed signs of resisting and knocking holes in the ceiling with revolver shots for emphasis. The billiard room was the only place of refuge and men hid under all the tables.

Minister Eberhardt was told that he might leave, but he remained. Lindberg and Hill were ordered to stay in the club. Each time they attempted to leave a rifle butt stopped them. At last Rivas got his prisoners rounded up. The most important of them were Roman y Reyes, General Moncada and the editors.

Rivas himself, with his pistol pressed against Moncada's body, dragged the future President toward the door.

"You coward!" Moncada snarled at him.

As the procession of captors and captives approached the door the agitation increased among the women, some of whom were the wives of the prisoners, for they expected their husbands to be killed.

Larga Espada tore himself loose from his escort and flung himself at the feet of the American Minister. As his captors dragged him away he threw his arms around the Minister's waist, and, his head under the tails of the Minister's evening coat, begged the protection of the United States. It was this incident, probably, which caused the report that he had draped himself in the American flag to claim asylum. Probably also it was the genesis of a rumor which spread for some hours that the American Minister had been assaulted and wounded.

After the prisoners had been removed the guard at the doors relaxed and the guests were allowed to leave. Minister Eberhardt escorted many of the terrified families home. Meanwhile President Solorzano, apprised of the incident, was the centre of an alarmed group at his private residence a few blocks from the Club.

Major Carter, who had turned out his little force

of constabulary to suppress disorder in the city, gave the President an extra guard of 50 men and advised him to go to the Loma, have the troops formed up and ask them whether they would stand by their President or be traitors. Major Carter even promised to go with Solorzano and shoot Rivas if necessary.

"Oh, but he is my brother-in-law," the President protested.

The comic opera reign of terror continued through the next day while the half dozen Liberals remained prisoners at La Loma. Alfredo Rivas addressed a letter to President Solorzano demanding the dismissal of the Liberal members of the government as the price of the release of the prisoners. Solorzano and his cabinet agreed to the terms and asked Minister Eberhardt to carry word of this to Rivas. The Minister made his way to the volcanic citadel and after a half hour's conference with Rivas took back word to the anxious President that the prisoners would be freed and the Loma turned over to the President's soldiers as soon as the cabinet changes became effective. President Solorzano and his cabinet signed the agreement at 8 p. m. August 29, and Rivas carried out his part of it. According to Major Carter, Rivas received $5,000 and a house in Managua as a reward for returning the Loma. The principal Liberals were cleared out of the cabinet.

But Roman y Reyes, even free, feared for his life, for he was the one against whom the Conservatives' hatred was chiefly directed. His hysterical wife had pleaded all day for the American Minister to save him. Finally he went to the Legation and was permitted to stay that night. The Minister considered it undesirable to give him permanent asylum and he and his wife spent the next few days at the homes of friends, most of them Americans.

In all this Emiliano Chamorro, the most aggrieved opponent of the coalition government, had not appeared. Apparently he was not even in the city, but at his ranch in Chontales across the Lake of Managua. There was a strong feeling in Managua, however, that Chamorro, too clever to be openly involved in such an escapade, had nevertheless inspired it. This feeling was shared by Minister Eberhardt who said a few days after the raid: "There were many indications that Emiliano Chamorro was back of this movement, managing it cunningly in the background to avoid being charged with direct complicity in it; that he was known to be very bitter at the State Department; that there were many who professed to believe that he was actively in touch with General Rivas, from whom some persons designated by him would take over La Loma ultimately, to continue the policy of heckling the Solorzano Government, preparatory to the assumption by Chamorro of power in Nicaragua."

In the midst of the alarums General Chamorro returned to Managua. This added further to the worries of the bewildered President. First he ordered Major Carter to force Chamorro to leave, then ordered him to post a guard at Chamorro's house. Word reached the President that Chamorro was planning to capture the Loma on a certain night and he sent Carter to Chamorro's residence at 2 o'clock in the morning. The major, reaching the house alone, found a crowd of two hundred excited men waving pistols and induced the General to send them home.

Minister Eberhardt advised Solorzano to give the Loma into keeping of the constabulary, but while the President was trying to make up his mind the Conservative press started a campaign of opposition to Carter, in which the kindest thing they said about him was that he was a grandson of William Walker, the filibuster of the eighteen-fifties. The President failed to act.

For several days Solorzano and Chamorro conferred actively, but their efforts to reach an agreement ended in a quarrel and once more General Chamorro left the city. When next Chamorro appeared it was to take the Loma for himself. With what soft and delicate touch he worked; and yet how firm and determined!

Before dawn of the morning of October 25 Chamorro and a small group of his followers toiled up the steep slope of the volcanic peak to a rear entrance of the citadel, that citadel where Zelaya had had Chamorro's father strung up by the thumbs. By pre-arrangement Colonel Padillo, an officer of the fortress and a strong adherent of Chamorro, opened the gate and the Chamorro group filed silently in. The invaders took over the machine gun positions and relieved the sentries before the sleeping garrison discovered that it was anything but the regular patrol making the rounds. Idolizing Chamorro as they did, the soldiers gladly accepted the new situation.

General Chamorro had handled the regular soldiery with ease but he had some misgivings about the American-commanded Guardia Nacional. So after breakfast he telephoned to Major Carter and asked what the constabulary would do if it was ordered to attack the Loma.

"I shall take orders from the President," Major Carter assured him.

"Well, if he does order you to attack us will you please call me up and let me know?" Chamorro requested. Then he laughed his boyish, chuckling laugh and rang off.

In the course of the morning, however, troops of Chamorro fired down on the constabulary and wounded one man. Later in the day patrols from the two forces encountered each other in the market in the centre of the city and in a brisk fight two of the constabulary and nine of the regular troops were killed. These conflicts apparently were not desired by Chamorro, and he gave his promise that his troops would not attack the constabulary. Around noon, however, Conservative troops who had occupied the upper part of the city leading to the Presidential Palace and the Loma threw up barricades in the streets and indulged in much firing toward the lower part of the city which was occupied by the police and by the troops still loyal to Solorzano. Two of the police were killed in front of the President's residence in the presence of Minister Eberhardt who had been called to the President's home for a conference and risked his life to get there.

No sooner had General Chamorro made himself secure in a military way than he set about to take control of the country. It was evident that he wished to become President and on the very day of the revolt Minister Eberhardt informed him that the Legation could pursue no other course than to support the constitutional government and that the United States would not recognize any government assuming power by force.

But Chamorro was too shrewd to flout openly the Conventions of 1923 which he had signed, with their unequivocal condemnation of *coups d'état*. He was planning far ahead, planning to skirt the prohibitions of that hampering treaty and become President in legal fashion.

A few hours after he had taken the Loma Chamorro served his demands on Solorzano. His object, Chamorro told the President, was to restore the Conservative party to the power which it had enjoyed before the elections of October, 1924, elections in which, he declared, the Conservatives had been beaten by fraud. To this end the remaining Liberals must be dismissed from the cabinet. But he wished Solorzano to remain as President. Specifically he demanded:

1. That the coalition compacts be broken and repudiated;

2. That the government be made entirely Conservative;

3. That full amnesty be granted to all participants in the recent military operations;

4. That the Government pay Chamorro $10,000 for the expenses of the uprising, and that in addition it pay the troops;

5. That General Chamorro be appointed General in Chief of the army.

This last condition of course was the crux of the whole affair. With the army under his command Chamorro would rule Nicaragua. There would be none to contend against him. The marines had gone, and the Guardia Nacional was as yet too young and too small in numbers to oppose successfully the skillful, powerful and determined Chamorro.

Solorzano, helpless in his private residence—hostile soldiers and belts of barbed wire separated him from the "White House"—sought in vain for comforting advice.

He called the American Minister into consultation. Frantic conferences were held with the Liberals. Some of the Liberals were disposed to resist Chamorro's demands, but as the passing hours only emphasized the plight of the Government, they were forced to admit that there was no option but to yield.

Adolfo Diaz called on the afternoon of the capture of the Loma and through him Solorzano sent word to Chamorro that he had decided to capitulate in order to avoid the shedding of blood. The next day the President and Chamorro signed an agreement embodying all of Chamorro's demands and Chamorro withdrew his troops from the streets. He had become dictator of Nicaragua at a total cost in casualties on both sides of 20 and was even paid in cash for his trouble.

And the State Department had on its hands another "situation" in Nicaragua where only a little while before everything had been arranged so beautifully. Secretary Kellogg, who that Spring had succeeded Secretary Hughes, found that he had acquired a Latin American problem in much the same way that Woodrow Wilson and William Jennings Bryan had acquired theirs in 1913. American cruisers again hung off the Nicaraguan shore.

The Liberals, who so recently had denounced the activities of the United States in Nicaragua, were as eager now to have the marines return. Their newspapers called loudly upon the United States to intervene, and propaganda that the United States would restore their rights by force was broadcast over Nicaragua. The Liberal party adopted resolutions denouncing the violation of constitutional order, invoked the Conventions of 1923 against a government by *coup d'état* and besought the good offices of the

State Department to effect a reconciliation between the Liberal and Chamorro factions.

But Chamorro had played his cards superbly. He was guarding President Solorzano like a queen bee. He obtained Solorzano's resignation but kept it in his pocket, to be used when the time was ripe. With the constitutional President of Nicaragua still holding office, albeit holding it nominally and disconsolately as a prisoner in his own home, the State Department could only reply to the Liberals that it could not act as a go-between for a political party and any foreign government.

Chamorro set about strengthening the army, and, with the constabulary also under his orders, put down revolts that rose here and there in the country.

Vice President Sacasa, at his home outside León, received a warning by telegraph one night in November that an attempt was about to be made on his life. With two companions he fled. It is said that only a few minutes after he left the house a raiding party arrived in search of him, looted the place, and then invaded a convent where dwelt Sacasa's two daughters. The daughters were taken away and held for a time as hostages. Dr. Sacasa and his companions rode all night on horses to the Gulf of Fonseca, where they took a launch to La Union, Salvador, and thence made their way to Guatemala.

Chamorro meanwhile controlled the Congress and he strengthened that control by having it declare void, on the ground of fraud, the election of 18 of its members. He immediately filled their seats with his own supporters. This thoroughly Chamorrist Congress thereupon charged Sacasa with plotting to invade the country and summoned him to return to face trial.

As the new year came in Chamorro's plans swept on toward complete fruition. On January 13 he had himself appointed Minister of War. On that same day Congress declared the vice presidency vacant, and voted a two year order of banishment against Dr. Sacasa, who had already arrived in Washington to fight for the presidency in a healthier atmosphere than he had left in Nicaragua.

Soon afterward a Senator from Managua conveniently resigned, and Chamorro was elected to fill his seat.

Then for the next step. The Nicaraguan constitution contains the following provision in Article 106:

"In case of the absolute or temporary default of the President of the Republic, the executive power shall devolve upon the Vice President, and in default of the latter upon one of the designates in the order of their election. In the latter case, should Congress be in session, it shall be its duty to authorize the intrustment of the office to the representative whom it may designate, who must fulfill the requirements for President of the Republic."

Chamorro had himself elected First Designate by his Congress. He had now finished with Solorzano. Congress first voted the President an indefinite vaca-tion, then accepted his resignation on January 16, 1926. Then it proceeded to proclaim Emiliano Chamorro President.

With a skill worthy a corporation lawyer, Chamorro had threaded his way through the loopholes of the supposedly airtight Article II of the Conventions of 1923 designed to prevent the very thing he had just accomplished. But although he had scrupulously observed the letter of the conventions, he had certainly trampled upon their spirit and Washington would have something to say about it.

CHAPTER XIII

UNCLE SAM SAYS THUMBS DOWN

NO one, of course, knew better than Emiliano Chamorro, ex-President and ex-Minister to Washington and now occupant once more of the Presidential chair, the importance to a weak Latin American republic of recognition by the United States. Such recognition was the basis of a country's financial credit, even if it had no other value. That was why Chamorro had gone to such pains to cover his seizure of power with a veneer of legality. He expected difficulty, but he hoped that the United States, which now seemed so anxious to keep out of Nicaraguan affairs, would accept the form of constitutionality with which he had surrounded his assumption of office and prefer not to remember the violence behind it.

And of one thing he felt sure—that the United States would not try to get him out by force. He was prepared to take a chance against any other means that might be employed against him. Long afterward, when Chamorro had had to confess his defeat, it became evident that his belief that Washington could be bluffed had been a factor in his decision to make himself President.

"Why did you do it? Why did you take the Loma when the State Department had told you you could not be President?" an acquaintance asked.

"I didn't think they meant it," said Chamorro earnestly. "They had taken the marines away. What was I to think?"

Chamorro is a good poker player but in this game the State Department had the cards and had the chips and at last intended to play them.

Chamorro immediately sought American sanction for his régime, through his friend, Dr. Salvador Castrillo, whom he had sent to Washington as Minister of Nicaragua in Solorzano's time. Secretary Kellogg replied on January 22, 1926, to Chamorro's overtures with such a beautiful example of a crushing diplomatic "no" that the writer cannot refrain from reproducing the message here. It read:

"Dear Doctor Castrillo: In your communication of the 19th instant addressed to the Secretary of State you advise that, President Solorzano having resigned his office, General Emiliano Chamorro took charge of the Executive power on January 17.

"The hope expressed in your letter that the relations which have been close and cordial for so many years between Nicaragua and the United States will continue and grow stronger has been noted with pleasure. The Government and people of the United States have feelings of sincerest friendship for Nicaragua and the people of Nicaragua and the Government of the United States will of course continue to maintain the most friendly relations with the people of Nicaragua. This Government has felt privileged to be able to be of assistance in the past at their request not only to Nicaragua but to all countries of Central America, more especially during the conference on Central American affairs which resulted in the signing of a general treaty of peace and amity on February 7, 1923, between the five Republics of Central America. The object of the Central American countries with which the United States was heartily in accord, was to promote constitutional government and orderly procedure in Central America and those Governments agreed upon a joint course of action with regard to the non-recognition of governments coming into office through *coup d'état* or revolution. The United States has adopted the principles of that treaty as its policy in the future recognition of Central American Governments as it feels that by so doing it can best show its friendly disposition towards and its desire to be helpful to the Republics of Central America.

"It is therefore with regret that I have to inform you that the Government of the United States has not recognized and will not recognize as the Government of Nicaragua the régime now headed by General Chamorro, as the latter was duly advised on several occasions by the American Minister after General Chamorro had taken charge of the citadel at Managua on October 25 last. This action is, I am happy to learn, in accord with that taken by all the

Governments that signed with Nicaragua the treaty of 1923."

Chamorro then sent Dr. Cuadra Pasos to Washington to intercede for him but this persuasive advocate was unable to swerve the Department an inch.

Meanwhile Chamorro himself was exerting efforts to the same end in Managua. Again and again he appealed to Minister Eberhardt, reciting the circumstances of Solorzano's election and the technical constitutionality of his own achievement of the Presidency. It became almost pathetic. Both Eberhardt and Chamorro are early risers. Chamorro used to call at the Legation morning after morning at seven o'clock to argue his case. Always the answer was a polite but decided negative.

Throughout this struggle with the American Government Chamorro remained on the most cordial terms with the American colony and even maintained friendly personal relations with the Minister. One night, at one of those frequent informal and charming dinner parties with which the international social group of Managua amuses itself, Chamorro lifted his champagne glass to Minister Eberhardt.

"To the grand republic of North America, to the President of the United States, and to the American Minister," Chamorro toasted guilelessly.

The American Minister raised his glass in turn.

"To the beautiful Republic of Nicaragua, and to General Chamorro."

And the General had hoped that he would make a slip and say "—to President Chamorro."

While Chamorro was still fighting doggedly Minister Eberhardt returned to the United States on private business. His farewell to Chamorro was to impress upon him once more that he would not be recognized.

In Minister Eberhardt's absence there came to the Legation as chargé d'affaires a tall personable, youngish man, Lawrence Dennis, who had handled intricate problems successfully in Honduras. He was a forceful character with little liking for diplomatic involutions and a belief that a straight line was the shortest distance between two points. His task was to get Chamorro out of the presidency, and he proceeded immediately to attend to it with energy and directness.

General Chamorro had never been talked to in his life as Dennis talked to him. At first Chamorro only laughed. "But why should I quit," he would say, "when I still have the money?"

For a time Chamorro did have the money. The American Collector of Customs and the American manager of the bank carried on as if the Chamorro administration were legitimate. Payments on the foreign debt were made without interruption and Chamorro received the surplus customs revenues. Besides, he had the ordinary revenues of the country and imposed forced loans as well.

But Dennis's persistence annoyed him. He came to dislike exceedingly being told by a man so much younger than he that he must give up the Presidency. Often Mr. Dennis would call up Chamorro by telephone and remark, "Good morning, General. Now, how about that resignation of yours?" And when he heard the explosion at the other end of the wire he would remind him, "But you know you will have to eventually. Better do it now."

That very night perhaps, Chamorro and Dennis would meet at the poker table at a party in some American home and Dennis would interrupt the General's draw with a casual, "Now, General, about that resignation I was speaking of—"

Chamorro gave up all hope of an amicable arrangement and cabled to Washington charging that Mr. Dennis had made statements that "disturb the public tranquillity and tend to throw us into anarchy." The American Chargé had told him, he asserted, that he intended making a campaign to enlighten the Nicaraguan people as to the necessity of forcing him from power and threatened that if he did not retire voluntarily the United States would compel him by force to retire. This of course was without effect and hurt Chamorro with the State Department rather than helped him.

Chamorro's seizure of the Presidency had been the signal for revolutionary disturbances against him. For a time he suppressed them as fast as they broke out. Early in May, however, on the East Coast, which always has been the cradle of revolutions, a Liberal force commanded by Luis Beltran Sandoval attacked Bluefields and captured it in a fight costing several lives. The Liberals imprisoned the Governor of the province and the local commandant and then broke into the East Coast branch of the National Bank of Nicaragua and took $161,000 in bank notes. The bank, although owned by Nicaragua, is an American corporation, so Mr. Rosenthall, the manager, protested to the Legation. Some $15,000 of the confiscated notes later found their way into the coffers of the Sacasa government.

Revolutionists swarmed over the Bluff and invaded the custom house administered by W. J. Crampton, a deputy collector. They riddled the custom house and Crampton's own residence with machine gun bullets and called on Crampton to hand over the customs receipts. This money, of course, was entailed to foreign creditors. Crampton, who was a veteran of the Spanish American war and hard as nails, resolutely refused to surrender the money and got away to the mainland with it in a launch. The Liberals took over the custom house and Colonel Ham protested.

Word of the Liberal revolt at Bluefields reached Washington within a few hours of its occurrence, and the same evening the cruiser Cleveland departed from Panamá for Bluefields. On its arrival there American forces were landed and proceeded at once to disarm the rebels remaining in the town and to post a guard at the Bluff to prevent further interference with the customs.

Chamorro declared a state of war to exist, and proceeded with great energy to suppress the uprising. Scores of his political opponents were imprisoned in various parts of the country and taken to Managua for safekeeping. The army was recruited in all haste. In one evening in Managua 600 men were taken off the streets. Houses were searched and the able-bodied males were impressed. Men went to war, on one side or the other, whether or not they had any interest in the proceedings.

The accepted method of recruiting soldiers in a country such as Nicaragua is to send armed parties through the towns and round up all men of military years who do not wear coats. Favorite recruiting places are the moving pictures and the *cantinas*, the little bars scattered through the outlying parts of the town where the lower class residents gather to drink the cheap and powerful *aguardiente*.

The conscripts are tied together with rope and conducted to their respective units. It is told that one local commander, receiving such a shipment of soldiers, wired to his general-in-chief: "Have received volunteers. Do you need the rope?"

On the East Coast, then predominantly Liberal, armed recruiting parties cruised up the rivers in launches towing banana barges which they had seized, stopped wherever there were groups of plantation workers and marched them aboard.

Uniforming the troops was simple. Red hatbands were given to the Liberal soldiers; blue ones to the Conservatives. The wise soldier obtained a ribbon of the enemy color at the first opportunity to substitute for his own if he was wounded or about to be captured. This was a form of insurance against an artistically inflicted death.

At first it seemed that Chamorro would suppress the revolt. He sent a strong force eastward and reoccupied Rama, Bluefields and the Bluff and other points late in May. After the rebels fled the marines withdrew and the normal status appeared to have been restored. So optimistic was Chamorro that he released 140 political prisoners. But as it developed, this was only a lull. The fighting on the East Coast had been merely the prelude to a long and sanguinary revolution which would cost Nicaragua some 2,500 lives and pile up $16,000,000 more of claims, and which would bring the United States into the country with 7,000 armed men.

Dr. Sacasa, after his flight from Nicaragua, had gone to Washington in December and there laid his problem before the State Department. He was received as a visiting Vice President, but Washington could do nothing for him as long as Solorzano remained President, even if only in name. When Solorzano abdicated in January, 1926, Dr. Sacasa set up what he considered to be the seat of the Nicaraguan Government in the Nicaraguan Legation in Washington, but failed to obtain recognition. In

May, when the revolt rose against the Chamorro
Government, the American Government permitted
him to buy munitions in the United States and ship
them to the East Coast of Nicaragua. The State Department was willing, it is said unofficially, to recognize him if he returned to Nicaragua, but it would
not agree to guard him once he was in that country,
and Sacasa believed that it would be suicidal for him
to enter Nicaragua without American armed protection. He remained for several months in Washington and New York. When he finally departed,
disappointed at his failure to win stronger support, it
was to go to Mexico.

Meanwhile Chamorro's intense military activities
had drained the national treasury and exhausted his
sources of money. He drew on the surplus of the
National Bank until its soundness was threatened.
The directors of the bank—and it will be remembered that American bankers still had places among
the officers and on the board—refused to pay further dividends. Chamorro then endeavored to sell the
bank and the railroad outright. This failed. Dr.
Sacasa published warnings in the United States that
such a sale would be illegal, since he was the rightful
President.

Sacasa reached Mexico City in June. He was received there cordially by members of the Mexican
Government and by the Liberal members of the extensive Nicaraguan colony in that city. He remained
there several months.

In August the fighting in Nicaragua flared up anew and with increased violence, this time in the western part of Nicaragua. Immediately there were reports, supported by evidence, that the Liberals were receiving assistance from Mexico. There were repeated and apparently veracious accounts of gun-running boats landing arms and Liberal troops along the Pacific Coast. Members of Liberal forces killed in battle were found by documents on their bodies to be Mexican officers on leave, according to Major Carter. Liberal troops had cartridges marked with the initials of the Mexican national arsenal. Some of them also had rifles which evidently had originated in the United States.

Chamorro, who thought he had smashed the revolution, now found himself opposed by outside forces which he had not taken into account. Munitions for his enemies were pouring into the country. He appealed on August 28 to the League of Nations, charging in a cablegram that Mexico was attempting by means of munitions of war and troops of its regular army to overthrow the Nicaraguan Government. He also protested directly to Mexico, where the charges were vigorously denied.

Proof that munitions nevertheless came from Mexico, whether or not with official knowledge, was afforded by one of the most bizarre incidents of the revolution.

On July 28 a tugboat of American registry named the Foam cleared from New York for San Diego with a crew of fifteen men, eleven of them Americans. It had been purchased by a Sacasa agent, it was established afterward. At sea the vessel changed course, and on August 12 it put in at Puerto Mexico. There, in the dark, a number of cases were taken aboard. The next day the Foam sailed.

"Shortly afterward we took on 20 passengers," said the second mate, telling months afterward of his adventure. "Two of these turned out to be Nicaraguan generals. One was a German captain and the rest Mexican gunners. As soon as the ship was at sea they broke out the ammunition and mounted a 37-millimeter gun on the forecastle. They also took complete charge of the vessel. The officers put on cartridge belts and automatic rifles. When we passed the boundary line between Honduras and Nicaragua they ordered the crew off the deck."

"They took down the American flag and raised the Nicaraguan flag," another seaman related in an interview in The New York Times. "From then on the soldiers stood day and night watches. We also were closely guarded."

As the voyage down the Nicaraguan coast progressed two towns were taken and barges belonging to a fruit company were seized.

On August 25, as the seaman told it, 150 men, "mostly generals," came aboard the Foam and about 80 of them were landed three miles north of Bragman's Bluff (Puerto Cabezas). Then the vessel mounted machine guns, steamed up to the dock under fire from the Conservatives ashore, and bombarded the town for an hour with her 37-millimeter gun. Before the Liberals captured Puerto Cabezas, "the Conservatives marched 17 political prisoners to a small house at the outskirts of the town and then turned a machine gun on it. From the vessel we could see its riddled walls." After the Liberals went into the town "they got drunk and killed 25 of their own men." One American, the manager of the Bragman's Bluff Lumber Company, was wounded in the head by a random bullet as he stood on the porch of his house.

For three weeks thereafter the Foam cruised up and down the coast, attacking small settlements, and at length set out to shell Bluefields. The vessel ran aground. The military personnel took off the guns and ammunition and the sailors were left ashore where they subsisted on beans, rice and coffee until rescued by an American destroyer.

Battles were fought in the North of Nicaragua, near the Gulf of Fonseca, and hostilities again broke out at Bluefields. The Governor of Bluefields declared his inability to protect noncombatants. A bombardment threatened the Bluff in a few hours and anxiety was acute, but on the next day, August 26, an American cruiser arrived and sent in a strong landing force. Other American war vessels were hastening to Nicaraguan waters. Rear Admiral Julian L. Latimer, commander of the Special Service Squadron, that aggregation of slowgoing, obsolescent cruisers which patrol the waters of Central America, set out from his base at the Panama Canal for Puerto Cabezas to take personal charge.

Fighting continued in all parts of the country. Chamorro defeated the Liberals on the West Coast, but the Liberals revived their strength in the East. They retook Rama, bombarded the Bluff and made a heavy although unsuccessful attack on Deer Island, at the gateway to Bluefields Harbor. Liberals molested a British ship and were driven off by an American cruiser. Two American adventurers and one German, fighting with the Liberal army, were killed in battle. Two free-lance American aviators, in the employ of the Conservatives, flew over from Managua and bombed the Liberal positions for a wage of $500 a month.

President Coolidge, from his Summer White House, placed an embargo on the shipment of arms and munitions to either side.

In the meantime the State Department had become convinced that Sacasa had enlisted Mexican assistance and it was now doubly worried about the affair in Nicaragua. It inaugurated definite action intended to bring an end to the hostilities by means of a memorandum on August 27 rebuking General Chamorro for having "brought disaster upon his country through the usurpation of the executive power" and threatening to intervene.

"Should events in Nicaragua continue their present course, which can only result in ultimate civil war and economic chaos and imperil the lives and property of Americans and other foreigners in Nicaragua," said the memorandum, "the United States Government will be compelled to take such measures as it may deem necessary for their adequate protection."

The memorandum called upon Chamorro to withdraw and suggested as a first step that a conference of the leaders of the rival parties be held.

There was a strong desire for peace throughout the country. The revolution was disastrous commercially as well as costly in lives. The prosperity which the country had enjoyed in the past few years had been checked. Stores were closed. Shipments of needed merchandise had been held up because of the uncertainty of payment. Private property had been seized for war purposes. Such industries as banana cutting, which bring money into the country, had been seriously impeded by the impressment of the workers into one army or the other and by the fighting along the rivers and ports of the East Coast.

Dennis in Managua and Latimer at Puerto Cabezas obtained the acquiescence of Chamorro and Moncada to the conference plan, and a 30-day armistice was declared. Chamorro even announced that he was willing to yield the executive power to a provisional government if an agreement could be reached at the conference. Dr. Sacasa, who had arrived in Guatemala by now, was invited to the conference, but declined on the ground that he had been invited as a revolutionist, a status which he repudiated. He sent delegates, however.

The cruiser Denver, lying in the harbor at Corinto, was the scene of the meeting of Conservatives and Liberals. Corinto was declared a neutral zone for the duration of the conference, and marines patrolled it to assure the safety of the conferees. Mr. Dennis was present to lend his assistance as a neutral chairman, but the United States was not officially a party. Indeed Mr. Dennis had only negative instructions: to do nothing which might commit the United States to any responsibility in connection with any settlement made at the conference.

The first session was held on October 16 and immediately a deadlock developed. The Conservatives insisted on a Conservative government, with Liberals merely participating in it; the Liberals insisted that Dr. Sacasa be the head of the government. There were discussions of a coalition under an impartial chief executive, but neither side could suggest a President whom the other would accept.

It became evident that the Liberals relied on support from Mexico and therefore preferred continuing the war to entering into a compromise in which they might be tricked. In a moment of anger on the fifth day of the conference Dr. Leonardo Argüello, one of the Liberal delegates, forgot himself and, in the midst of a denial that the Liberals had any understanding with the Mexican Government, declared that "if Mexico aided us, it is because there is an interest in

Mexico in establishing a Liberal Government in Nicaragua." Afterward Dr. Argüello had access to the minutes and removed that sentence.

Mr. Dennis tried to save the conference. He held a private meeting one night with the Liberal delegation at the American consulate and, making clear to them that he was speaking only for himself and not for the State Department, explained to them that it was extremely unlikely that the United States would permit the success of any movement which had assistance from Mexico. The Liberals felt too confident just then to accept this unofficial counsel and the conference broke up on October 24 without agreeing on anything.

Chamorro knew now that it was hopeless for him to contend further and on October 30, the day on which the armistice expired, he deposited the executive power with Senator Sebastian Uriza, who had been elected designate by the Congress which Chamorro controlled. Thus Chamorro was out, but he was still trying to hold the government through his friend Uriza.

The State Department, quite understanding the situation, was no more disposed to recognize Uriza than it had been to recognize Chamorro. But something had to be done. Revolutionary activities were again breaking out. From the point of view of the American Government, there had to be a stable government in Nicaragua, and one which the State Department could recognize. The first task of Lawrence

Dennis had been to get rid of Chamorro. The second, it appeared, was to find a President to take his place.

The logical man for the State Department of course was Don Adolfo Diaz, who had coöperated with it so fully in earlier crises. He would be a good choice for Nicaragua as well in its present distraction of hatreds and jealousies, for he was the least ambitious personally and the least intransigent politically of the Conservative leaders. Mr. Dennis set about with vigor and dispatch to make him once more President. In Managua it is quite generally believed that the Chargé did so on explicit instructions from Washington. The State Department has denied this, and so has Mr. Dennis. But of Mr. Dennis's activities in bringing about the selection of Diaz there can be no question. They necessarily were known to a wide circle in Managua.

It was not easy. The very moderateness of Don Adolfo made him unacceptable to many of the embattled Conservatives. Chamorro, still the strong man of the party, wished to temporize. But no time was to be lost. The grey old Legation was as busy as a beehive with politicians coming and conferring and going. Marines were pouring into the country now, and that strengthened Dennis's hand. He evidently knew that Washington would back him up. Determined measures were required.

Dennis wrote to Cuadra Pasos and to Chamorro. He telephoned to Martin Benard, a wealthy Chamorrista, and others of the Granada Conservatives and served what amounted to an ultimatum on them. They acceded to his demands and on November 10 an extra session of Congress was called. Efforts were made on the instance of Mr. Dennis to give the Congress the appearance at least of constitutionality. The eighteen Senators and Deputies who had been expelled under the domination of Chamorro were invited to resume their seats. Only three of them came; the others, it is said in Managua, were restrained by fear. Six of the eighteen were represented by alternates who had been elected in 1924. Nine were altogether absent or unrepresented.

Events then moved with extraordinary speed and precision. Nicaraguan Congressmen are paid $15 a session, and they love to string out their legislative affairs. But this time there was no dawdling. On November 11 they designated Adolfo Diaz for the presidency by 44 votes out of a total membership present of 53. Two members voted for Solorzano and the remainder cast no ballots.

President Diaz was inaugurated on November 14, with the American Chargé attending. On November 17, the United States extended formal recognition to the new government. Soon afterward, President Diaz appointed his friend, Emiliano Chamorro, Minister to the governments of France, Great Britain, Spain and Italy—a delightful position and a tactful removal of this clever gentleman which was immensely pleasing to the American Government.

Diaz immediately set about to salvage his disrupted

country. He extended an olive branch toward the Liberals by promising a general amnesty if they would abandon the revolution, and by offering cabinet posts to members of the Liberal party. He informed the State Department of his overtures and Washington enjoyed a few days of hope that a peaceful end to the difficulties and disturbances of the past year was at hand. The American Chargé again lent his good offices in the service of harmony and transmitted to General Moncada peace offers which included a diplomatic post for the General. Moncada declined to discuss a reconciliation without the authority of Dr. Sacasa, and this brings us back to the political claims of the Liberals.

Dr. Sacasa, who had been absent from the country of which he claimed to be President throughout the year in which his adherents were fighting to displace a usurper, returned at this moment to Nicaragua. He had tarried in the United States, then in Mexico, then in Guatemala. Among the Liberals it is said that the American Government, when it learned of Sacasa's dealings in Mexico, brought pressure to bear on the Government of Guatemala to prevent Sacasa leaving the country. The writer has had no means of establishing the accuracy of this assertion and can only state it for what it is worth in justice to Dr. Sacasa.

At any rate Sacasa and the adherents who were with him departed from Guatemala on a schooner and reached Puerto Cabezas on December 1, after

Diaz had been installed as President and recognized by the United States. On the same day he was inaugurated by his supporters there as "Constitutional President of Nicaragua." He organized a cabinet in which General Moncada was Minister of War and announced that he would undertake military action against the Diaz Government.

CHAPTER XIV

THE BOGEY OF BOLSHEVISM

SO at the waning of the calamitous year of 1926 Nicaragua had two Presidents and each of them could prove title to the office.

Adolfo Diaz had come to the presidency through the constitutional means of being designated by Congress in the absence of a President and Vice President. Dr. Sacasa had assumed the presidency as the constitutional successor of a President who had resigned in the midst of his term. Sacasa, it was true, had been adjudged in default by Chamorro's Congress when he left the country, but that departure was under duress; he fled to save his life.

Dr. Sacasa was justified in feeling that his life was in danger if he returned to Nicaragua. But personal peril is as normal a penalty for political prominence in Nicaragua as mass handshaking is in North America. Even the conciliatory Diaz has had to face the danger of assassins. Five weeks after he had taken office for the last time he was attacked late one night in his automobile by men with *machetes* who killed his driver and wounded Diaz himself on the foot. It is impossible to believe that such indomitable men as Chamorro and Moncada, for instance, if they had been in Sacasa's shoes, would have let that critical year go by without finding some way to get into Nicaragua.

If Dr. Sacasa had arrived in his country and proclaimed himself President before the United States committed itself to Diaz, the State Department would have been put to it to find adequate reason for not recognizing him. But now that the United States had at last settled upon a President with whom it could deal, Sacasa was indeed an optimist to believe that it could be brought to reverse itself. He might be right, but he could not now be President.

In that year during which both the State Department and Dr. Sacasa had hopefully dallied another element had come into the situation and had come to be, for the American Government, the dominant element. The State Department, with micawberish optimism, had permitted the Nicaraguan affair to drift into a test of prestige between the United States and Mexico at a time when their relations already were uncomfortably strained by a controversy over Mexico's oil and land laws.

Sacasa normally was sympathetic with the United States and with its basic aims in Nicaragua. His years of residence in the United States were pleasant memories to him. But he had known that he must have help from outside his country if he was to defeat the Conservatives. He took it where he could get it, in Mexico. So it was that Mexico alone recognized Sacasa when he set up his government at Puerto

Cabezas, and it recognized him almost as promptly as the United States had recognized Adolfo Diaz. Honduras and Salvador had followed the lead of the United States in the matter of recognition. Costa Rica and Guatemala refrained from recognizing either one.

The first act of President Diaz, taken the day after he was inaugurated and two days before his government was recognized by the United States, was to address a communication to the American Legation which was the occasion of fanning the ill-feeling between Mexico and the United States perilously near to a war, increasing the alarm in other Latin countries at American intentions and inspiring unfavorable comments on American policy throughout the world. In this communication he complained that the Mexican Government was actively intervening against his government and called on the United States to protect it. It read:

"Upon assuming the Presidency I found the Republic in a very difficult situation because of the attitude, assumed without motive by the Government of Mexico in open hostility to Nicaragua. It must be clear to you that, given the forces which that Government disposes of, its elements of attack are irresistible for this feeble and small Nation. This condition places in imminent risk the sovereignty and independence of Nicaragua, and consequently, the continental equilibrium on which the Pan Americanism is founded which the United States has fostered with such lofty spirit.

"Naturally the emergency resulting from these conditions places in peril the interests of American citizens and other foreigners residing in our territory and renders it impossible for a Government so rudely attacked to protect them as is its duty and as it desires.

"For these reasons and appreciating the friendly disposition of the United States toward weak Republics and the intentions which your Government has always manifested for the protection of the sovereignty and independence of all the countries of America by morally supporting legitimate Governments in order to enable them to afford a tranquil field of labor for foreigners which is needed for the stimulation of the growth of the prosperity of these countries, I address myself to you in order that, with the same good will with which you have aided in Nicaraguan reconciliation, you may solicit for my Government and in my name the support of the Department of State in order to reach a solution in the present crisis and avoid further hostilities and invasions on the part of the Government of Mexico.

"I desire to manifest to you at the same time that whatever may be the means chosen by the Department of State, they will meet with my absolute confidence in the high spirit of justice of the Government of the United States."

The United States declined to step in and informed Diaz on December 8 that the fact that the American government had recognized him did not imply that the United States had assumed any obligation to protect his government by physical means but that "the United States Government was prepared to lend him such moral encouragement and support as are ordinarily due constitutional governments with which the United States maintains friendly relations, when those governments are threatened by revolutionary movements." Further than this the United States was not willing to go.

President Diaz felt that the United States was letting him down. He expressed his growing anxiety together with some interesting implications of a pre-election understanding with the United States in an interview with the Associated Press in which he said that he had accepted the Presidency "expecting that the United States would aid Nicaragua to restore order and secure peace."

"I am confronted with the question," he continued, "if the aid which I expected is not received, whether it will not be better in order to save lives and the industries of Nicaragua to deal with President Calles direct now. I cannot believe, however, that the United States Government will stand aloof and allow Mexico to overthrow a Nicaraguan government recognized by the United States and recognized under the conditions which existed.

"The Nicaraguan government can quite easily

dominate any revolution by Nicaraguan Liberals alone, but a Nicaraguan Government supported by 90 percent of the people could not permanently withstand a revolution made by ten percent, aided by arms, money and supplies and military personnel furnished by the Mexican Government."

But the American administration, even if it could not see its way clear to give Diaz the assistance he asked and to which he evidently believed he was entitled, nevertheless treated the situation in a way to bring down on its head the distrust, opprobrium and sarcasm of many in Latin America and Europe, and even in the United States, and almost to get the country into war. Soon after receiving the Diaz appeal of November 15, the State Department made its substance public and enlarged upon it to raise what the Associated Press called "the spectre of a Mexican-fostered Bolshevistic hegemony intervening between the United States and the Panama Canal."

That old fear of interference in the canal region which had turned the eyes of the United States to Nicaragua so many years before was active again. To quote further the Washington dispatch telling of the alarm in the State Department:

"While there is no sign as yet that radical theories similar to those of the Russian soviet régime have taken any deep hold anywhere in Central America, the Washington Government cannot fail to be deeply concerned as to the purpose of Mexican interference, because of the geographic position of these countries,

intervening as they do between the United States and
the Panama Canal."

Protest rose from all Latin America on the morrow
of the tactless accusation. Indignation meetings were
held in widely separated capitals.

Europe, so used to having a reproving American
finger shaken in its face for its international sins,
interpreted the incident as pleasantly illuminating
the international morality of Pennsylvania Avenue.
Europe, as reflected in the comments of its editors,
conceived that the United States was now making
war on Nicaragua if not on all Latin America. It could
quite understand the United States being imperialistic,
but it could not understand the United States being
so and pretending that it was not. To Europe it was
a very neat exhibition of plain, old-fashioned hypocrisy. Among the unruffled realists of Downing Street,
the Wilhelmstrasse and the Quai d'Orsay there were
chuckles at the embarrassing predicament into which
the United States had floundered.

A few commentators, more acute than the ordinary, saw America reluctantly being "drawn by the
magnet of political and economic interests into the
disputes of Central America."

"The United States is finding out, as we found out
long ago, how slippery is the slope of imperialism—
a slope where the best intentions prove of no avail
and where force of circumstances is always in charge,"
the Spectator of London remarked. Building the Panama Canal, this interpretation continued, was as se-

rious a step in imperialism as was the treaty made by the East India Company with the local Rajah in Bengal. Now to make good the position into which America had gradually slipped, the whole of Central America was to come within the sphere of influence of the United States.

The Mexican Government at first declined to treat seriously the charges of the Nicaraguan President and the American Secretary of State.

"This is pure professional jealousy on the part of the United States," remarked General Obregon when he first heard of them. "She has been accustomed to foment uprisings and revolutions in the countries of Central and South America and naturally she does not wish to see this profitable trade slipping away from her."

After some days, however, President Calles was goaded to make public a reply in which he characterized "the propaganda about Mexican Bolshevism" as "a new lie to discredit Mexico."

"What sound mind could shelter the idea that Mexico, a country in process of organization, without an army for conquest, without even a shadow of a navy, would plan to threaten the defenses of the Panama Canal or the defenses of other countries?" the Mexican President asked.

For weeks the recriminations flashed back and forth, whipping ill-feeling to a dangerous point.

There was a tremendous outburst of anti-American feeling in the Mexican Chamber of Deputies when the oil laws, opposed by the United States, went into effect at midnight of January 1. Excited speakers boasted of the brave blood of the ancient Indians and the Spanish conquerers and talked boldly of war with the Colossus of the North.

"This country must protest with all energy against the excesses of dollar diplomacy," thundered Soto y Gama, the agrarian leader. "What the United States has done in Nicaragua is not an act of the sovereignty of North America against a weaker country, but is the action of a group of capitalists, of oil men, magnates of the dollar, as lending strength to a tyrant and traitor to his country in order to sustain himself in power with the help of foreign soldiers who are killing his brothers. I do not believe there will be war between Mexico and the United States, but I should like to know what the United States is seeking—another Maine?"

The Diaz Government meanwhile kept returning to the attack. On December 11 President Diaz issued a long manifesto coupling the charges that Mexico was intervening on the side of the revolution with a new overture of peace toward the Liberals.

He followed this soon with a long statement "To the American and Foreign Public," asserting that millions had been expended by the Calles government to overturn his own régime.

"Nicaragua does not want to be a European colony, nor does it want to be a satellite of Mexico," he said. "From the fate of Mexican domination it sees its only salvation in the protecting hand of its great North American brother. . . . All the nations of Central America are at this moment trembling in the presence of the military aggressions of the irresponsible and immoral Government of Mexico directed against Nicaragua and menacing all of Central America."

Late in the quarrel Dr. Sacasa took a hand by denying that the Liberals had a compact with Mexico or had received military aid from the Mexican government, in a statement at Puerto Cabezas. Nicaragua needed "a friendly and just alliance with and the cooperation of the United States," he said, but could not agree to a tutelage which injured her dignity and sovereignty.

"I am in perfect accord that the United States offers Nicaragua and the other Latin American nations greater commercial advantages than Mexico or any other nation," said the claimant to the Presidency.

"What awakens fear are the proceedings employed for quite a number of years against Nicaragua and the other small republics of Central America," he told the press. "It is not an American national policy beneficial to Americans as a whole but rather a policy for the exclusive benefit of a certain group of bankers.

"We wish a frank and dignified understanding between Nicaragua and the United States—an understanding between the greater commercial and financial interests of two sovereign entities.

"We do not wish offenses which, under the pretext of defending American capital, are committed against our country, flagrantly disregarding our weakness, rights and decorum.

"The financial policy—let's call it 'the dollar policy' —which has been perfectly defined in the recent political technique of the United States, has occasioned for the United States more harm than her greater competitors ever could. The United States has unnecessarily made herself feared instead of being a protective promise."

To Linton Wells, staff correspondent of The New York Herald Tribune, he made a statement at about the same time concerning the financing of the revolution. At the end of January it had cost the Liberal government more than a half million dollars. Of this money, Dr. Sacasa said, $15,000 was from the funds of the National Bank taken in the raid on Bluefields; $100,000 was given by cabinet members from their personal funds and $300,000 was from the issuance of bonds—*bonas del patriotísmo Centro Americano* —subscribed by supporters of the Liberals in the United States, Mexico and Central and South America. At that moment, Sacasa reported, the funds of the Liberal government had dwindled to $10,000 but more money was pouring in in response to appeals.

But strong as was the feeling in other countries aroused by the hints of the State Department of Bolshevist Mexican machinations against the United States in the canal region, it was no more significant than the reaction of a large body of public opinion in the United States. If the State Department intended, as a considerable portion of public opinion believed, to influence the American public against Mexico at the height of the quarrel over the oil and land laws, it failed most spectacularly. The public certainly was stirred but it was stirred against the State Department. A cry arose, from many conservative newspapers as well as from the liberal ones, for light on what the administration was about in Latin America. The disquietude in the American mind was increased as marines once more landed in force in Nicaragua and were employed in such fashion as to handicap the military activities of the Sacasa government.

Congress, which has resounded so many times to attack on the policy in Nicaragua, took up the new crisis with almost as much feeling as had the Mexican Congress.

Senator Burton K. Wheeler of Montana, a Democrat, launched the attack on January 3 with the introduction of a resolution alleging that the United States was supporting by force of arms a usurper in the Presidency of Nicaragua and declaring it the sense of the Senate that American marines should be withdrawn from Nicaraguan soil and American warships recalled from Nicaraguan ports. Before the week was out six more American war vessels and 600 more marines were dispatched to Nicaragua and the embargo on arms to the forces of Diaz was lifted.

On January 4 President Coolidge, through the mouth of the "White House Spokesman," eliminated any pretense that the American interests being pro-

tected by marines in Nicaragua were merely the ordinary ones of lives and property by disclosing that a
determining factor in the present American policy
was the protection of American rights to build a canal
across Nicaragua and to establish a naval base in the
Gulf of Fonseca, acquired under the Bryan-Chamorro
treaty of 1916. Thus the American Government conceived that its national interests were menaced by
what it professed to believe was an effort of the labor
government of President Calles to set up a Bolshevist
control in Nicaragua and thus drive a wedge between
the United States and the Panama Canal.

The hand of the administration was somewhat
strengthened a day later by news that the British and
Italian diplomatic officers at Managua had appealed
to the American Legation for protection to their nationals, whom they considered to be in imminent peril,
an action which naturally brought the Monroe Doctrine into the discussion. Unofficially, the public was
given to understand that American bluejackets and
marines would protect European as well as American
lives and property.

"The importance attached to this announcement,"
wrote Richard V. Oulahan, chief of the Washington
Bureau of The New York Times, in interpreting the
day's developments, "lies in one construction placed
upon it, that the British and Italian governments recognize that the United States has a special sphere of
influence in Nicaragua under the Monroe Doctrine,
which invests this Government with the responsibility

of protecting foreign as well as American interests. It is the understanding that the Government will claim that its course in sending bluejackets and marines to Nicaragua was the result of the appeal of foreign diplomatic representatives for protection."

President Coolidge presently summoned Democratic Senate leaders to the White House for a conference in which he outlined the Nicaraguan situation from the viewpoint of the American government and asked the support of the Democrats in the administration's efforts to deal with the crisis. The Democrats moderated their attacks. Nevertheless the excitement in Congress continued. On the following day, January 7, Senator William E. Borah, liberal Republican and Chairman of the Foreign Relations Committee, had a long talk with the President in which every phase of the dispute was covered. He left the White House still frankly hostile to the administration's course.

"I am opposed to our taking part in the controversies in Nicaragua or the Central American countries," Senator Borah said in a public statement issued after he had returned to his office. "But if we are going to take part, then we ought to take part on the side of the constitutional authorities. If there is anybody in Nicaragua who is constitutionally entitled to be President of Nicaragua, it is Sacasa."

The Senator's statement reviewed the elections of 1924, the Chamorro *coup d'état*, the flight of Sacasa and the election of Diaz by Congress and concluded: "Diaz is president in violation of every provision of the Constitution and in violation of the five-power treaty in Central America and is held there by sheer force of foreign arms."

Unexpectedly and dramatically President Coolidge stepped from behind the screen of the White House spokesman on January 10 and related in a message to Congress the steps taken by the United States in Nicaragua since 1912, upholding the legality of President Diaz's election, defending his own policy, accusing Mexican officials of conniving at gun-running expeditions to Nicaragua and hinting that that country was seeking to jeopardize American interests in the canal region.

"I have the most conclusive evidence," said the President, "that arms and munitions in large quantities have been on several occasions since August, 1926, shipped to the revolutionists in Nicaragua. Boats carrying these munitions have been fitted out in Mexican ports, and some of the munitions bear evidence of having belonged to the Mexican Government. It also appears that the ships were fitted out with the full knowledge of and, in some cases, with the encouragement of Mexican officials and were in one instance, at least, commanded by a Mexican naval reserve officer.

". . . The proprietary rights of the United States in the Nicaraguan canal route, with the necessary implications growing out of it affecting the Panama Canal, together with the obligations flowing from the investments of all classes of our citizens in Nicaragua, place us in a position of peculiar responsibility. I am sure it is not the desire of the United States to intervene in the internal affairs of Nicaragua or of any other Central American Republic. Nevertheless it must be said that we have a very definite and special interest in the maintenance of order and good government in Nicaragua at the present time, and that the stability, prosperity and independence of all Central American countries can never be a matter of indifference to us. The United States cannot, therefore, fail to view with deep concern any serious threat to stability and constitutional government in Nicaragua tending toward anarchy and jeopardizing American interests, especially if such state of affairs is contributed to or brought about by outside influences or by any foreign power. It has always been and remains the policy of the United States in such circumstances to take the steps that may be necessary for the preservation and protection of the lives, the property and the interests of its citizens and of this Government itself."

Mexico immediately issued a denial of the Coolidge charges and intimations in a statement broadcast from Mexico City by Foreign Minister Aaron Saenz.

" . . . it is evident," he said, "that Mexico has no interests whatever in Nicaragua nor political views of any kind, nor any aims of territorial expansion, nor any Mexican properties or commercial interests to protect. Therefore Mexico in this regard has nothing to do in that country and naturally she only entertains spiritual feelings akin to all the countries of the same culture."

Two days after the unexpected message of President Coolidge, Secretary of State Kellogg appeared by invitation before the Senate Foreign Relations Committee and submitted to questioning concerning the validity of the claims of Diaz and of Sacasa to the Presidency, and of other phases of the dispute. The Secretary also submitted a lengthy memorandum intended to support the assertion that Bolshevists were moving through the medium of Mexico to attack American interests in the Caribbean.

In this memorandum the Secretary quoted various communistic declarations to the effect that American imperialism must be broken down, an example of which was the following paragraph from a resolution of the Third Congress of the Red International of Trade Unions in July 1924:

"To unite the national struggle against American imperialism in individual countries in a movement on a scale of the whole American continent, embracing the workers of all countries of Latin America and the revolutionary forces of the United States. Mexico is a natural connecting link between the movement of the United States of North America and Latin America; therefore, Mexico must be the centre of union."

Secretary Kellogg's memorandum also related in

some detail the activities of the All-American Anti-Imperialist League created by American communists, according to the Secretary, "to carry out the instructions of Moscow in the matter of organizing Latin America against the United States." Quotations from a report of the Anti-Imperialist work told of the League's sending agents into Mexico and other Latin American states.

Kellogg's action in making public these data was commended as helping dissipate the fog which had enveloped the motives of the State Department but it certainly failed to confirm the Department's veiled charges of "a Mexican-fostered Bolshevistic hegemony" threatening the canal region. Indeed it went much further toward proving that Mexico had been the field of operations of agitators from the United States.

The reasoned view of the whole muddle held by thoughtful persons in Latin America was well reflected by an editorial in La Nacion of Buenos Aires: "Evidently the President of the United States has not been able to carry conviction with his message, neither to the Federal Congress nor to the world, about the necessity of having adopted such extreme measures which in themselves constitute an injurious attitude toward the ideals and sentiments of international justice professed by all civilized countries. No acts against Americans justified military intervention without first exhausting all diplomatic measures and resources which the United States would have applied in the case of any other nation not so weak as Nicaragua.

"President Coolidge, in the matter of protecting the rights of his country before a weak Central American nation, practically establishes a doctrine of acting in an unwarranted manner on mere disquieting or vague threats of injury to his country's potential rights. It is difficult to suppose that such a doctrine, which all international opinion condemns, could secure the approval of American citizens and their representatives in Congress, whose rousing protests have been raised with impressive authority to safeguard the prestige of the United States before the world and before history."

In the United States the State Department's earlier hysteria was quite widely set down to a bad case of nerves and little more was heard of the Bolshevist phase of the matter.

Discussions settled down to a common sense basis. Senator Borah, in an extensive speech in the Senate on January 13, pleaded for the right of Nicaragua to manage its own affairs and suggested as a solution of the present confused issues that the United States ask President Diaz to call an election at which the Nicaraguans could choose their President.

"I understand perfectly, of course," said the Senator, "not only the right but the duty of the United States, or of any other power, to protect the lives of its citizens or their property at whatever place they may find themselves or their property may be located. . . . It is only when that doctrine is used for the purpose of establishing a policy which reaches far beyond the mere protection of their rights or their property, and which interferes with the sovereignty of a people or which results in carrying on war against a people, that I find myself in discord with some of those who assume to apply these policies."

President Coolidge found an opportunity to disavow imperialistic motives and to promise that the marines would be withdrawn as soon as possible at the presentation of credentials by Alejandro Cesar, new Minister of Nicaragua, on January 20.

"Although American forces have, with the consent and at the request of your Government, been landed in order to safeguard the legitimate interests of the United States and the lives and property of its citizens," President Coolidge told the Minister, "this state of affairs should not continue longer than is necessary. The United States . . . has no selfish ends or imperialistic designs to serve. Least of all have we any desire to influence or dictate in any way the internal affairs of your country."

Subsequently Senator Borah proposed that his committee visit Mexico and Central America to see for themselves the conditions there, but this project was rejected by his colleagues of the committee. The current Congressional crisis over Nicaraguan relations was past and President Coolidge and Secretary Kellogg, chastened perhaps, proceeded on their course.

There was no shadow of doubt that Mexico had been the centre of gun-running into Nicaragua. It is probable, as Diaz and Coolidge and Kellogg maintained, that Mexican officials looked leniently on the shipment of munitions to Sacasa and in some instances participated in it. Mexico's sympathies inevitably would be and will be with the faction opposed to the United States in any important and clear cut controversy because of the natural ties of common origin, common culture and common language. Mexico wished Sacasa to win, and had Sacasa established himself as President of Nicaragua over the executive whom the United States had chosen to champion and assist, there would have resulted a weakening of North American influence in the canal region, and a consolidation of Latin influence which might have embarrassed the United States in the Caribbean.

It must be conceded that the blazoning of the charges against Mexico—particularly the charges that Mexico was acting as an ally of Russia against America's interests—served a useful purpose. It evoked enormous public concern about the relations of the United States with Mexico and doubtless played an important part in swerving those relations from a path which seemed to be leading toward conflict.

CHAPTER XV

NEUTRAL ZONES AND INTERVENTION

WHILE the storm was beating about the Latin American policy in the United States, American naval forces in swiftly increasing numbers were pouring into Nicaragua. They operated at first with scrupulous neutrality as between the warring factions, but little by little they found themselves pushed by the shifting circumstances into the position of allies of the Diaz Government, ready at the last to take the field openly against the Liberals to force a peace which would leave Diaz in the Presidency.

In a way the marines and bluejackets of this new intervention were reënacting the drama of 1909–1910 when the United States had played such a conclusive part in the revolution of Adolfo Diaz and his partisans against José Santos Zelaya. The events opened in 1926 in the same setting—the palm-fringed harbors, the broad lagoons and the trade-laden rivers of the East Coast.

The American forces operating in Nicaragua and in the waters bordering it were under the command of Admiral Latimer, a jaunty and impeccable officer with a gift for being liked and an ability to hide profound thoughts behind his good-natured countenance which had won him the title "Rosie Poker Face" among his friends of the service. He already wore laurels as a sea-going diplomat and the State Department trusted in his ability to handle as well as could be handled the baffling complexities in Nicaragua. He fulfilled this confidence by interspersing his military duties with tactful essays toward compromising the quarrel between the Conservatives and the Liberals; it was no fault of the Admiral that these efforts were not successful.

The procedure of a naval force called to referee a revolution in a subordinate country is as much a matter of routine as a sailor's washday. First a cruiser or two arrives off a port in consequence of actual or suppositious danger to foreigners or their property. Then a landing force is sent ashore to suppress or prevent disorder, to provide a guard for the foreigners and their property, and if there is prospect of fighting between the native factions to forbid them holding their battle where they might endanger foreigners and foreign interests. Such procedure is of course a flagrant violation in actuality of the sovereignty of the country which is indulging in the revolution, but it is a normal, accepted practice of all strong countries having nationals in weak countries and is the only method yet devised for affording the protection in a concrete crisis which all sovereign states concede is their duty to their citizens.

Admiral Latimer's marines and bluejackets had

begun to carry out this ritual on the East Coast during the struggle of Chamorro and the Liberals, months before Diaz became President. The first landing was at Bluefields where a neutral zone covering 9,000 square miles was established. Fighting was prohibited in this extensive area by mutual agreement between the two field commanders of the opposing Nicaraguan forces. Next, marines were disembarked at the Rio Grande Bar, one of the principal outlets of the Cuyamel Fruit Company, a big American banana concern, and of American lumber companies having mahogany concessions in the interior. These were followed on December 23, after the election and recognition of Diaz, by the landing of marines and sailors from the cruisers Denver and Cleveland and the declaration of a neutral zone at Puerto Cabezas where Sacasa had established his government on December 1. Similar steps were taken at other points along the Mosquito Coast until there were in all six neutral zones in that part of the country alone.

The motive officially stated for the establishment of these neutral zones was "for the protection of American lives and property." Appeals for protection in view of the disturbances or fear of disturbances had poured into the State Department from dozens of Americans on the East Coast ever since the Liberals had begun their efforts to unhorse Chamorro, and they grew more insistent as the revolution against President Diaz took serious form. Mahogany firms reported interference with their work of getting out logs; fruit companies feared that their boats and barges would be commandeered, fears which sometimes were borne out by actual seizures. The La Luz y Los Angeles company wrote that its gold mine was threatened and that forced levies of merchandise had been made on its stores. The Standard Fruit and Steamship Company complained of disturbances in its Bragman's Bluff division at Puerto Cabezas, where the company had an $8,000,000 investment. From Bluefields came a score of appeals from the various American interests centred there.

Bluefields has many foreign residents, most of them American, and is the headquarters of several large foreign companies operating on the East Coast. Puerto Cabezas is even more American than Bluefields. It is an industrial village of some 1,200 population, situated on a broad, flat plain overlooking the Caribbean. It looks and is precisely like a lumber mill village in some southern state in North America. It is operated like a tiny principality by the Standard Fruit Company and its subsidiary, the Bragman's Bluff Lumber Company, which possess vast banana and lumber lands in the interior, tapped by a small privately owned railroad. Logs from the interior are manufactured into lumber at a large sawmill at the edge of the village.

This American company owns the town and everything in it. The inhabitants, American families from American villages, live in quantity production wooden houses rented from the company, buy their clothing and groceries from the company's store, and find their relaxations in a club built by the company. One would never dream that he was in the tropics but for a few mangy mango trees, and the warning to watch out for sharks and baracudas if he bathes in the inviting sea.

From the margin of the American settlement the native town of Bilway, 100 feet wide and two miles long, stretches parallel with the seashore. It is a filthy street of Chinese and German stores interspersed with half-breed bars and brothels. The population is largely *"mestizo,"* a mongrel of Mosquito Indian and Jamaican negro, and the languages range from bad Spanish and degenerate Mosquito to Oxford English.

When there have been disturbances on the East Coast the Americans of Puerto Cabezas have had cause to be alarmed, for their town is so situated as to be peculiarly defenseless and open to fire from all sides. It was at the edge of this town, in a large frame house, that Doctor Sacasa and his advisers set up their government.

The Liberal government and its troops were ordered to disarm, or abandon the zone within 24 hours, immediately on the arrival of the American forces. There was indignation among the Liberals. Dr. Sacasa sent a protest by radio asserting that his small Presidential guard and his private residence had been surrounded "with bellicose display" and cited the following memorandum to him signed by Lieutenant Commander Spencer S. Lewis, commanding the landing forces.

"Confirming my conversation of this afternoon, the following territory is hereby declared a neutral zone: Puerto Cabezas and Bilway, including the outskirts, for a distance of two miles. There will be no carrying of arms, ammunition, knives, etc., in the neutral zone. There must be no recruiting or any other activities carried on in the neutral zone which have any bearing on the prosecution of hostilities. Dr. Sacasa and his forces may leave the neutral zone by 4 p. m. the 24th of December 1926, by water, with their arms if they so desire. Otherwise they must disarm and deliver such arms to the Cleveland's landing force commander. The radio station may send only plain messages and these messages must have no bearing on the prosecution of hostilities."

Sacasa chose to disarm and retain his capital. Said he in his protest:

"The consequence of the occupation was the disarming of my guard and the detention of part of my war elements, which were detained even before the expiration of the time limit given in the notification. All my movements are impeded and even those of my boats. I am prohibited and relegated to indefinite inaction. Foreign capital is not and never has been in danger. Hence I must understand that the declaration of a neutral zone for the protection of foreign interests is only an apparent reason, but that the real motive is for protecting the de facto government of Adolfo Diaz."

His assertion that Admiral Latimer had established a censorship (it included supervision of dispatches of American correspondents to their newspapers) was denied by the State Department on December 30, only to be confirmed a day later with the additional information that the censorship had been removed.

Friction was inevitable with American marines and bluejackets taking charge of every outlet and every important settlement in the area in which the Liberal army was operating.

There was trouble over taxes. The Sacasa government sought to collect revenues in the territory which it controlled, just as the Conservative revolutionists had done in 1910 with the support of the American forces. Accordingly it imposed an export tax on mahogany logs coming out at the mouth of the Rio Grande. These logs were owned chiefly by American companies, which of course protested that they already were taxed by the Diaz government. The United States upheld the mahogany men and decreed that no taxes should be paid to Sacasa.

There was trouble when an American detachment dumped rifles and machine guns and 2,000,000 rounds of ammunition on their way from Mexico to the Liberal army into the Rio Grande. Various denials, partial denials and explanations of this action were given in Washington and at length the State Department admitted that some of the ammunition had been "lost."

The landings along the Coast frequently imposed handicaps on the Liberal forces in the field, an imposition which the Liberal government considered deliberate notwithstanding that a legitimate reason of protecting foreign lives and property could be given for every zone established.

In the closing days of December one of the big battles of the revolution was fought at Pearl Lagoon, a few miles south of the mouth of the Rio Grande. The Conservative army was badly beaten. Hundreds were killed in four days of fighting. The wounded were gathered up by American naval forces and many were transported to Bluefields on fruit barges. The disorganized remnants of the Diaz force fell back into Bluefields, freed by the neutral zone regulation of the danger of pursuit, and took refuge there. A week after the battle Pearl Lagoon was made a neutral zone. It was said on the spot that the Conservative soldiers found the neutral zones welcome asylums when weary, for they could hide their weapons in the brush, come in to such a hospitable area as Rama and rest, then return to the fighting.

The establishment of the zone around Puerto Cabezas was of theoretical advantage to Sacasa in that it made his capital secure from attack by Conservatives throughout the revolution, but it was hardly more than theoretical, for Moncada had so thoroughly defeated the Conservatives in that region that there was little possibility of Sacasa being attacked in his own capital.

Admiral Latimer devoted much of his energy to an endeavor to bring about peace. He enjoyed the confidence of Moncada and found Sacasa willing to abandon any personal ambitions for the sake of an honorable compromise. Minister Eberhardt, at Managua, similarly was endeavoring to guide events toward a settlement, but he naturally was bound by the policy of the State Department which was committed to President Diaz's administration.

President Diaz proposed specific terms of peace on January 15. The terms included an agreement to hold free elections, to be supervised by Americans, in 1928; the establishment of a mixed claims commission of equal Conservative, Liberal and American representation to pass on damage claims growing out of the revolution, and the purchase of the arms of the Liberals by the Nicaraguan Government. But the fundamental condition was that Diaz should retain the Presidency until the end of the term, December 31, 1928. He was willing that Liberals should participate in the government during this period.

In making this overture President Diaz asserted that American coöperation was "in many ways the keystone of the structure of Nicaraguan welfare and prosperity," and once more paid his respects to Mexico with the remark that "the decision of the American Government to check Mexican intervention . . . will spare Nicaragua the horrors of Bolshevism, lawlessness, religious persecution and general retrogression." The Liberals, he said, "being cut off from their Mexican military allies, are without means of carrying on their movements to ultimate success." Furthermore he proposed, when peace was attained, to obtain a large loan in the United States for the construction of a railroad to the Atlantic Coast.

Word came from Sacasa that he was willing to relinquish his claims to the Presidency, but he also wished Diaz to step out, the Presidency to be filled in the meantime by a third man chosen at a special election.

The proposal of each party was quite inacceptable to the other. Nor would the Diaz government listen to mediatory appeals made by Costa Rica and Guatemala. The good offices of Costa Rica were rejected because, as Diaz said, Costa Rica had refused through fear of Mexico to recognize his government. The efforts of Guatemala were politely suppressed in a note intimating that the revolution was a private fight.

These peace manœuvres had taken place while the Liberals were immobilized on the East Coast. Now suddenly the Liberals by vigorous military activity produced a situation which presently would force the United States to abandon even the pretense of neutrality between the opposing military forces and to impose peace through the threat of throwing the marines into the field against the Liberals.

Moncada, blocked at every point on the East Coast

⤜ General José Maria Moncada ⤛
President of Nicaragua

by the neutral zones, had turned his attention to the western part of the country and was leading his ragged army, recruiting it as he marched from any band which would join, across the jungles, mountains, rivers and sun-baked plains toward the heart of the Conservative strength. His army was virtually without supplies, because American naval detachments held most of the points through which supplies could come to the East Coast. It lived off the country, on beans and rice and fresh-killed cattle. It grew to a strength of 3,000 men. Women, some of them carrying rifles, trudged along with their husbands. Half grown boys marched beside their grandfathers.

But before the threat of Moncada had developed seriously, another Liberal army in the northwestern part of Nicaragua began heavy operations. Early on a Sunday morning this army, under General Parajon, attacked and seized the city of Chinandega, an important commercial centre of 11,000 population on the railroad only ten miles from the port of Corinto. Heavy Conservative forces were in the vicinity and for several days the armies battled back and forth in and around the city. Twelve blocks in the centre of the city caught fire and were destroyed. Hundreds of men on both sides were killed and the right of way of the railroad was black with the flopping, squawking vultures which grow fat on Central American fields of honor.

In the midst of the first day's fighting two American free lance aviators, Lee Mason and William S.

Brooks, who were employed by the Diaz Government as Nicaragua's aviation corps, flew over the town and hurried back to Managua with word of its capture.

News of the Liberals' blow caused great alarm in Managua, for it cut the country's main artery of communication and isolated the capital. There was another spasm of recruiting; reinforcements were rushed to the vicinity until 4,000 Conservatives under General Bartoloméo Viquez were massed around the burning city.

Next day the aviators flew back, carrying homemade bombs, to coöperate with Conservative ground forces which were preparing an attack on a hamlet near Chinandega held by Liberal troops. They were fired on heavily by Liberal soldiers on the ground and rifle bullets punctured parts of their planes. Brooks afterward wrote a graphic account of his adventure for The New York Times. Telling of his attack on Chinandega, he said:

"After I had figured out where the sharpshooters were hidden I heaved a bomb at them. The traffic jam that followed probably was the worst ever known in Chinandega. Men and women and children dashed up and down the streets, through the squares and back again. They seemed to be crazy, they ran so fast and aimlessly."

There was heavy fighting on Wednesday and Thursday in Chinandega, where a small force of Conservatives was trapped and was fighting valiantly, behind barricades of barbed wire and giant cactus, to

hold out until partisans outside the town could force
their way in. To quote Brooks again:

"The bloodiest fight was in front of a church. The
attackers kept running down the streets leading to it.
Three blocks away they filled the thoroughfare; two
blocks away they were running a yard apart, and in
the last block so many stumbled that only a man or
two ran frantically up to the walls. They fell there.

"This happened several times while I circled above.
The machine guns in the church were taking a heavy
toll.

"The Conservatives seemed to be having dog fights
in nearly every square and there was nothing I could
do. Little groups of men, colored like flakes of confetti, kept rushing together as though little whirl-
winds were at work down below. After a few minutes
most of the flakes would be swept around the corner,
but a few always remained on the white, dusty
street."

Brooks flew to Corinto trying to summon help for
the bitterly fighting Conservatives. When he returned—

"—the men were still rushing at the church, but
the flakes of confetti, except those lying on the streets,
were all gone. The Conservative flag was flying from
many buildings. The town surrendered next day."

Grotesque soldiers, these scrawny little Nicaraguan
conscripts, with their dirty shirts of all colors and
their flopping straw hats. Comical on parade, yet
capable of desperate and senseless courage.

Mason and Brooks afterwards were accused of starting the Chinandega fire, but their account was that
the city was blazing when they first saw it. The Liberals served notice that they would not be responsible
for the fate of the aviators if they should be captured
and the State Department was somewhat embarrassed
by their activities, for they had not taken an oath of
allegiance to Nicaragua and still were technically entitled to American protection. The exploit of Mason
and Brooks at Chinandega afterward was utilized
in propaganda against the conduct of the marines
in Nicaragua in a way to give the impression that
the destruction wrought at Chinandega was the work
of marine aviators.

The outburst of hostilities in the West not only
brought a new threat to the Diaz government, but it
carried the war toward a new set of foreigners and
their property.

Admiral Latimer immediately extended the neutral
zone system to the West Coast. More marines were
disembarked at Corinto and the railroad was reopened
to the capital. León and Chinandega and other points
along the railroad were occupied, and though the
railroad itself was not neutralized (it was a vital part
of the military system of the Diaz government for
the transportation of men and supplies) fighting was
forbidden within 2,000 yards of it. The guarding of
the railroad was predicated on the necessity of keeping open for foreigners in the interior an avenue of
retreat to the coast. On January 6, 160 marines from

the cruiser Galveston arrived in Managua, the first to be seen in the capital since the withdrawal of the Legation guard in 1925. They marched through the ugly avenues, cheered from the sidewalks, to the Campo de Marte and turned into the very barracks where their predecessors had lived for so long.

But even with the United States behind him, with the marines operating as his allies by protecting his line of communication, Don Adolfo Diaz was heartily sick of his task. Now more than ever he wished to be rid of the thankless presidency if the United States would let him. He revealed his eagerness to step down in an interview with the Associated Press.

"If the United States should think best that I give way to some one else as a means of furthering the best interest of Nicaragua, I shall do so immediately," said the President.

"So long as I am President, and also under subse-sequent administrations, I think the United States marines should remain in Nicaragua. This is the only means of preventing revolution and guaranteeing un-interrupted progress of the coast-to-coast railroad which I plan, paved highways, and educational sys-tems allowing the Nicaraguans to realize their natural physical advantages and possibilities of development during peace time."

This offered a way out, for the elimination of Diaz, whom they regarded as the beneficiary of the Cha-morro *coup d'état,* was the one point on which the Liberals were immovable. Sacasa himself already was on record as willing to give up his personal claims to the office. Conversations again were held by Admiral Latimer and Dr. Sacasa at Puerto Cabezas. But the American Government, as it was demonstrated later, was determined that Diaz should complete the term. Not only was it committed to Diaz. It had good reason to fear that the confusion which certainly would attend any effort to install a substitute in the place of Diaz would make a very bad matter worse.

On February 14, five days after the Diaz interview, the assertion that he was willing to resign was repudiated in a statement by Foreign Minister Cuadra Pasos, who said that the attitude of the President had been misinterpreted.

"The Government of Nicaragua does not believe possible any peace agreement, the fundamental basis of which might be the withdrawal of President Diaz," the Foreign Minister announced.

"The Liberal party, without legal or moral justification, has plunged the country into disastrous war. President Diaz, as director of Conservative party policy, has desired to bring about peace by methods of conciliation, persuasion and moderation; unhappily he has failed in these efforts because of the intransigency of the Liberals. His enemies have obliged him to impose pacification with arms. . . . The military operations of the Government have been everywhere triumphant and today the revolutionary groups of the East and West have been dispersed. Now there is in arms only General Moncada with a column of men in a precarious situation in the forests of the mountains between Matagalpa and the East Coast. As soon as he sallies forth into the open and inhabited country, where our forces can give him battle, his army will be destroyed. . . . The peace which we can not obtain by friendly overtures we may have eventually to impose by force of our arms, but when peace is once firmly established President Diaz will be able to work out his benevolent and honorable program of conciliation to which the Conservative party is committed."

To one who understands how interviews are given and how they sometimes afterward are disclaimed, and in view of the known sentiments of President Diaz, it is obvious that pressure had been brought to bear between the time of the interview and the statement of Cuadra Pasos. There would be no compromise, though Diaz himself desired one heart and soul.

CHAPTER XVI

A BRITISH CRUISER AND GREAT ADO

IF the Conservative Government actually was as confident as it professed to be of the early destruction of Moncada's army, that optimism was not shared by residents in the region toward which he was marching.

For while Cuadra Pasos was announcing prematurely the expected victory of Conservative arms, Moncada and his men toiled out of the East into the rich valleys and verdant mountains of North Central Nicaragua and prepared to capture Matagalpa.

This little city of 5,000, lying in a saucer-like depression in the mountains and often veiled by low-lying clouds, is the commercial metropolis of its section of the country and also is an important centre of foreign interests. The principal industry in the city is a coffee cleaning establishment owned at the time of the revolution by two resident Americans, W. H. De Savigny, who acted as American consular agent, and his son, Blair De Savigny. The principal retail store was owned by Guillaume Hueper, German consular agent.

On the slopes of the hills outside the city at the end of trails festooned with wild orchids drooping from dying trees, are some two score rich coffee plantations. A dozen of these are owned by Americans, another dozen or two by Europeans of various nationalities who live the lives of landed proprietors in their pretty little manors. They conduct a pleasant and cultivated social life in company with their charming Nicaraguan neighbors of the higher class. At times they meet in Matagalpa for dinner-coated receptions and dances.

As the Liberals drew near in that February, the plantation owners came into the city to avoid the perils of wandering groups of soldiers, some of whom were bandits who had joined Moncada or were operating entirely independently for the fun and the looting.

The plantation owners were in danger even in the city. Moncada coveted Matagalpa because it was the centre of a cluster of roads, one of which was the principal highway in the country and ran directly to Managua. A battle for possession of the town almost certainly would have culminated in fighting in the streets and from house to house. Even now there were disorders. Early one morning De Savigny was found bruised and dazed in the street in front of the consulate, apparently the victim of an assault, of which neither he nor anybody else could give a clear version.

Information came that Moncada would make an attack in the moonlight. There was a Conservative army near the city. There also was a small detachment of marines. The Americans and other foreigners consulted with the marine officer, and, according to their account of the conversation, he showed no disposition to prevent the battle.

"Hell, that's what you're here for!" one of the hotter headed Americans exclaimed.

An account of the situation was telephoned to the American Legation in Managua; marine reinforcements were rushed northward, and Matagalpa and the territory immediately surrounding it were declared a neutral zone. Both armies heeded this ruling and moved away, and the threatening battle was averted.

Moncada's objective was Managua and he manœuvred steadily though slowly toward the capital. The Conservatives had the men and the munitions to stop him, but they had no military leader who could cope with the schoolmaster who was opposing them. They desperately needed Chamorro, and he was out of the country.

All this time the American Government was maintaining an outward show of neutrality. The marines and bluejackets scrupulously avoided friction with the contending armies. It was the boast of the naval command that from the beginning of the revolution no American had fired a shot toward a Nicaraguan, or struck a blow. This was a record which was kept unmarred until late in April when a train, carrying a marine guard, was fired on and the fire returned, the first of several such incidents, and when marines repulsed an attack on a village and killed three of the attackers, who were wearing Liberal hatbands. And on the West Coast and in Central Nicaragua, as on the

East Coast, it was literally true that there were foreign interests to safeguard at every point where marines were posted or a neutral zone was proclaimed. There are few places of consequence in Nicaragua where there are not foreign interests.

It was an explosive situation, for every moment of the day and night offered the acute possibility of a major clash between the marines and some band of Nicaraguans which would pitchfork the American forces into the actual hostilities, for all their sedulous avoidance of it. The condition of the country was anarchy, no less. Groups of outlaws and of deserting soldiers, still carrying their weapons, roved about the sparsely populated regions, winning their livings at the point of the gun.

Washington kept pouring marines and more marines into Nicaragua. On February 21 the Navy Department announced that 5,414 men were on duty in the Republic or en route there. They were established in every section of the country ready to repel any attempt of armed forces to take any important point, thus, as it worked out in practice, barring the Sacasa armies from all large towns. As February neared its end preparations were under way to establish a marine aviation unit in Nicaragua, and Brigadier General Logan Feland, of distinguished service in Belleau Wood, was on his way to Managua to take command of the forces on land.

But still, with all its advantages, the Diaz Government was unable to suppress the revolution, and at last the State Department was forced to give overt assistance to the Conservatives by selling them munitions on credit at a reduced price. A contract was entered into on February 25 for the sale of 3,000 Krag rifles, 200 Browning machine guns and 3,000,000 rounds of ammunition. The Nicaraguan Government gave a series of notes of $5,000 each bearing 6 percent, the first of which was to mature on January 31, 1929. The total price of the military supplies, including interest, was $217,718.

This transaction was announced a month later by the State Department with the explanation that the munitions were urgently needed to maintain law and order and suppress revolutionary activities which not only threatened the constitutional government of Nicaragua but also the lives and property of Americans and other foreigners.

"It will be recalled," the Department added, "that a similar transaction was entered into early in 1924 with the Obregon Government in Mexico after its recognition by this Government and during the de la Huerta revolution."

The announcement caused another flurry of criticism in the United States Senate. The extraordinary activities of the United States in Nicaragua intensified the normal suspicion of American intentions. "Why do we need 5,000 men in Nicaragua if we are merely protecting American lives and property?" was a question constantly asked both in the Senate and in the editorial columns of the North American press. Senator Borah and other critics kept hammering away at the Coolidge-Kellogg policy, demanding explanations which explained.

That portion of the American public which is interested in the foreign relations of its government was startled on the morning of February 24, 1927, to read in newspapers that the British Government was contemplating sending a war vessel to Nicaraguan waters. Great Britain had kept hands off Nicaragua ever since the United States had established its own predominance in the Republic in 1910 and taken upon itself the responsibility of protecting foreign interests. For reasons not fully explained it chose to take measures looking to the protection of its nationals by its own forces in 1927. That of course put the Monroe Doctrine on the front pages.

British interests in Nicaragua are next to American in extent. There are about 200 British nationals in the country and there are British investments of approximately $2,500,00. English merchants had lost goods worth about $2,000 in the destruction of Chinandega. English owners of coffee plantations, like American, German and Italian owners, were fearful of hostilities in the vicinity of their holdings. So long as hostilities were in progress there of course existed a certain danger to life and property.

On February 23 Secretary Kellogg announced to the press that he had received a cablegram from Minister Eberhardt in Managua inclosing the following communication delivered to him by Harold Patteson, British Chargé d'Affaires in Nicaragua:

"I have the honor to inform Your Excellency that in the absence of guarantees from the Nicaraguan and United States Governments for the protection of the lives and properties of British subjects in the event of further street fighting, incendiarism and pillage, in the threatened districts of this republic, His Britannic Majesty's Government are reluctantly contemplating the dispatch of a man-of-war to the Western coast of Nicaragua.

"It is with pleasure that I am instructed to inform Your Excellency that His Majesty's Government thanks the Government of the United States once more for its assistance and still continues to rely thereon."

What had happened was that the British official had called on President Diaz at the beginning of the year and asked whether he could give guarantees for the protection of British lives and property. The President had replied that because of the aid being received by the Liberals from Mexico he could not guarantee protection without the immediate aid of the United States. The Chargé thereupon called on the American Minister and asked what protection the United States could give. He did not regard the American assurance as sufficiently conclusive, and when Moncada's march appeared to imperil his countrymen he called for a warship.

The British Ambassador, Sir Esme Howard, on instructions from his Government, also called on the American Secretary of State and informed him of the threat to English citizens in Corinto, León, Managua, Granada and Matagalpa, as reported to London by Mr. Patteson, and reminded the American Government that Great Britain expected the United States "to extend to British subjects, and especially to those in the places above mentioned, the same measure of protection as they afford to United States citizens in the districts now threatened by revolutionary disturbances."

The State Department prepared a reply which assured the British Government that "the American armed forces which have been landed in Nicaragua for the protection of American and foreign lives and property will be pleased to extend to British subjects such protection as may be possible and proper under the circumstances." Before this reply was delivered the British Ambassador officially informed the Department that the British cruiser Colombo had been dispatched to Corinto, and should arrive there on February 26.

"His Majesty's government feel that the presence of a war vessel may have a moral effect and would be a base of refuge for British subjects," said the Ambassador's note of information. "It is of course not intended to land forces and the commanding officer will be instructed acordingly."

This explanation was treated by Secretary Kellogg

as entirely satisfactory, in view of the British assurances that no troops would be sent ashore. By the time the Colombo reached Corinto President Coolidge also had expressed himself in similar vein, with the added intimation that the policy of the United States remained in opposition to permitting any European government to land troops in the Western Hemisphere for the purpose of collecting debts. It was further authoritatively stated that "there was every indication in administration circles that the dispatch of the British cruiser was not considered as a step in contravention of the Monroe Doctrine, nor, in fact, in opposition to American policy in Central America."

The Colombo arrived in due time, remained in the harbor of Corinto a few days and departed. Indeed there had been nothing for the British vessel to do when American warships were plowing the seas on both sides of Nicaragua and American marines were posted throughout the Republic,—"sufficient to blow it to ruin overnight," as Senator Borah remarked. And so complacent was the American Government that a suspicion arose that there had been a previous agreement in the matter between England and the United States.

Even the well-informed and non-speculative Washington Bureau of The New York Times noted that "there was some evidence that this correspondence (between the British and American Governments) may have been preceded by informal conversations of a satisfactory character, although officials declined to discuss that question."

Dr. T. S. Vaca, agent of Dr. Sacasa at Washington, immediately interpreted the incident as collusion.

"It is ridiculous and too absurd to believe," he said, "that England would make the least move in the Caribbean region without previous and full accord with the United States, particularly in Nicaragua, where intervention now has grown far beyond its stated aims. The coöperation of the British Chargé d'Affaires was obtained from the beginning to ask protection for his subjects to the American Minister in order to justify the landing of marines."

Much of the Central American press shared this view, and it even was broached in American newspapers. The interpretation of collusion is not substantiated by any evidence now available and is probably untrue. But the Colombo did serve to create a diversion by dragging the Monroe Doctrine by its heels into the midst of the controversy over Latin America.

CHAPTER XVII

PEACE BY THE THREAT OF WAR

WHEN the Foreign Minister of Nicaragua had asserted in the middle of February, 1927, that the withdrawal of Adolfo Diaz would not be considered as a part of any peace agreement he had added that when peace once was established President Diaz would be able to work out "his benevolent and honorable program of conciliation to which the Conservative party is committed."

The President's benevolent program, it soon appeared, rested on his hope that the United States itself would guarantee peace and justice in Nicaragua by means of a control over that country's affairs more intimate and more extensive even than it already exercised. It was a hope for unequivocal intervention, and for salvation by dollar diplomacy. President Diaz expressed it in great detail on February 24 in a carefully prepared communication to the North American Government proposing a "Treaty of Alliance" between the two governments establishing a protectorate over Nicaragua—for the same reasons, stated in almost the same terms, which had moved him to ask the United States to take over the country in 1911, which he had repeated in 1914 in his request for the application of the Platt Amendment to Nicaragua, and which he had suggested the day after he took office for the last time in 1926.

There was implied in his appeal a rebuke to the American Government for its indecision, for its policy of trying at the same time to intervene and not to intervene, of spasmodically interfering in Nicaragua's affairs, then backing out, a policy which President Diaz felt did not satisfactorily serve the interests of either nation.

"The treaty we desire would secure for us from the United States two fundamental guaranties, one of incalculable benefit for Nicaragua and the other of great advantage for the American nation," wrote President Diaz in his proposal.

"The first guaranty would assure to us our sovereignty and independence, and the uninterrupted maintenance of a government adequate for the protection of life, property and individual liberty. The second guaranty would assure to the American people their rights under the Bryan-Chamorro treaty to build an interoceanic canal through Nicaragua and to a naval base in this country.

"In return for these guaranties, which would sound the death knell of *coups d'état* and revolutions in Nicaragua and open to its people new vistas of peace and prosperity, my Government would concede to the United States the right to intervene in Nicaragua, whenever it might be necessary, in order to make effective the guaranties mentioned above.

"As matters now stand, we have today, as we have had frequently in the past along with several of our Central American neighbors, the intervention of American armed forces in our territory directed exclusively for the protection of American and foreign lives and property. Such interventions are in their essence *de facto,* and in their scope uncertain and most inadequate for the achievement of ends associated with our interests.

"We have taken due account of these facts of our history, and we see ourselves obliged by the unhappy conditions—not theories—of our political existence to contemplate periodically within our territory these fortuitous *de facto* American interventions, which only safeguard imperfectly American and foreign lives during our spasmodic civil disturbances and which leave our fundamental ills unremedied.

"We have, therefore, reached the conclusion that we want to derive for ourselves some definite and permanent advantage from American intervention, which we have thus far found inevitable, and at the same time transfer it from its somewhat vague *de facto* basis to a well-defined *de jure* status with clearly stated responsibilities and apparent benefits for the intervener and the intervened. . . .

"We have in mind most particularly coöperation along three lines to enable us (1) to effect the financial and economic rehabilitation of our country with the aid of an American financial adviser and a receiver general of our revenues; (2) to preserve throughout the country peace and guarantee the security of individual rights and liberties under our Constitution and laws, as well as the observance of the provisions of the treaty; (3) to improve the public health and general welfare of Nicaragua with the assistance of specially selected American experts. We should like to include adequate stipulations, either in the treaty proper or in a special convention with the United States annexed thereto, to make possible effective American coöperation toward the end just mentioned."

The solution of the first problem, involving the economic regeneration of the country, President Diaz wrote, necessitated a large loan, a step which would "require absolutely the coöperation of the American Government."

"We believe," he continued, "that our situation calls for and warrants a financial operation involving some $20,000,000—first, some $7,000,000 for the refunding of our debt; second, some $3,000,000 or $4,-000,000 for the settlement of claims arising out of recent disturbances, in which the losses of private property of Nicaraguans and foreigners have been enormous; third, a loan to bring our total indebtedness to not more than $20,000,000 for the construction of a railway to the Atlantic. . . .

"In return for the advantages accruing to Nicaragua from such a loan we are prepared to accept any measure of control by an American financial adviser and receiver general which the American Government might consider proper. We should thereby have the certainty that our country would not be exploited in a predatory manner by foreign capital."

The second problem in which the assistance of the United States was sought was that of establishing and maintaining peace and of assuring "the permanence of adequate constitutional government affording guaranties for all." To this end, said President Diaz:

"We need a well-organized, trained and equipped constabulary, which would be strictly nonpolitical and the only armed force in Nicaragua. Our present armies would be disbanded and all arms turned over to the constabulary. . . . In order to bring into existence the constabulary force required by our situation, we need the aid of an American military mission to direct and train this corps during a period of some ten years or more, while a capable body of Nicaraguan officers was being formed to perpetuate the organization so created."

The State Department rejected the proposal. However earnestly it might have wished to be once for all in position to direct Nicaragua's affairs above the table rather than under it, and to have done with constantly explaining its activities, it did not care to increase the already hot fire raining on its Latin American policy by adopting any such measures as were contained in the Diaz proposal. Interestingly enough, however, in this same period President Coolidge began considering measures looking to the actual construction of a canal across Nicaragua, and in accordance with his wishes projects for making new surveys were brought up in the Senate; the building of the canal was advocated from the double viewpoint of its commercial utility and its part in American national defense.

But the State Department, while it would not grasp the solution which President Diaz extended, was being forced day by day to a realization that it had to do something radical. Although the Diaz Government was straining every nerve to break the Liberals in the field, and although the extensive forces of the marines and bluejackets served as his allies without technically compromising their neutrality, Moncada's army was a growing menace. Like the giant Antæus, whose strength increased each time he was thrown to the ground, Moncada was thriving on the "defeats" which were being optimistically reported to the capital.

Everyone wanted peace—Conservatives, Liberals, Americans—but there lacked the final push to obtain it. There was an earnest effort early in March. A mission of three prominent Liberals, accompanied by marine officers and with an American flag flying at the front of their car, drove through the Conservative lines and the Liberal outposts and found Moncada in the wilderness near Muy Muy, well south of Matagalpa and measurably nearer Managua at the conclusion of his latest "defeat." The effort failed because Moncada considered himself to be under the orders of Sacasa, from whom he was isolated.

Yet the conference produced a surprising expression from Moncada. He was informed of President

Diaz's proposal of a defensive alliance with the United States, and favored it, although he opposed the project of a new loan as an "enslavement" of his country. Not only did he favor American intervention, Moncada said. He believed that both Diaz and Sacasa should be eliminated, that a new election, supervised by the United States, should be held, and that in the interim Nicaragua should be ruled by an American military governor. There must be an end to the fighting; it was ruining Nicaragua, but it was beyond his authority to negotiate peace.

The delegates returned unsuccessful, but with the feeling that a settlement was nearer. It only required one decisive act of the United States to bring it about.

In April President Coolidge turned his back on the indecision of the past and initiated that act. He could hardly have hoped for the measure of success, both for Nicaragua and the United States, which ultimately crowned it. Henry L. Stimson, New York lawyer, one-time Secretary of War and as such fully conversant with the basic American strategy in the Caribbean, was dispatched to Nicaragua as President Coolidge's personal representative.

His mission, as announced by the State Department, was to get information from Minister Eberhardt and Admiral Latimer on the entire situation in Nicaragua "to bring back for the use of this Government, which they cannot very well give us through correspondence." Nothing further as to his functions was announced. His only other instructions, according to

Colonel Stimson himself, were that if he should find a chance to straighten the matter out, President Coolidge would like him to do so.

As Colonel Stimson hurried south to Panamá, then up the Pacific Coast on a racing cruiser, the fighting went on in Nicaragua. Another series of victories was announced by the Conservatives: Moncada and a little band of survivors were surrounded one day—in flight toward the border of Honduras the next. Meanwhile Moncada had slipped on south to the vicinity of Boaco, a cattle-raising centre only 40 miles from Managua. Another crushing "defeat" and he would be in the capital.

For several days Stimson absorbed the views of people of varying beliefs and drew on the wealth of knowledge which Eberhardt and Latimer had acquired. The bland and unruffled lawyer brought a prestige that was denied the Minister and the Admiral. He personified Coolidge directly. To the Nicaraguans he was divine revelation. It was as if the heavens of Washington had opened and a messenger had issued forth in a chariot.

Colonel Stimson found everyone with whom he talked convinced of the necessity of American supervision of the elections if there was to be a fair choice of President. He was insistent that Diaz finish out the term; otherwise there would be dangerous if not fatal confusion. He found that if a new President were chosen at that time it must be by the vote of the Congress, and no Congress then existed. An acceptable decision was impossible of course from the "rump Congress" which had elected Diaz, even if that Congress could be called back into existence, and the war prevented the fair election of a successor to that Congress. Besides, Colonel Stimson felt, there was no real danger to the Liberals in the continuance of Diaz in the Presidency because of his proven magnanimity toward his political opponents.

But first of all there must be peace. Stimson and Eberhardt and Latimer worked day and night to bring about a settlement, for every day meant lives and the further weakening of American prestige. On April 22 President Diaz, after conferences with the American representatives, proposed the following terms to the Liberals:

(1) Immediate general peace and delivery of arms simultaneously by both parties into American custody;

(2) General amnesty and return of exiles and return of confiscated property;

(3) Participation in the Diaz cabinet by representatives Liberals;

(4) The organization of a Nicaraguan constabulary on a non-partisan basis, to be commanded by American officers;

(5) Supervision of 1928 and subsequent elections by Americans who would have ample police power to make effective such supervision;

(6) A temporary continuance of a sufficient force

of American marines to secure the enforcement of peace terms.

Liberal leaders in Managua transmitted these terms to Dr. Sacasa at Puerto Cabezas, and informed the presidential claimant that Stimson would be glad to confer with him, or with his representatives, in Managua. Sacasa declined to go to Managua, as he had declined to go to Corinto, but he appointed as representatives Dr. Rudolfo Espinosa, Dr. Leonardo Argüello, his minister of foreign affairs, and Dr. Manuel Cordero Reyes. An American destroyer picked them up at Puerto Cabezas and rushed them through the Panama Canal and up the Pacific Coast. They arrived in Managua on April 29.

The conference opened informally and auspiciously. Stimson's very naïveté in the situation confronting him was a source of strength. He was starting from scratch. He was unshakable. One of the American correspondents noted with amused appreciation that he even clung to the awful pronunciation of "Nica-ragew-a" with no notice of the soft accent with which Nicaraguans themselves spoke the name of their country. It was a sign of his stability.

"I believe Mr. Stimson is the finest man possible for the mission and that justice will be given to the Nicaraguan people through his efforts, due to his open, unbiased and understanding attitude," said Argüello.

In the long hours of patient discussion which followed, the Liberals struck once more on the point of

Diaz's retention of the Presidency. Because of his moderateness he was the least objectionable to them of any Conservative, even though they believed that he had been a guiding spirit in the Chamorro *coup* of 1925 and held his office as a direct result of that. But Diaz himself was an issue; the symbol of what they were fighting. They could not in honor sign any agreement which left him in the Presidency, they told Stimson.

"If Diaz would only change his name!" exclaimed one of the despairing Liberals.

The conferences ranged over other ground—the possibilities of a supervised election and the necessary guarantees of its fairness—and reached approximate agreement on all but the one point—Diaz. Even the attitude of the Liberals toward the United States was gone into. The Liberals disavowed hostility to American interests, and denied that they had any understanding with Mexico contrary to such interests. They went so far as to admit, according to Colonel Stimson, that the United States had a legitimate zone of interest and influence extending as far south as Panamá and that "they considered this fact natural and beneficial in its results to Nicaragua." But always the American mediator and the Liberal delegates came back to the issue of Diaz and there stuck.

The Liberals revived their suggestion of a neutral temporary President. An excellent theory, but a futile dream.

"I am quite clear that in the present crisis no neu-

tral or impartial Nicaraguan exists," Stimson reported with perfect accuracy to the State Department. "Moreover, any attempt by the Nicaraguan
Congress to elect a substitute for Diaz under the forms
of Nicaraguan law would almost certainly, in the
present situation, become the occasion of further bitter factional strife."

At length the Liberal delegates suggested that they
be permitted to get in touch with Moncada. Stimson
gladly agreed and included with their letter to the
field leader an invitation of his own to come to Managua for a conference, together with a copy of the
Diaz peace proposals. Three marine officers took the
messages through the lines of the two armies. Moncada
accepted Stimson's suggestion and sent word on May 3
that he would meet him early the next morning at
Tipitapa, a village 15 miles from Managua, on the
Tipitapa River which connects the nearby lakes of
Managua and Nicaragua. The village at that time was
on the outpost line of the Conservative army defending the capital on this narrow neck of land. A 48 hour
truce was declared and 500 marines moved into position along the river between the hostile armies.

So on May 4 the peace conference began. Colonel
Stimson, with the Sacasa delegates and accompanied
by Minister Eberhardt and Admiral Latimer, motored
out along the shore of the lake and at the village they
met Moncada and the three marine officers. The latter
were a weary party, for they had traveled down from
the mountains through most of the preceding night.

Now an important thing had been happening to Moncada while he was battling his way toward Managua. He was leading the forces of Sacasa in an effort to confirm in the field Sacasa's claimed title of constitutional President of Nicaragua. As he again and again had eluded defeat and driven ahead, his men had come to idolize him. The Nicaraguans so love a military leader! Sacasa, safe in Puerto Cabezas all this time, had faded into the background. Moncada still described himself as a subordinate of Sacasa, but whether he wished it or not, he had supplanted him. He with his army was carrying on the actual revolution, the only agency by which the Liberals could hope to achieve the power they claimed. He now *was* the revolution. Whatever decision was to be made, it was the men who had fought who would make it.

There were pleasant greetings—Moncada has a charming personality and an air almost as gracious as that of Diaz—then the Liberal commander retired into the dingy inn with the Sacasa delegates to learn about the preliminary negotiations. Fifteen minutes later he emerged.

It was at the height of the dry season and the sun beat down on the suffocating plain. Stimson and Moncada sat down together in the shade of a large black thorn tree beside the parched bed of the river. They spoke for a half hour, Moncada in hesitating but precise English. Moncada's attitude was that of Sacasa's delegates. He would agree to all of President Diaz's terms, which were the terms of the United States, except the one point of Diaz's continuance in office. He felt that he had a chance to win against the Conservative armies, and he could not ask his men to yield on the one point which had become their battle-cry.

But Stimson had one overwhelming argument in reserve—the United States marines. He threatened to throw them in.

Now there is a point of history which is completely known only to those two men who sat there alone.

Stimson's own account of their conversation permits the interpretation that he made this threat at the suggestion of Moncada, who wished peace but felt that he could not bring his army to accept it unless they knew they would have to fight the United States if they refused.

" . . . though he might outmanœuvre and sometimes beat Diaz's armies," said Colonel Stimson in his brief account of Moncada's conversation with him in his "American Policy in Nicaragua," "he frankly admitted that neither he nor any Nicaraguan could, without the help of the United States, end the war or pacify the country; so that the situation would necessarily grow worse each month. If I would assure him that we insisted on Diaz as a necessary condition to our supervision of the election, he would not fight the United States. He said he did not wish a single life to be lost on that issue between us. If I would give him a letter to that effect, he would use it to persuade his army to lay down its arms.

"In short, the gist of the situation was that while

he felt he could not, in view of past history, voluntarily make such a settlement, if our government was ready to accept the invitation of the Nicaraguan Government to supervise the election of 1928 and insisted on Diaz finishing out his term as a condition of that acceptance, he would yield to that decision and do his best to persuade his army to do so."

Colonel Stimson called his secretary and dictated the following letter for Moncada to take back to his subordinate chieftains:

Tipitapa, May 4, 1927.

General José Maria Moncada,
Tipitapa.

Dear General Moncada: Confirming our conversation of this morning, I have the honor to inform you that I am authorized to say that the President of the United States intends to accept the request of the Nicaraguan Government to supervise the election of 1928; that the retention of President Diaz during the remainder of his term is regarded as essential to that plan and will be insisted upon; that a general disarmament of the country is also regarded as necessary for the proper and successful conduct of such election; and that the forces of the United States will be authorized to accept the custody of the arms of those willing to lay them down, including the government, and to disarm forcibly those who will not do so.

Very respectfully,
Henry L. Stimson.

"I included the last sentence not as a threat to Moncada's organized and loyal troops, who, I was confident, would follow their leader's direction," wrote Mr. Stimson, "but as a needed warning to the bandit fringe who were watching for any sign that we were not in earnest in order to indulge their taste for pillage once the government troops had laid down their arms and there remained no force in the country other than the Americans able to restrain them."

Moncada departed within the lines of his soldiers to discuss the peace terms with his leaders and the armistice was extended.

A practical agreement was reached on May 5, although there were a few gestures yet to be accomplished on the Liberal side. Moncada came into Managua escorted by a platoon of marines to renew his conversations with Stimson. After the meeting he gave the following interview to the Associated Press:

"The view seems certain that the United States is prepared to take the field against us if the fighting continues, and I am prepared to order my troops to lay down their arms, turning them over to the United States troops. As continuation of Diaz is essential to the United States program we are unable to resist, but we are not signing any peace agreement bearing such a provision.

"We are forced by a greater power to cease our fight, but as peace will be the result I shall devote my effort to help in restoring order, so that the Liberals may gain legitimate and honest control in the 1928 elections, which will be supervised by the United States."

Because of the ambiguity of Mr. Stimson's own account—he does not mention Moncada's visit of May 5th—the testimony of Admiral Latimer, who was collaborating intimately with Stimson and Eberhardt in the peace settlement, is doubly important. In a hearing before the Senate Foreign Relations Committee in February, 1928, Admiral Latimer was questioned in some detail on the means used to bring Moncada to terms.

"—did you understand, and did Moncada understand from the statement made by Mr. Stimson, that if he did not acquiesce in the continuance of Diaz until an election was held, force would be used to disarm him and compel him to acquiesce?" Senator Swanson asked.

"Yes," responded the Admiral.

"You understood it, and so did he?"

"I had no doubt of it."

Moncada returned to his army after his second conference with Stimson and on the next day President Diaz proclaimed immediate general amnesty to political prisoners and exiles, announced that freedom of the press would be restored as soon as the disarmament was under way and agreed to the suggestion of Moncada for the appointment of Liberal military governors in the six provinces of strong Liberal political complexion.

The delegates whom Sacasa had sent still refused to accede to the term embodying Diaz's continuance in office and so telegraphed him. He replied with a message of commendation for their rejection of an ultimatum which was humiliating and said he was leaving the decision of the army to Moncada. His message concluded:

"I sincerely deplore the fact that the Government of the United States, departing from the principles of justice and forgetting the true interests of a weak country in order solely to sustain a régime born of a *coup d'état,* has not only violated and broken into pieces the constitution of the Republic but also the Central American treaty signed in Washington, D. C. For this reason it is entirely impossible for us to accept said régime, to say nothing of the respect which is due our honor and the national dignity."

For the second time, on May 11, Stimson, Eberhardt and Latimer motored out to Tipitapa for a conference with Moncada. General Feland of the marines accompanied them. Moncada asked for assurance on certain points raised by his chieftains and Stimson dictated a letter for him in which he said:

"In seeking to terminate this war, President Coolidge is actuated only by a desire to benefit the people of Nicaragua and to secure for them a free, fair and impartial election. He believes that only by such free and fair elections can permanent peace be secured for Nicaragua. To insure this in 1928 he has consented to the request that American representatives selected by him shall supervise the election. He has also consented to assign American officers to train and command a nonpartisan national constabulary for Nicaragua which will have the duty of securing such a fair election and of preventing any fraud or intimidation of voters. He is willing also to leave in Nicaragua until after the election a sufficient force of marines to support the work of the constabulary and insure peace and freedom at the election."

Colonel Stimson added in his letter a reference to the measures which were being taken to assure equitable conditions and pledged once more the impartiality of the United States in the task it had undertaken. General Moncada dictated a statement in reply expressing the confidence of the Liberals in the good faith of North America. Then he returned to his army. He telegraphed next day that eleven of his generals—all of them except one—had agreed to lay down their arms.

The Diaz Government had undertaken to pay each soldier, Government and rebel alike, $10 for each serviceable rifle or machine gun surrendered. A loan of $1,000,000 already had been negotiated in March with the Seligmans and the Guaranty Trust Company, and it was used largely for this purpose. The distribution of the money was as thoroughly safeguarded as possible, to see that it got to the men and was not appropriated by the officers, and marines in trucks set out to gather in the arms. Thousands of leaflets giving notice of the disarmament were scattered in the remote regions by marine airplanes. Eight hundred more marines were ordered to Nicaragua to assist in the policing of the country until it should be on its feet once more, and the revival of the Guardia Nacional, the nonpartisan constabulary, was begun immediately under Colonel Robert Y. Rhea of the marine corps.

The roads were cluttered with straggling lines of *mozos* who only a little while before had been soldiers and now were trudging toward the capital, or toward their neglected little patches, still cheering for "la revolucion" which had just blessedly ended. With them plodded their women folk, patient, placid, expressionless, barefoot creatures laden with bags and babies and pots and pans.

Moncada entered peaceably the capital which he had tried so hard to win by force of arms. As his car passed, the tattered bits of his old army waved their red-scarfed hats at him and yelled deliriously.

There was enthusiasm even in Managua. One never would have dreamed that it was the capital of a Conservative government. Men and boys leaped and shouted alongside the hurrying car. A toy saluting cannon roared; homemade skyrockets, bundles of powder tied to bamboo tips, sizzled and banged through the crowd at all angles and miraculously put out no eyes.

Moncada and his staff, still wearing their pistols, set up headquarters in the city's principal hotel, as if they indeed had conquered Managua, while the Indian servant girls giggled and whispered with excitement at the presence of greatness.

There was a banquet in Managua at which Admiral Latimer was a guest. General Moncada proposed a toast to the Admiral in cordial respect to his fairness and his efforts to bring peace to Nicaragua. He regretted that he had no power to confer a decoration in the name of the Republic. He drew a little plush box from his pocket and said, "Admiral Latimer and I are both members of one great society devoted to peace, a society founded 1927 years ago by the great Prince of Peace, and I propose, in the name of the Liberal party of Nicaragua, to confer on him the emblem of that great society." With that he opened the box, took out a little gold cross, one which he, a Catholic, had worn through all his battles, and pinned it on the Admiral's breast, above the ribbons of his military service.

Over at Puerto Cabezas Dr. Sacasa still declined to accept the situation. He issued a statement which proved to be his valedictory: "Our determination to stand aloof from the Government of President Diaz remains unchanged, because national dignity demands it. Confronted with Mr. Stimson's intimation to disarm it, my army, whose endurance and valor nobody denies, can only sacrifice itself or submit to the strength of a foreign power. . . ."

Soon afterward he departed from Puerto Cabezas with his followers, stopping first in Costa Rica, where great popular enthusiasm was evinced for him.

Later he settled with his wife and daughters in Guatemala and resumed the practice of medicine.

Colonel Stimson was signally honored by the leaders of both parties. As soon as possible after the completion of his work he prepared to return to the United States. On May 15 he telegraphed to the State Department a résumé of the situation and a happy picture of common men who had been soldiers hurrying to their homes.

"The civil war in Nicaragua is now definitely ended," he said. ". . . I am bringing with me the formal request of the Government for American supervision at the 1928 election. I believe that the way is now open for the development of Nicaragua along the lines of peace, order and ultimate self government."

The next day two marines, Captain Richard B. Buchanan and Private Marvin A. Jackson, were killed when a band of guerrillists attacked a marine post guarding the railroad near León. They were the first of twenty-six to be killed by hostile bullets in the long struggle of the United States to give Nicaragua the honest election to which both parties were now pledged.

CHAPTER XVIII

FIGHTING A BAMBOO WAR

THAT fight between natives and marines which was Nicaragua's farewell to Colonel Stimson was the presage of a bloody year for the marines and for a portion of the Nicaraguan people, but neither Colonel Stimson nor any other American was to be blamed for attaching little significance to it. The mediator returned to the United States justifiably proud of having stopped at last a ruinous war and pointed the way to an amicable solution of a complex problem which was honorable to all parties concerned, including the United States.

The one danger now, and it did not appear serious, was from the "bandit fringe" of Moncada's army, as Colonel Stimson well knew. Moncada, in his trek across Nicaragua, had been joined by several bands of guerrillas who operated partly or altogether independently of him, and for gain as much as for patriotism. The sparsely settled northern area of Nicaragua has from time immemorial been infested with these wandering gangs, living by cattle rustling, coffee stealing and miscellaneous thievery. Normally they slip at will back and forth across the border between Nicaragua and Honduras, which here is an imagi-

By the Author

~ WHERE THE MARINES WERE FIGHTING ~
Airplane View of the Mountainous Jungles of Nueva Segovia

nary line running across a tortured territory of jungles and mountains. Many of these marauders are from Honduras, and the leaders are of various Central American nationalities.

When the disarmament of the Conservative and Liberal armies had first been decided upon there had been fear that some of these undisciplined bands would drift away with their arms and carry on individual wars in the remote parts of the country. But when Stimson departed there was every indication that this danger had been overrated. Even Cabulla, renowned for years as a guerrilla leader, was reported to have disarmed. Whether he disarmed or not, he was shot to death, and a woman with him, by a captain and a small group of marines soon after Colonel Stimson left Nicaragua. The marines' account of this was that they had gone to Cabulla's house to warn him against further terrorizing villagers as he was to alleged to have done when drunk. Cabulla was in bed. He started to draw a pistol, they said, a woman in the house attacked the captain, and the marines shot both of them.

But there was peace now in Nicaragua, after all. There had to be peace. The whole structure of future tranquillity in Nicaragua, of security to American interests, and of American prestige in Latin America rested on the fulfilment by the United States of its promise to see that the country had a genuinely free and fair election, the promise under which the Liberals had laid down their arms and sacrificed their hope of gaining the power by force. Such an election could not be held unless the country was free of disorder. When Colonel Stimson sailed for home there was no indication that there was or would be a situation which 3,100 marines could not master easily; indeed it was planned to decrease this force to 1,000, which it was felt would be sufficient to handle the election.

So the State Department, breathing easily for the first time in months, and at last emerging from the storm of criticism which had so ruffled it, took steps toward carrying out its part of the Diaz-Stimson terms. In June Colonel E. R. Beadle of the marine corps was sent from the United States to take permanant command of the Guardia Nacional—with the rank of Brigadier General of Nicaragua and subject to the orders of the President of Nicaragua—and build it up into a nonpolitical organization which in time would be the Republic's army and police force. A month later President Coolidge announced the appointment of Brigadier General Frank Ross McCoy to be supervisor of the Nicaraguan elections. The Diaz Government and the State Department began the joint work of framing an electoral law, to take the place of the old Dodds law and make the power of the American supervisor so absolute that neither party could by any trick corrupt or steal the election. Only once since the first intervention—when the marines were withdrawn in 1925—had Nicaragua seemed so perfectly settled on the path to stability and prosperity.

As was noted a few pages ago, Moncada had reported to Stimson on his final return to his troops that all but one of his dozen generals had accepted the terms of disarmament. That one was Augusto C. Sandino. He was one of the least conspicuous of Moncada's leaders, but he had no record of banditry behind him and was not to be classed with such ruffians as Cabulla. He had come down from the mountains along the border of Honduras with a tatterdemalion army of several hundred men and allied himself with Moncada in the march toward Managua, fighting effectively but with little regard to orders.

Sandino at first promised to disarm his men, according to an apparently genuine letter from Sandino to Moncada, written at Boaco, on May 9th, informing the Liberal general-in-chief that he was going north to Jinotega, where he had recruited many of his men. This letter was as follows:

"Esteemed General: I take pleasure in informing you that having arrived at this place I have found myself in a difficult position due to the fact that all my followers have not joined me, since I have found but a few chiefs, the rest of my troops having gone to Jinotega, the place whence they came. For this reason I feel that remaining at this place will avail me nothing, all of my followers having disbanded.

"I have decided to go to Jinotega again to assemble

my men in order to collect all the arms. In this case I shall remain there awaiting your orders.

"I likewise delegate my rights in order that you may arrange the matter as may suit you best, informing me of the result at Jinotega, which I shall occupy with my troops.

"The disbanding of my men is due to their not finding anything to eat and for this reason they have left. However, I assure you that as soon as I arrive they must all come where I am and then I shall collect all the arms."

Admiral Latimer was concerned at the delay in completing the disarming which Sandino's move implied, but he and the marines under him were eager to complete their mission in Nicaragua by peaceable means and orders were given that Sandino be not disturbed. General Moncada was apprehensive and went to Jinotega to intercede with his former aide, accompanied by Sandino's father, a man of the upper middle class living near Masaya. At Matagalpa Moncada and the elder Sandino sent an emissary on to Jinotega. Sandino sent back word that he would see them the next afternoon, but instead took the unmarried men of his band, numbering about 40, left his hundred married soldiers free to return to their homes, and started toward the wild border of Honduras. There he was turned back by Honduran troops.

Presently there came word that Sandino and his band were filtering through the narrow trails of the thickly forested mountains of Nueva Segovia and

Jinotega provinces. Gradually he was building up his band into what eventually became an army of a thousand brave, hardy men who knew every trail of this patternless wilderness of jungles, peaks, ridges and rockstrewn cliffs. But long before he had raised such a force as this Sandino declared war on the Americans.

First he sent to the marine major at Matagalpa a threat to capture the town. Presently he was engaged in a long exchange of letters and telegrams with Captain G. D. Hatfield, commanding 37 marines and 40 members of the constabulary in Ocotal, chief town of Nueva Segovia. Sandino's letters were in fairly good Spanish and often revealed a vein of humor. They seemed more the braggadocio of a mischievous young man than the serious productions of a desperate leader of a patriotic cause. He and the marine captain cajoled, threatened and insulted each other. Each dared the other to come out and fight. Sandino called on the marines to lay down their arms. He decorated a letter with a crude drawing, which later became his official seal, of a guerrilla soldier brandishing a *machete* over a prostrate marine and signed himself:

"Your obedient servant, who wishes to put you in a handsome tomb with flowers."

It was purely a war of words. Hatfield was forbidden by higher authority to seek battle with Sandino, and Sandino hesitated to throw himself against the well-armed marines.

During all this *fracaso*, while Sandino moved about

in the mountainous jungles at will, the marines patiently waited for him to subside of himself. But in June Sandino's activities became of so serious a nature that they could not be ignored. He captured and held the managers of German and French concerns near Ocotal for $5,000 ransom, and finally released them after taking money and goods worth $3,500. Then with a force of some fifty men he invaded the gold mine of Charles Butters, an American, at San Albino, where he had worked as a clerk until he joined the revolution. The mine, according to Butters, was worth $700,000. Sandino drove off his former co-workers without harming them, took out what gold he could and appropriated dynamite for the manufacture of bombs.

At this, Admiral Latimer determined that Sandino must be eliminated and ordered the marines to proceed against him. Early in July Captain Hatfield sent Sandino an ultimatum demanding that he lay down his arms by July 15 or sustain an attack by marines. Sandino from behind a ridge of mountains sent back a defiant reply:

"Your communication has been received and understood. I will not surrender and will await you here. I want a free country or death. I have no fear and rely on the patriotism of my followers."

Sandino quickly followed this with a second and tremendous answer.

Captain Hatfield and his small force were established in the two-story adobe city hall of Ocotal, in the centre of that quiet town of 2,000. The town was spread out in a valley rimmed by mountains so that it was subject to attack from all sides, and the marines necessarily made no pretense of trying to hold more than their own headquarters. Across the open square on which the city hall fronted was the church. There the constabulary was installed with a machine gun in the belfry.

At one o'clock on the morning of July 16 a marine sentry, patrolling 100 yards from the city hall, saw a shadow in a row of bushes. The shadow, startled by the approach of the marine, fired, and while the marine raced back to the headquarters a fusillade blazed out all through the town. Sandino was attacking in force and according to an elaborate plan. His men had filtered through the streets and the courtyards of the houses and were closing in on the marines from every direction.

A group got into the courtyard in the rear of the city hall and killed a marine. Wave after wave of the Sandinistas tried to cross the square before the building and were caught by the fire of machine guns and rifles pouring from the barricaded windows, and by the flanking fire of the Guardia Nacional in the church tower. Lieutenant Thomas G. Bruce of the constabulary, a first sergeant of the marine corps, lay in the street behind a machine gun and sprayed the attackers.

It was evident that Sandino had determined on wiping out the marine garrison at all costs as a

terrible lesson to the Americans. A squad of Sandinistas got into the house next door and tried to set
fire to the city hall, but Hatfield heard them and
dispatched them with his pistol.

The battle wore on with hardly a lull through
the morning and into the afternoon, waged with
bravery and stubbornness on both sides. A tropical
hurricane drenched the scene but did not stop the
fighting. The issue possibly would have been disaster
for the marines, except for the providence that two
scouting marine aviators flew by, saw the engage-
ment, and hurried to Managua for help. Five planes
loaded with bombs and armed with machine guns
hastened to Ocotal with Major Ross E. Rowell in the
lead and at 3 p. m. dived down on the attacking
Sandinistas through the rain and unloosed their bombs
and bullets. Thirty minutes of this and the last of the
attacking force had disappeared into the mountains
and forests. Major Rowell and his aviators bombed the
fastnesses in a hope of breaking up the survivors and
punishing Sandino so decisively that they would hear
no more from him.

In fourteen hours of hard fighting the marines had
suffered only one dead and two wounded, and the
Guardia had lost only four wounded. Reports of 300
Sandinist casualties were given out. The actual
number killed was under 40 according to residents
of the town. Certainly one, and probably more, innocent natives were killed accidentally.

Where Sandino had posted himself during the fight

was not definitely determined. The *jefe politico*—
the chief official—of Ocotal reported to President
Diaz that Sandino was at the edge of the town,
directing the movements of his men. The marines
believed that he remained behind the nearest ridge of
hills and entrusted the actual carrying out of the
attack to a subordinate.

Four days later marine aviators reported concen-
trations of rebel groups at various points in the
vicinity of Ocotal and while reinforcements were
being hurried overland to Captain Hatfield's tired
and nerve-racked little company, Sandino, still defiant, sent out a proclamation stating his motives for
attacking Ocotal:

"First, to show that we continue protesting and
defending the constitutionality of Dr. Juan Sacasa,
former Liberal President.

"Second, to disprove the idea that we are bandits.

"Third, to prove that we prefer death to slavery,
for the peace obtained by Moncada is not the peace
that can give liberty to men, but a peace that puts
men under the domination of others."

The one to be held responsible for the attack,
Sandino continued, was President Coolidge, who had
bolstered up Adolfo Diaz.

"Whoever believes we are downcast by the heavy
casualties misjudges my army," he wrote, "for today
we are more impatient than ever to seek out the
traitors of our country, determined to die if we
cannot secure complete liberty for all men."

On the day in which this proclamation became known Secretary of the Navy Wilbur received the most optimistic report from Admiral Latimer.

"Conditions in Nicaragua today are better than when the revolution started," said the Admiral. "The recent activity of Sandino has no political bearing or significance."

There was indeed hope that there would be no more fighting. A strong column of marines and constabulary under command of Major Oliver O. Floyd was sent in pursuit of Sandino with instructions to avoid a conflict, but to force him out of the country by gentle, constant pressure. Major Floyd was unable to carry out these instructions literally, for the insurgents set ambushes through which he had to fight, but he drove straight through the heart of the guerrilla country and occupied the village of Jicaro, which Sandino had denominated his capital under the name of "Sandino City." The marine command felt justified, on the strength of this, in considering that Sandino was no longer a serious impediment to the peace of Nicaragua and the fulfilment of the American plans for the election. In August General Feland returned to the United States with many of his men, and the reduced Second Brigade was left in command of Colonel Louis Mason Gulick.

For many weeks it appeared that the judgment of the higher officers in Nicaragua had been correct. There still was occasional activity, much of it purely banditry. A marine was killed in September in an attack on the town of Telpaneca in Nueva Segovia by Carlos Salgado, a guerrilla chief. But Sandino himself had dropped out of sight.

In the Fall, however, marines began to hear frequently from the natives of a place called El Chipote —it means "the back-handed slap," in Spanish slang—where Sandino had taken refuge and built a fortress.

In mid-October there was a miserable tragedy. A marine plane piloted by Lieutenant L. A. Thomas with Sergeant Frank E. Dowdell as observer crashed from some unknown cause in the densest region of Nueva Segovia. Aviators in an accompanying plane saw Thomas and Dowdell run from the wreck, apparently unhurt, and then saw the plane burst into flames. They dropped a map. The grounded aviators disappeared in the brush and were never seen again by their comrades. But long afterwards friendly Indians told how Thomas and Dowdell had been betrayed by a native who offered to guide them, had been attacked with a *machete* and finally had been killed by a band of Sandinistas in a cave where they had taken refuge.

Ground patrols hunting for the aviators encountered heavy fighting and narrowly escaped from cunning traps. From time to time in the succeeding weeks there were marine casualties. In the Winter Colonel Gulick located Chipote and quietly laid plans to take his men off the defensive and subdue the guerrilla leader by an attack on his stronghold.

Chipote was a mile-high mountain overgrown with forests looming above the valleys at its base like the prow of a titanic battleship. Its flanks extended back fifteen miles and in the center of this triangle was the house in which lived Sandino, surrounded by a small picked bodyguard. The prow of the mountain was studded with trenches and machine gun nests, and at the top were quarters for men and storehouses for supplies. Sandino, the neighboring Indians said, had boasted that it never could be taken. A little to the south of the peak flowed the Coco River, and through the valley to its west trickled the tiny Jicaro.

On the bank of this latter river, in the shadow of Chipote, stood Quilali, a village of a score or two of houses, some of them adobe with red tiled roofs and some rude shelters of wooden slabs roofed with bamboo and banana leaves. A few miles up the Jicaro was the Butters mine at San Albino, where Sandino's men now operated an ingenious armory in which they made trench mortars out of sections of iron pipe and fashioned bombs by enclosing stones, glass and bits of iron with a dynamite charge in rawhide.

On New Year's day of 1928 Sandino became a world figure. On that day news trickled into Managua in fragmentary messages picked up by aviators of a dreadful fight in the shadow of El Chipote—of five marines killed and 23 wounded and their comrades besieged in a village while relief columns tried to force their way through the treacherous trails to rescue them.

It was war at last—a bamboo war as oldtime marines humorously call such tropical fracases, but the bitterest and bloodiest campaign in which Americans had participated since the World War.

The Americans involved were a strong combat patrol of marines and Guardia Nacional, accompanied by a large convoy of pack mules. Their objective, it was learned months afterwards, had been Chipote and their mission to eliminate Sandino. A half mile south of the village of Quilali, they were ambushed where the narrow trail, clinging to the side of a cliff, turned the shoulder of a mountain. The marine commander, Captain Richard Livingston, was wounded and put out of action in the first volley. Lieutenant Moses J. Gould, commanding the Guardia, also was slightly wounded. He took command. Frightened mules dashed away or rolled down the side of the cliff. The insurgents, armed with automatic rifles and handmade bombs, directed a heavy fire on the column from their concealed positions in the brush above the trail, but Gould got the column through, carrying their dead and wounded, and drove off the attackers.

But the forests around Quilali were alive with Sandinistas. The insurgents, as the marines glimpsed them, were dressed in khaki clothing; they were well armed and showed evidence of a training far better than is usual in Central American bush fighting.

On January 1, a reinforcing column commanded by Lieutenant Merton A. Richal forced its way to Gould's beleaguered force, after a series of heavy engagements, in one of which Lieutenant Richal was shot through the face but continued trying to direct his men after he was blinded. Thomas G. Bruce, who had fought so daringly at Ocotal, was killed. Four other marines were wounded. The two columns joined and got into Quilali, where for a week they withstood intermittent firing from the hills overlooking the town, completely cut off, and with eight seriously wounded men to care for.

Their predicament, however, afforded the opportunity for one of the most gallant and skilful exploits in aviation. Gould begged help for his wounded by means of messages, strung on wires stretched between poles and picked up by airplanes with grappling hooks, and by panel signals spread in the main street of the village. Four of the wounded certainly would die if they were transported on mule back, even if the force could elude the surrounding Sandinistas.

Lieutenant C. Frank Schilt, a brilliant aviator, volunteered to try to get the men out by plane. The only possible landing place was a narrow road through the town, only 300 feet of whose length was available as a runway. Gould and his men set to work with their bare hands demolishing the houses on either side and, facilitated later by shovels and picks dropped from a plane, widened this space to 70 feet.

Then Schilt, with a brother aviator hovering over-
head and trying with his machine gun to keep down
the fire from the surrounding hills, dived down into
the town time after time, ten trips in all, evacuated
all the wounded and brought in a relief officer. For
this he was awarded the Congressional Medal of
Honor.

It was the beginning of a bitter, baffling campaign
extending into the Summer in which the marines, reinforced repeatedly until at last there were 5,700 in
the country, struggled against difficulties which cannot be appreciated by one who has not seen that terrain, to capture Sandino, to kill him, to drive him
out of the country, to induce him by negotiation to
lay down his arms, to eliminate him in any way possible. He and less famous guerrilla chiefs now had
three provinces, Nueva Segovia, Jinotega and Esteli,
clustered in the northwestern corner of Nicaragua,
in an uproar. He threatened Matagalpa province as
well. Under such conditions it would be impossible
for an election of unchallenged freedom and impartiality to be held, and thus the whole American program was threatened.

A thousand marine reinforcements were rushed to
Nicaragua, and General Feland again was sent to take
command. Major General John A. Lejeune, commandant of the marine corps, went with him to inspect
conditions. Admiral David Foote Sellers, who had
succeeded Latimer as Commander of the Special Service Squadron, hurried to Nicaragua.

This new upflaring of hostility came at a most embarrassing time. It was the eve of the Pan-American Conference at Havana, which the United States earnestly hoped would be a feast of harmony but which already had threatened to produce a controversy about Nicaragua. Indeed the controversy did come in the form of an insistent effort by elements critical of American Caribbean policy, notably the delegates of Mexico and Salvador, to have the question of intervention in Latin America threshed out on the floor of the assemblage, but Charles Evans Hughes thwarted the attempt with a masterful effort of shrewdness and winning oratory.

Furthermore Congress, where assaults on the administration's Latin American policy were epidemic, was in session. The deaths of American youths in Nicaragua, together with reports of the slaughtering of Sandino's men, gave the issue a biting edge. Senators and Representatives again demanded to know what the United States was doing in Nicaragua.

The State Department endeavored to quell the outbreak with a brief but accurate statement:

"In connection with the announcement of the Navy Department that additional marines are being sent to Nicaragua, it will be recalled that under the arrangement effected by Colonel Stimson, both sides to the internal conflict then going on agreed to lay down their arms, and that they did so with the exception of a comparatively small body of men under Sandino, which has since been augmented by lawless elements who have continued to pillage a remote section of the country.

"These men are regarded as ordinary bandits, not only by the Government of Nicaragua, but by both political parties in that country. The Government of the United States fully intends to coöperate with the constabulary of Nicaragua effectively to establish order throughout that country and make possible the holding throughout the country of a free and fair election which we have undertaken to supervise."

This did not in the least halt the attack. The charges of imperialism and dollar diplomacy, of warfare for Wall Street bankers, familiar since the first intervention, resounded again, and in the same phrases. Coupled to them this time were charges of murder and spoliation practiced against the Nicaraguans by Americans with bayonets.

There was a new crop of resolutions. Senator Borah demanded information concerning the naval forces employed in Nicaragua and the number of individuals on both sides killed. Senator King sought by resolution to test the right of the President "to employ the armed military and naval forces of the United States to carry on belligerent operations in foreign countries in cases where Congress has not declared a state of war to exist or authorized the employment of the military and naval forces in or against such countries."

Resolutions for the withdrawal of the marines

were seriously advanced and the naval appropriations bill was held up while the administration and its critics struggled. Senator Borah, however, opposed the withdrawal because of the commitments of the United States involved in the Stimson agreements at Tipitapa. The opposition subsided. The administration was left with its hands free.

Outside the halls of Congress the Nicaraguan situation was debated with hardly less asperity. A large section of the American press was puzzled, critical and sarcastic. Europe again had its derisive attention directed toward American difficulties in the Caribbean. Student leagues in many places in Latin America denounced the United States. Liberal and radical organizations, some of them sincere, others apparently using Sandino as a convenient hook on which to hang their own propaganda, some of them with no conception of what it was about, stormed at the war of mighty America on a band of penniless natives who as these persons conceived it were asking only the right of their country to run its own affairs.

Denunciatory speeches were made at the corner of Wall and Broad Streets in New York. The White House was picketed by men and women protesting against American rule in Nicaragua, carrying such signs as "Wall Street and not Sandino is the Real Bandit," and calling for the withdrawal of the marines. The pickets were driven off and 107 were arrested. Opponents of the policy even obtained the names of marines going to Nicaragua for duty and mailed them appeals to refuse to fight Sandino but to join him in his "war for freedom."

While all this was happening, marines were extending their posts throughout Nueva Segovia, Esteli, and Jinotega, in the face of extreme hardship, trying to invest every place of consequence and even every crossing of important trails so as to protect the centres of population and immobilize Sandino and his bands. They were tormented by ticks, fleas and mosquitoes, they fell ill of the various fevers which infest the tropics, and they were in constant danger. Hardly a week went by without a patrol running into an ambush, or discovering a knot of Sandinistas or of plain bandits and attacking them. There were feats of extraordinary bravery by marines, constabulary, and Sandino's men. Marines performed acts of courage and self-sacrifice out in the bush which would have brought them glory in a popular war.

Marine planes gave Chipote a tremendous strafing by bomb and machine gun; ground patrols toiled cautiously up its sides and found it deserted. Rumors came in from the natives that Sandino himself had been killed and among the marines there was rejoicing—albeit restrained, for the news was too good to be true.

For several weeks after the bombing of Chipote in January the marines had no inkling of Sandino's whereabouts and ventured pardonably to hope that he had died or that his force had disintegrated and he was done. At enormous effort they had driven.

roads into the wilderness of Nueva Segovia and massed men and supplies in the area which once had been his playground.

Then with his characteristic suddenness and unpredictability Sandino swung southward at the head of a body of 150 mounted troops into San Rafael del Norte, an important town in the vicinity of Jinotega. From there he slipped down past the town of Jinotega, avoiding the marines who were on guard there, and took possession of the large coffee plantation of Charles Potter, one of the finest in Nicaragua, situated in the mountains 15 miles north of Matagalpa.

Potter was an English citizen. He was in Matagalpa at the time and the only person on the plantation besides the native help was the superintendent, a German. Sandino spent the night in the ranch house, with a bodyguard on watch. He and his men ate. He treated the superintendent courteously, appropriated what cash was on the plantation, took fresh mules, supplied his men with blankets and clothing from the commissary on the place, all to the value of about $1,200 for which he gave a receipt, swore in recruits from among the plantation workers and jauntily departed. That of course occasioned another call by the British Chargé upon the American Minister for information as to whether his people would be protected, and more references to the Monroe Doctrine.

The dozens of foreigners in the district as well as many Nicaraguans flowed into Matagalpa for protection. Some even drove to Managua, and there were

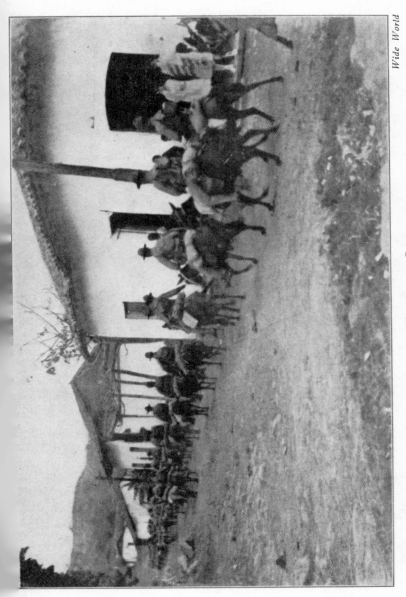

Wide World

~ OFF ON A HUNT FOR SANDINO ~
United States Marines, Mounted on Mules, Leaving Matagalpa

alarming rumors that Sandino intended to plunder and murder the American civilians.

Why Sandino did not come into Matagalpa the next night is known only to himself. He might well have captured it and have done as he liked with its rich booty and the lives of the many foreigners. It was guarded by only 45 marines who would have been hard-pressed to hold their own headquarters. He contented himself with leaving a threatening, sarcastic note for the American commander.

As soon as word of the raid reached Managua, a battalion of marines was rushed to Matagalpa in commandeered automobiles and confidence was restored, although for a few days the city was in a state of siege. The marines combed the mountains about Matagalpa but found no trace of Sandino. He had slid away again into the fastnesses near the border of Honduras.

As weeks passed with no news about the rebel leader, and as hostile activity faded away, the marines were encouraged again to believe that at last their difficulties were over. Nueva Segovia, Esteli, Jinotega and Matagalpa were now patroled and garrisoned so thoroughly that it did not appear possible for Sandino to inflict further damage or create further difficulties. *Mozos* returned to their garden patches; the countryside resumed its usual activities. Managua, León, Granada, Corinto, Masaya, Rivas, all the important centres in Western Nicaragua, even where from the first there had been no disorder, had their marine garrisons. Another thousand marines were sent down in March, but it was not felt that they would have any but routine garrison duty until election time drew near.

Then suddenly it happened again. In April a band of insurgents appeared in the gold mining region of the East Coast and on April 12 they raided a mine of the American-owned La Luz y Los Angeles Company, of which Diaz once had been an official. They took away with them George B. Marshall, an American citizen, the manager of the mine, and some $12,000 in cash and goods. The invading group was led by Giron, a Guatemalan, one of Sandino's chief lieutenants. Giron was followed by three more groups, one of which was headed by Sandino himself. The last one was a nondescript aggregation of ordinary looters not connected with Sandino but profiting by cleaning up after him.

The first news of the raid was accompanied by frightened rumors that a half dozen Americans and English had been captured and taken away to be beheaded. Subsequently it was learned that all had escaped except Marshall. Natives who had seen Marshall after the raid said that he was being well treated and was being utilized, because of his technical knowledge, to extract gold from neighboring mines. He has been given up for dead, presumably the victim of fever.

The mine itself was blown up with dynamite and the elaborate mills above the ground were destroyed. Too late, a battalion of marines was rushed from the western slopes of Nicaragua, through the Panama Canal to the East Coast district to reinforce the single company of marines which was stretched out all down the Mosquito coast. They drove through the whole area, gaining momentary contact with hostile groups occasionally, but when they completed their movement Sandino again had disappeared utterly and was not to be heard from again for many months.

With the delayed but effective policing of the East Coast, the entire country was at last under marine occupation and disorders ceased almost entirely. Whether or not Sandino, or some other leader, may stir up disorder again, the marines accomplished their mission. The election was held in complete peace, even in the remotest crossroads in the hills.

CHAPTER XIX

THE ENIGMATIC SANDINO

AND what manner of man was this Sandino, that he could cause such grief to the marines and such embarrassment to the American Government and threaten the peace settlement between the Liberals and the Conservatives?

Certainly he was not merely the bandit which he was officially considered to be by the State Department, by the Nicaraguan Government, and by the leadership of the Liberal party in Nicaragua. Neither was he the "George Washington of Central America" as a United States Senator once referred to him.

At the best and at the worst he was a young man of more than average learning, experience and character, endowed with an extraordinary personality with which he inspired the simple Indians of the mountains to heroism and devotion, and himself motivated to some extent, in the later period of his activities at least, by a wild patriotism. Certainly, too, he was touched with megalomania. He was a *poseur*. He loved to posture and declaim before his men and before the outside world.

And, although himself not a bandit in the ordinary sense—General Lejeune paid him that compliment ungrudgingly before the Senators after his return from Nicaragua—his red and black banner with its death's head was the rallying point of veteran desperadoes and despoilers of the northern mountains. Sandino as well as the unquestioned bandits whose assistance he apparently welcomed lived off the country. There was indeed no other way for them to live. Some of the marauders simply took what they wished as they always had done. Sandino "requisitioned" what he needed, and punctiliously left signed receipts for the comfort of his involuntary contributors. Toward the last he humorously presented certificates stating that "The Honorable Calvin Coolidge, President of the United States of North America, will pay the bearer $————," inserting the amount at which the levied goods were valued.

There was nothing in his birth or upbringing to mark Sandino for even an evanescent fame. He was born in May, 1893, at Niquinohomo, a village near Masaya, and hence was 34 years old when he blazed on to the Nicaraguan scene. He was half Indian. His father was a small coffee planter, an ardent Liberal who had been imprisoned for his politics. He was of slight stature, with a full brow and a strong jaw and cheeks of decidedly Indian cast. His eyes were sympathetic, and piercing.

In his youth he went to Mexico and worked at Tampico for the Huasteca Petroleum Company, an American corporation. He returned to Nicaragua and before joining Moncada's army was a timekeeper at the Butters mine at San Albino which he later occupied.

Sandino had a gift of oratory which he used with effect on his men. He was apt at coining heroic phrases—"Death is only a moment of discomfort not to be taken seriously"; "God and our mountains fight for us"; heartening thoughts in hardship and danger which his soldiers loved to repeat. He seems to have stirred his immediate band to an ardor akin to religion.

Sandino did not drink, and he forbade his men to drink before the attack on Ocotal, a practice entirely contrary to the usual Central American rules of war. He swore those who joined his forces to submit completely to his will and to fight without other pay than food, clothing and ammunition.

And as to Sandino's objects, he seems to have had none except to expel the American invaders—the "pirates" as he liked to call them. Unless there was truth in the charges heard everywhere in Nicaragua, but never with evidence to support them, that the factions trying for their own political ends to prevent the American supervision of the election were assisting him. He himself, by all accounts, had no ambition for political place, but promised that he would withdraw into obscurity when the marines and American influence had been driven from the country.

The only firsthand account of Sandino after he began hostilities against the Americans was given by Carleton Beals, a correspondent for The Nation, of

~ SANDINO AND HIS STAFF ~
The Guerrilla Leader Is the Second Figure From the Left

New York, who crossed the border from Honduras into Nicaragua in an adventurous and hazardous journey, and visited the guerrilla chief at San Rafael del Norte just before he descended on the foreign plantations near Matagalpa. Sandino evidently impressed Mr. Beals as a man of sincerity and intense conviction. In their interview Sandino repeated the charges so often made by opponents of American intervention in Nicaragua. He attacked the Diaz régime as the tool of the American Government, anathematized the American bankers, condemned the sale of the canal rights and asserted that eighteen years of American meddling had plunged Nicaragua into economic misery.

Sandino's message to the Americans after destroying the La Luz mine two months later was in the same tone.

"The most honorable resolution which your government could adopt in the conflict with Nicaragua," he wrote in a message left at the mine, "is to retire its forces from our territory, thus permitting us, the Nicaraguans, to elect our national government, which is the only means of pacifying the country. With your government rests the conservation of good or bad relations with our government and you, the capitalists, will be appreciated and respected by us according as you treat us as equals and not in the mistaken manner which now obtains, believing yourselves lords and masters of our lives and property."

That was Sandino's last gesture until after the

election. His importance at the time was overes-'timated. The fact that his men were killing American troops and defying efforts to suppress them naturally made him a front page newspaper figure. Notwithstanding the extraordinary propaganda in his favor, some of it extravagantly false, which flowed out from Honduras to all of Latin America, to the United States and to Europe, he did not represent public opinion in Nicaragua. He had the sentimental sympathy of great numbers of Nicaraguans, but the voluntary support of only a few. He was regarded with a certain sympathy by many foreigners, for he was an under dog making a terrific fight. I have heard foreigners in fear of an imminent attack on their plantations discuss him with something akin to admiration. But few people in Nicaragua were really interested in throwing the Americans out of the country, even though they might not love them. To the more intelligent persons of both parties, Sandino was a lively danger to Nicaragua's hard won opportunity for a just peace. Toward the last even some of his supporters outside the country urged him to cease fighting because his warfare, instead of driving the marines from the country, was insuring that they would remain.

It is not easy to weigh Sandino or his movement, but this is certainly true—that his chief significance was that he served as a focal point for all the undoubted dislike and jealousy and distrust in Latin America for the United States.

"No, he can't accomplish anything tangible," one of Sandino's chief advocates told me one evening when I was seeking to learn the purpose of Sandino. "But every time there is a battle, every time marines are killed, the attention of the United States and the world is drawn to what is going on in Nicaragua. That is why he keeps on fighting."

The marines did a much better job of their war with Sandino and the desperadoes who took advantage of the disorder which he produced to prosecute their private depredations than they received credit for in the United States.

There was a general inability to understand why several thousand marines with airplanes, machine guns and mountain artillery could not more quickly eliminate an obscure little guerrilla chief and his ragged band of Indians. To one who knew the difficulties of the country in which the marines were operating, difficulties which were of enormous advantage to the native warriors who knew every hidden trail; to one who knew the bravery and the ferocity of Sandino's men, there could be only admiration for the fortitude and dogged courage of the marines and wonder that their losses were not more extensive than they were.

There was hardly a contact between marines and rebels which did not produce outstanding feats of valor; too many instances of heroism and self-sacrifice to catalogue here. The aviation unit, under command of Major Rowell through all the heavy fighting, performed with such efficiency, energy and intelligence over country so hazardous that a motor failure meant probable death, that one wondered how the ground forces ever could have mastered the situation in time for the elections without the aid from the air.

Next to the difficulties of terrain, the chief handicap to the marines in their campaign against Sandino and the other chieftains in the North was their inability to get information of Sandinist activities which they could trust. Sandino apparently knew in advance every move the marines would make and could set his ambushes accordingly. The marines seldom knew what Sandino would do until after he had done it. The marines of course were almost entirely dependent on information given them by natives. If a native was intelligent and friendly toward the marines, the information he gave was likely to be correct. If he was unfriendly, if he was a partisan of Sandino or afraid of reprisals by the Sandinistas, the information would be incorrect. It was rarely that the marines could know whether or not they were being betrayed. More than one column, guided by a supposedly friendly Indian, found itself being led into an ambush. The marines, so often deceived, frequently disbelieved truthful information when they did get it.

At the very time Sandino was resting on a British plantation a few miles north of Matagalpa, the Navy Department was congratulating itself over a message stating that Sandino was leaving the country and that "in so far as Nicaragua is concerned, he is finished and is simply trying to escape."

One accusation levelled continually at the marines in Nicaragua was that they were abusing the natives, and that of course was the most serious charge that could be laid at their door. There were sufficient instances of the killing or wounding of noncombatants, women among them, to give color to such charges. But statements that the marines were engaged in a campaign of ruthlessness, of murder of natives and destruction of their homes, were grossly untrue and unfair. Such instances as occurred, if not accidental, were exceptional and in violation of explicit orders. Indeed, the marines leaned over backward in their endeavor to harm no one not actually engaged in hostilities and in so doing imposed handicaps on themselves in their efforts to stamp out rebel and bandit activity.

The marines were in an aggravatingly anomalous situation. They were carrying on a fair-sized military campaign in a country with which they were at peace; with an indefinite and seldom recognizable faction of a population which they were assigned to protect.

The military disadvantages of such a position are obvious. When an army is operating in a country which is officially hostile all the inhabitants are considered to be hostile. Military law is supreme. Persons suspected of inimical activity can be locked up. Information can be wrested from the people by methods akin to the third degree of the police station. But the marines, at war in a friendly country, were under obligations, which they understood and in general observed, to guard the people and all their civil rights. And there was no way of telling with assurance that a specific native was an enemy unless that native attacked them. It was a common practice for members of Sandino's army to hide away their rifles, remove their red and black hatbands and boldly enter towns where marines were posted. One can understand with what chagrin the marines learned that members of Sandino's command on their march toward Matagalpa had thus entertained themselves at a native dance within hearing of the marines garrisoned at Jinotega. The marines could have done nothing even if they had known about it. They might have suspected certain of the dancers, but they would not have dared take action.

The marines interfered to a remarkably slight extent in the civil life of the country—far less than many Nicaraguans wished them to. Immediately after the peace of Tipitapa, when the ordinary police power of the country was broken down, the marines performed a certain amount of civil police work in order to check the rampant disorder; but in all cases they delivered their prisoners to the civil authorities of the Republic for disposition. No Nicaraguan, not even those suspected of being Sandino agents, was tried by a military court. Several persons believed to be assisting Sandino were arrested and questioned, however. One of these was Toribio Tijerino, of New

York, former consul general of Nicaragua, one of the most active critics of the intervention and a sympathizer with Sandino. On Mr. Tijerino's visit to Nicaragua in the Summer of 1928 it was suspected that he would endeavor to get into contact with the rebel leader. He was picked up by marines, questioned at marine headquarters in León, and released. He was indignant at his detention, and marine officers were annoyed that they had no authority to hold him.

The marines were under detailed instructions to apply no unnecessary violence in making arrests, as evidenced by the following order issued from the headquarters of General Feland on May 31, 1927.

"Force Order No. 16.

"1.—The following is published relative to the arrest and detention as prisoners of civilians in Nicaragua and will be strictly adhered to by the naval forces ashore in Western Nicaragua, viz:

"2.—When the arrest of a civilian is made no more force will be used than is absolutely necessary to require such person to submit to arrest.

"3.—When the offense committed by the civilian whom it is desired to arrest is not of a serious nature and the arrest is resisted, extreme measures such as shooting, killing or wounding such person with a deadly weapon will in no case be resorted to to effect the arrest except where it is apparent that the life or limb of the person or persons making the arrest is in danger.

"4.—In the detention of a civilian prisoner by the

naval forces on shore in Western Nicaragua no more force will be used than is absolutely necessary to insure the detention of such prisoner.

"5.—In case the offense committed by a civilian prisoner for which such prisoner is being detained is not of a serious nature, such as a misdemeanor, extreme measures such as shooting, killing or wounding such prisoner will not be resorted to to prevent the escape of such prisoner, except under the conditions as specified in paragraph 3 above.

"6.—In case the offense committed by a civilian prisoner for which such prisoner is being detained is of a serious nature such as a felony, extreme measures such as shooting, killing or wounding such prisoner with a deadly weapon to prevent escape will only be used when all other means of prevention have failed or when as specified in paragraph 3 above.

"7.—When shooting is resorted to in making the arrest of a civilian prisoner or prisoners, the shooting will be so directed as to disable and not to kill such prisoner or prisoners, except as specified in paragraph 3 above. Shots to disable are usually directed at the lower extremities of a person.

"8.—In case the shooting, killing or wounding with a deadly weapon of a prisoner either in making an arrest or in preventing an escape is resorted to, due regard must be paid to the number of lives of innocent bystanders which would be endangered by such shooting or killing or wounding.

"9.—In all cases of killing or wounding of civilian

prisoners in Nicaragua by the naval forces a board of investigation or an investigating officer will immediately be ordered to investigate the circumstances connected therewith by the senior officer present at the post where it occurs."

The marines continued throughout their tenure in 1928 to exercise an unobtrusive watchfulness over the movements of the people. For instance, if one boarded a train the last person he saw as the train pulled out was a marine making a note of the passengers. On the other hand the marines were constantly besieged by civilians wishing them to settle every imaginable kind of private quarrel and were constantly having to impress on the Nicaraguans that their function was not to interfere in people's private affairs. These appeals of the Nicaraguans were eloquent of their confidence in the justice of the Americans as contrasted with the justice of their own local officials.

To a remarkable degree the relations between the marines and the inhabitants were cordial and friendly. The marine officers participated in the social life of the upper classes in the cities where they were stationed and became so much a part of the life of these localities that there was a tendency for officers located in Granada for instance to develop decidedly pro-Conservative feeling, and for those in León to lean strongly toward the Liberals. This quite natural sympathy, born of propinquity, sometimes had unfortunate results because of the obligation of the marines to preserve impartiality in the period between the peace of Tipitapa and the election, and it was necessary to remove one officer for over-enthusiastic utterances favoring the Liberals at a dinner in León.

The enlisted men, to a slight extent in Managua, but markedly in the small towns and villages of the hinterlands, also enjoyed friendly relations with the native population.

Navy doctors and pharmacists on duty with the marines in the jungles treated the natives without charge and were a valuable conciliatory influence.

There were exceptions of course to these harmonious relations. There was for instance the young officer in command of a small garrison in a remote town who found that his sleeping quarters were on a level with the bell-tower of the church a few feet distant. Now there is nothing most Nicaraguans enjoy more than making a noise. They especially love church bells, and hammer on them at all hours of the day and night. They do not ring them decorously and solemnly, but two men, each with a sledge, pound on them with all their speed and power and create enough clamor to exorcise devils.

After this lieutenant had been awakened at untimely hours on two or three successive mornings he made out a schedule of times at which the bells could be rung and issued a warning that if they were rung at any other hour he would shoot the ringers from his bedroom window. The priests of course protested to headquarters. The lieutenant was transferred and is still getting official letters about the incident. The writer, having suffered for six months from fire-crackers, saluting cannon, hack gongs and wandering free-lance orchestras, not to speak of church bells, is inclined to sympathize with the lieutenant.

One of the evils of an extensive occupation such as the marines conducted in Nicaragua is the in-evitability of unfortunate incidents. No organization of any sort, military or civil, composed of several thousand men is without sadists, ignoramuses and tact-less blunderers and the marine corps, needless to say, had representatives of these types.

Over a cafe table the writer has heard an officer who had spent many months in the bush speak with almost emotional affection of the simple Indians among whom he had lived, of their loyalty, generosity and hospitality, of their response to kindly and courteous treatment. Over the same table on another night he has heard another officer, on leave from the jungles, boast of how he "ran" his district by tolerat-ing no nonsense from the "spigs."

Undoubtedly, human nature being as it is, there were instances of abuse of natives in the remote re-gions. Mr. Beals, after his interview with Sandino, brought out reports of several such instances includ-ing what were described as wanton murders of prison-ers. Official reports of the marine corps list only one unjustifiable killing of a native by a marine. That was the shooting of a man by an intoxicated marine in Matagalpa in December 1927. The marine received a dishonorable discharge and a sentence of ten years in prison. On several occasions women were shot in the course of engagements between Sandinistas or bandits and marines. A typical incident of this sort is described in the following report from the commanding officer of a marine patrol which had a contact with a hostile group at Cuje in December, 1927:

"The bandits were divided between a group of five houses and a separate house some 300 yards further up on the ridge line. A sentinel was sleeping alongside of the separate house, in front of Corporal Tucker's patrol, with a dog sleeping at his feet. The dog scented danger and awoke the bandit sentry by barking. There were some 25 bandits in this house alone.

"The separate house was not demolished as one woman living there had been accidentally killed during the fire fight, and a small boy wounded. These and the three wounded bandits were left there with several other women who were found in the other houses."

Another patrol leader, telling of creeping up toward a house on whose veranda were a score of men wearing Sandino's colors, wrote in his report: "I was seen at the same instant and all hands broke for cover after a large well-dressed native yelled, 'Los marinos!'

"I had a hand grenade in my hand but the presence of two women and several children made it impossible to throw it. I therefore raised my pistol and killed the man who had shouted as he reached the corner of the house. At this signal, as prearranged, the patrol deployed along two sides of the fence and opened fire, rushed the house and pursued by fire the enemy.

"One of my groups which had deployed on the west side of the house shot a woman through the left shoulder who was running up the hill behind the men. When she screamed I noticed her and ordered cease firing. The woman was not badly hurt as she continued running holding her shoulder."

Besides a few such incidents as these there were a number of killings as a result of attacks by drunken natives on marines or of attempts to escape after serious crimes, killings which the marine command considered justifiable.

Contrary to certain propaganda circulated in the United States, the marine aviators did not engage in a campaign of bombarding towns. One town, and one town only, so far as the writer was able to learn, was bombed in the Autumn of 1927. From that time on the flyers operated under orders forbidding the bombardment of towns and counselling care not to endanger innocent persons. They adhered so faithfully to this policy that they knowingly sacrificed an opportunity to end Sandino's career, because he was in town.

That incident occurred early in February when Sandino, with a large body of mounted men, came from the north into San Rafael del Norte. There among other residents was Sandino's wife, Blanca. Mr. Beals had arrived from the vicinity of Quilali for his interview with Sandino and was then in the town.

A flight of marine planes, headed by Major Rowell, flew over San Rafael, saw the streets filled with armed men and horses and strongly suspected that Sandino himself was there.

"I was close enough to shake hands with him," said Major Rowell, a few days afterwards. "We flew so low the propellor wash knocked hats off the men in the streets."

The aviators contented themselves with a close inspection of the Sandinist band, departed without firing a shot or loosing a bomb, because it was an inhabited town, and hurried back to Managua to report their discovery.

Certainly whatever mistakes were made and whatever cruelties may have been practiced by individual members of the force far out in the wilderness where there was little danger of their becoming known to the higher officers, both General Lejeune and General Feland were sincerely committed to a policy of mercy and consideration. General LeJeune, in his expressions of his attitude, put it on practical as well as humanitarian grounds.

"If we treat the natives kindly they will be our friends," he said. "If we treat them unkindly they will be our enemies and we merely will have that many more people to fight."

One of General Feland's first acts when he arrived in Nicaragua in January, 1928, in company with

General Lejeune, was to issue a memorandum to the force on the treatment to be accorded to natives and their property. The text was as follows:

"Orders to avoid the use of physical force, the inflicting of physical or excessive mental suffering or what is spoken of as 'being hard with the natives' have been frequently given and have been impressed upon you constantly by your seniors. I am glad to say that all of you have accepted and have been guided by the spirit of these orders.

"But I do not want a single officer ever to feel that those orders are a blind, that they are not meant strictly, and that you might be justified, away out in the bush, on being a little 'rough.' This is not true. We do mean the orders literally.

"Use all the force in your power against outlaws with arms in their hands. But against the native population, or against prisoners, the use of physical force to get information cannot be justified, except in the unlikely, but possible case that it means the life or death of your men. Any abuse by the use of our power in any instance will in the long run defeat our purpose.

"The purpose of this letter is to impress on you the fact that conciliatory methods will help us, harsh methods would injure our mission.

"No hesitation would be felt in dealing with any officer who fails to carry out the policy of conciliation or to impress it on all his men."

There is no possibility of this order being marine

corps propaganda designed to quiet fears at home that the marines were abusing the natives. The writer learned of it only in May, when a Nicaraguan told him of it, and obtained the text from General Feland only after considerable persuasion. It became known at that time because General Feland reissued it, probably because of charges that an officer in command of a patrol near the Honduran border had maltreated natives in an effort to extract information. This officer was tried by court martial.

At the same time that he reissued the memorandum General Feland quoted with approval an order issued by Colonel Robert N. Dunlap, commanding the area of the North where the fiercest part of the campaign against Sandino was waged. Colonel Dunlap's order read in part:

"Remember that when a bandit group is moving from one area to another the only bandit property—stores etc.—in existence is that which the group carries with it. Therefore do not destroy anything when in contact with this group except that possessed by the bandits. All else belongs to innocent people.

"Because you are fired on from a house do not destroy it unless you can prove it is the house of those doing the firing.

"In general do not destroy property, stores or houses except those known to belong to bandits or known to be bandit hangouts. These places are usually to be found in the mountains off the main trails and concealed. When found, such places give unmistakable evidence of being bandit centres and their destruction is necessary and desirable."

A unique and unpremeditated opportunity to check up on reports that the marines had been devastating the countryside was afforded the author in an unscheduled airplane trip over most of the places which had figured in the operations of the Winter and Spring of 1927–1928. Swinging low and circling close over towns, villages and isolated houses—for the airplane was one of a combat patrol searching for Sandinistas—the writer saw everywhere the homes intact and the people going about their peaceful occupations with little heed to the planes which had become familiar to them through almost daily visits during many months.

With two exceptions there was no sign of the "blackened ruins" and general destruction which had been so often described. One of the exceptions was the ruins of two or three wooden buildings at Murra. These, the writer was told afterward by marine officers, belonged to the Pittsburgh Exploration Syndicate and had been burned by Sandino after the American manager and his wife had fled. The other was Quilali. Quilali was not destroyed, as had been reported, but it suffered damage. It was a deserted village and under the fire of Sandino's men when marines fought their way into it at New Year's 1928. It was in this town that Lieutenant Schilt landed his airplane and removed the seriously wounded. For this purpose the marines had widened the road through Quilali by pulling down the flimsy structures on either side. Afterwards an emergency landing field was constructed at one end of the town, for which other houses may have been wrecked. The remainder of Quilali, constituting its greater part, appears to be undamaged as viewed from a height of 200 feet.

All in all, conceding the mistakes which were made, Brigadier General Williams was only telling the truth in the memorandum which Secretary of the Navy Wilbur presented to the Senate Foreign Relations Committee in February, 1928, when it was investigating the use of the navy in Nicaragua:

"I wish to emphasize the fact that the American naval forces in Nicaragua have executed a very difficult duty with great tact and forbearance," said the general's memorandum. "They have used force only where absolutely necessary and have interfered as little as possible with the happiness and well-being of the inhabitants. A great mass of the Nicaraguan people have welcomed the American naval forces and have been glad to avail themselves of the protection which these forces insure. The steps that have been taken since the Stimson agreement are those considered necessary to prepare the country so that a fair election may be conducted in 1928."

At the best the Sandino revolt, whatever its motives, was a beastly and a bloody and above all a futile and needless business. It cost the Nicaraguans some two hundred lives. It disrupted the normal existence of hundreds of noncombatants in the northern wilderness. It rolled up more damage claims which presumably will be presented to the Nicaraguan government and add to the country's foreign debt. It was costly to the United States, too, in money as well as in men. Perhaps $2,000,000 will cover the cost to the United States of that war which was not a war. Secretary of the Navy Wilbur reported to the Senate that the Department had expended $3,536,000 in maintaining the expeditionary force in Nicaragua from May 4, 1927, the day of the Tipitapa conference, to April 16, 1928. That, it was explained, was $1,530,000 more than the marines would have cost if they had been kept at home stations.

CHAPTER XX

HAVING A FLING AT "LOS YANQUIS"

JUST as Sandino's little war against the marines
was getting well under way there came another
and equally unexpected difficulty to increase
the cares of the Americans who were trying to
straighten out Nicaragua's affairs. A powerful element in the Conservative party decided that it did
not wish the election supervised after all.

The Conservatives had been eager enough to in-
dorse the program of American supervision when it
was the one means of stopping the war which the
Liberals were waging against them—but the war was
over now. The reason for their change of front was
obvious. They feared they might be beaten at the
polls. Since they at that time were in power, they
might look forward to controlling the 1928 election
by the historic Nicaraguan methods of intimidation
and higher mathematics if the procedure of the past
could be followed. But if the election was to be the
free and impartial one to which both the American
and Nicaraguan Governments were pledged by the
peace of Tipitapa they could not be at all sure of
the result.

Emiliano Chamorro, who recently had been evicted

from the Presidency partly as a result of the disapproval of the Washington Government, presently was disclosed as the leader of the anti-supervision movement. He was not acting through pique or desire for revenge. Chamorro does not harbor malice. He was acting to prevent the defeat of the party of which he was the chief figure, the party which had been in control during the seventeen years since the United States had assisted in dispossessing the Liberals.

Chamorro as usual wished to be President. This time again he was not permitted to be.

During the struggle between Diaz and Sacasa and the months immediately following the peace imposed by Colonel Stimson, General Chamorro had been in Europe as Minister of Nicaragua. He left Europe in the Autumn of 1927 and went first to Washington to sound out the State Department on the subject of his projected candidacy for president in 1928. The Department informed him bluntly that if he ran and was elected he would not be recognized. The Secretary of State presented him the following written statement:

"On January 1, 1929, the Government of the United States will be confronted by the necessity of deciding whether it can consistently recognize the incoming administration in Nicaragua as the constitutional government of that country. While the United States is not supporting or opposing any political candidate, it is most desirous that there should be no question at that time as to the eligibility under

the Constitution of the person who may have prevailed at the Presidential elections, since it wishes to
extend the fullest and most sympathetic coöperation
to the new government.

"In these circumstances and in view of the reports
that General Chamorro contemplates becoming a
candidate for the Presidency of Nicaragua in the
1928 elections, the Government of the United States
has no choice but to point out that it regards General
Chamorro as ineligible under the provisions of the
Nicaraguan Constitution to the office of President
of Nicaragua during any part of the term commenc-
ing January 1, 1929.

"Article 104 of the Nicaraguan Constitution pro-
vides that—

No citizen who holds the office of President,
either as the duly elected incumbent or accidentally,
shall be eligible to the office of President or Vice
President for the next term.

"General Chamorro unquestionably held the office
of President de facto from January 17 to October
30, 1926, thus bringing himself within the prohibition of Article 104 of the Constitution and Article
2 of the general treaty of peace and amity of February 7, 1923, thus making it impossible for the
Government of the United States to regard him as
eligible to the office of President of Nicaragua for
the term beginning January 1, 1929, or to recognize
him as the Constitutional President of Nicaragua if

he should claim or attempt to occupy the office during any part of said term."

At the same time General Moncada also went to Washington "to obtain assurances," as he expressed it, "that the United States will fulfill the promises made to me by Mr. Stimson." His real object was to learn whether the United States considered him eligible to the Presidency. Conservatives in Nicaragua had asserted that his participation in the Sacasa revolution had ruled him out under the Washington Conventions of 1923. The State Department decided, however, that Moncada was eligible, since the revolution of which he had been a principal part had not resulted in the overthrow of an established government. It gave him to understand that he would be recognized if elected. Secretary Kellogg made public the following expression of his attitude:

"As I have said before, the United States is not going to select any candidate for President of Nicaragua, either Conservative or Liberal. Neither is the United States going to back or use its influence for the election of any particular person. The United States is going to do its best to see that there is a fair, open, and free election where everybody who is entitled to vote has an opportunity to do so. This has been made perfectly plain. Of course, following the Constitution of Nicaragua and the treaty, the United States cannot recognize anybody who is not qualified under the Constitution to hold the office."

This was true. As the events of the next

year demonstrated, no government ever has made a promise in greater sincerity or carried it out more scrupulously. But it was long before Nicaragua could be persuaded of this.

In the course of his visit to the United States General Moncada renewed the acquaintance which he and Colonel Stimson had begun under the historic black thorn tree at Tipitapa, and was a guest of the Colonel at lunch. General Chamorro was not so favored. His feelings were hurt, and it was months before he got over it. He returned to Nicaragua late in November reconciled to the shelving once more of his presidential ambition, but professing, at least, to believe that the American Government would favor Moncada in the election. Rumors began filtering among the Conservatives that Colonel Stimson had made some mysterious promise to Moncada under the thorn tree. Conservatives began recalling every instance in which marines had shown friendliness to Liberals, ignoring the instances, probably as numerous, in which marines had had cordial contacts with the Conservatives.

There was an outward show of validity to some of the contentions of the Chamorrist Conservatives. Adolfo Diaz was of course ineligible under the constitution of Nicaragua, and since the State Department had ruled that Chamorro likewise was ineligible, the two most important men in the party were relegated to the sidelines.

"They have decapitated the Conservative party,"

Chamorro complained, "yet they will let Moncada, who also led a revolution, run for president."

Thus the opposition to the American program of supervision took form.

The Liberals meanwhile were as anxious to have supervision as the Chamorrists were anxious to avoid it. It was their only chance to regain the power. And so, curiously enough, the positions of the two historic parties in relation to the North American Government were suddenly reversed. The Liberals were now supporting the American program as enthusiastically as the Conservatives had supported it in 1910, and the Conservatives were fighting it just as the Liberals had fought it when the Conservatives first came into power. The Liberals themselves endeavored to confirm the charges of the Conservatives that they would profit by the favoritism of the United States. They lost no effort to give the impression that they now were the pets of the State Department, thinking that this would perhaps influence the American supervisors in their favor, and also that it would influence the voters at the polls to support a candidate who was sanctioned by the big brother in the North.

The first step in the program of supervision was the enactment of a law placing the election under complete American control. The United States had had unfortunate experience in the case of the plebiscite over Tacna and Arica where General Pershing had had insufficient authority, and it intended to avoid another such fiasco. To accomplish this it was

360 DOLLARS FOR BULLETS

necessary to supplant for the period of American supervision the permanent electoral law of Nicaragua, which had been written originally by Professor Dodds in 1922 but weakened by the Nicaraguan Congress so that control of elections still pertained to the party in power.

The Diaz element in the Conservative party accordingly framed, in collaboration with State Department officials, a "transitory provision" to remain in force during the registrations and election. It provided for a bi-partisan national electoral board containing a Conservative and a Liberal and presided over by Brigadier General Frank Ross McCoy. It put General McCoy in complete control of this board by providing that the board could not meet without his presence, or the presence of a substitute chairman also chosen by the President of the United States; that no action of the board would be valid without his concurrence; that he should have a double vote in case of a tie; and that in any situation which he regarded as an emergency he alone could constitute a quorum and transact the business of the board. It provided also for departmental and cantonal boards, and for boards in each of the 432 voting precincts in the Republic. Each of these boards also was to be bi-partisan and presided over by an American citizen. The national board would canvass the election and certify the result to Congress, which, under the Nicaraguan constitution, has the duty of proclaiming the result of the elections. This central structure of the supervision was buttressed with carefully contrived subordinate provisions intended to make American control absolute.

The transitory provision immediately was nicknamed by the Nicaraguans "the McCoy law"—la ley McCoy. It came up in the Senate early in January and was passed unchanged without difficulty. General Chamorro was saving his ammunition for the lower house of Congress, which he controlled. The McCoy law had been referred to a committee in the House of Deputies. On January 13 this committee brought the opposition into the open by reporting out a substitute bill which pulled the teeth of the McCoy law and would have reduced the American supervisor to the futile status of observer. The House approved the committee report and four days later tentatively passed the substitute bill.

The issue split the Conservative party. President Diaz was pledged to the supervision and had to push it through. He apparently did his best and was thoroughly indignant when intimations came from American sources that he was not exerting himself to the utmost in behalf of the bill. His chief ally was Dr. Cuadra Pasos, the Foreign Minister, who was then in Havana as the leader of the Nicaraguan delegation to the Pan-American Conference. Cuadra Pasos had been Minister to Washington and was reputed to be a supporter of the general American policy in Nicaragua. It was Diaz and Cuadra Pasos on one side and Chamorro on the other.

The situation was deadlocked when General McCoy arrived in Managua on January 23, and began at once to add his persuasions to those of Minister Eberhardt and the Legation Counsellor, Dr. Dana G. Munro. McCoy came with as fitting qualities and background as any one whom the United States could have sent. He had served in Cuba and the Philippines with General Leonard Wood. He had a fair knowledge of the Latin mind and a sympathetic understanding of the people with whom he had to deal. The Nicaraguans at once gained the impression that they had a just man to deal with.

But with his arrival the Chamorristas only intensified their efforts to evade supervision and prosecuted their campaign with all the deviousness of which the Nicaraguan political mind is capable. Their principal argument was that the transitory provision was unconstitutional. The American officials brought forward Nicaraguan jurists to state that it was constitutional and suggested to General Chamorro that it was a little strange that he should display this sudden passion for constitutionality when he himself had overridden the constitution whenever he found it in his way. Chamorro took advantage of the Sandino revolt to contend that there obviously could not be a free and fair election with the northern departments in a state of war. He shrewdly suggested that these departments be ruled out of the voting; that would have delighted him because they were a region of Liberal voting strength. The Americans would not hear to it. Then Chamorro advanced a valid objection to the program of supervision as then arranged: The agreement of President Coolidge and President Diaz provided only for the election of 1928; if the Liberals won they would be able to maintain themselves in the saddle indefinitely unless succeeding elections also were supervised. He offered to permit the McCoy law to go through if the American Government would sign a treaty providing for supervision of the next four or five elections. The American officials could not promise that any such treaty would be ratified in the United States, and, besides, they knew that the Coolidge administration would not wish to tie its successors to the continued intervention which such an agreement would imply.

The discussions went on for weeks without result. All day long there was a stream of political callers at the Legation. Driven from one argument, the Chamorristas would advance to the next, and when they had gone through them all they would return to the first and start all over. Sometimes they would vary the discussion by trying to draw some expression of preference from McCoy and Eberhardt as to which candidate they would prefer the Conservative party to nominate. Again and again the Americans told them that it made no difference to the American Government who was nominated; that the candidate chosen in the election would be recognized by the United States, so long as he was a man not barred by the Nicaraguan constitution or the Central American Conventions.

"That is for you alone to decide," Minister Eberhardt would insist. He would point through the open door of the Legation to a dilapidated hack standing at the curb, with its driver dozing on the box.

"Nominate that cab driver if you like," he would exclaim, "and if he is elected the United States will recognize him."

The Nicaraguans simply could not believe it.

At the end of such a session Eberhardt and McCoy would mop their perspiring brows and shake their heads at the futility of argument—and next day they would go through it all again.

Meanwhile the Conservative and Liberal newspapers were revelling in mutual denunciation. The Liberal organs clamored for the deportation of Chamorro, and the Conservative said Moncada should be sent from the country. Each side thunderously accused the other of financing Sandino's revolt. A lemonade stand in Managua's principal park burned one night and the Liberal press charged that it was the work of Conservative conspirators who wished thus to discredit the Liberal administration of the city.

The supporters of the American policy staved off a final vote in the House of Deputies and obtained a recess until Dr. Cuadra Pasos should arrive from Havana and help in the fight for supervision. At

Havana the Foreign Minister had supported Charles
Evans Hughes's efforts to keep the intervention question out of the discussions and collaborated with State
Department officials in drafting changes in the original transitory provision intended to eliminate any
question as to its constitutionality without lessening
its effectiveness. The United States sent a cruiser
to hasten the journey of Cuadra Pasos. He reached
Managua on March 5—a day later than planned.
The cause of the delay was a spike, maliciously
driven, which derailed the regular train preceding
the special on which the Foreign Minister was riding.

Cuadra Pasos threw himself into the struggle on
the side of President Diaz and the Americans. The
Senate passed his amended draft but the result in the
House was extremely doubtful. Strenuous efforts were
made to win over the Chamorristas in the lower body,
and at times General Chamorro himself seemed to be
at the point of yielding. From day to day the final
issue was put off until the Americans were wearied
of delay. On March 12 General McCoy and Minister
Eberhardt, with the assent of President Diaz and Dr.
Cuadra Pasos, held a final conference with the leaders
of the House of Deputies and issued an ultimatum.
They demanded a final vote—yes or no—before ad-
journment on the following day. They were willing
to permit modifications of the transitory provision
in order to save the face of the Chamorrist opposition, so long as such modifications did not lessen the
force of the law, but it must be settled at once. If

the vote was favorable, then General McCoy would proceed to the erection of the supervisory machinery; if it was unfavorable, the American Government would find some other means than a law of Congress as the basis of its supervision. One thing was certain, the United States intended to supervise the election. Sandino could fight, politicians could balk—the American Government would not be deflected. Its honor, its good faith with the Liberals, its prestige before the world were at stake. There had come at last an end to hesitation and timidity. Mr. Coolidge and Mr. Kellogg had now set their teeth in a definite and clearcut policy directed toward a definite and discernible goal and would not be shaken from it. Their representatives in Managua told the Chamorristas that they preferred that the supervision be by the will of Congress. If that could not be—

The next day was the tensest that Nicaragua had known since the end of the revolution. When Congress met, the shabby-genteel National Palace, erected by Zelaya and still unfinished, was surrounded by a cordon of constabulary under command of marine officers who were officers of the Guardia Nacional. This was not intimidation, as some persons professed to view it, but a precaution against disorder normally taken when a hard-fought matter is before the Congress of Nicaragua. No one was admitted to the building who did not have business there. A great crowd of Liberals massed in Dario Park, across the street from the palace and cheered for "la ley McCoy" and "el Presidente Coolidge." One of their generals started haranguing them, and an American officer of the Guardia persuaded him to desist and the crowd to disperse for fear the gathering might lead to a riot. In the steamingly hot little Hall of Deputies Chamorro Conservatives, Cuadra Pasos Conservatives and Liberals argued and expounded all day. The Liberals, who in their time had railed at the tyranny of the "Yanquis," extolled the United States now as the rescuer of the Republic from revolution and the protector of its liberties. They pointed to Cuba as visible proof of the magnanimity of North America.

A Cuadra Pasos Conservative got to his feet.

"What would become of us if our little nation did not have a great nation like the United States to restrain us from our own mistakes?" he asked. "Intervention by the United States is an absolute necessity. The North American Government asked us what was the best way to obtain peace and order in this country. The answer was 'a free election.' The Conservative party agreed to this. Let us have it."

An undercurrent of bitterness was evident. There were men in that hall whose sons had fallen in the fighting of less than a year before. There was now a double struggle—a fight for supremacy between the Liberals and the Conservatives, and a fight among the Conservatives for control of their own party. There was a gust of anti-American feeling. Alejandro Arcia, a Chamorrist of Managua, referred to the utterances of President Coolidge at Havana.

"I do not know whether President Coolidge is a faker," he shouted, "or whether the cables lie to us when they quote him as saying that he will not transgress the laws of weak nations. Yet here is President Coolidge's representative trying to pass a law which is contrary to our constitution."

A tropical sun beat into the room through the very window from which the aviator Lindbergh had addressed an adulating crowd two months before, when the Nicaraguans had hailed him as "the eagle without talons."

"We have got nothing from intervention except disastrous wars," Arcia continued. "There is Sandino fighting the Americans, and that is God's punishment upon them for their intervention. The blood of North Americans is running in the northern departments. It is a judgment of God."

There was a burst of cheering when he sat down, but there also were murmurs of resentment among other deputies. Even the majority of the Chamorrists asserted that Arcia had "foamed over," and Chamorro himself afterwards rebuked the deputy for his immoderation.

Late in the session a recess was taken and Chamorro conferred with his followers. They returned to the hall in uncompromising mood. Just before the vote telegrams urging them to defeat the American project arrived from organizations in other Latin American countries and were handed around among the deputies. At dusk the House voted down the McCoy law, 23 to 17, and adjourned sine die. All of the Chamorro-faction except one voted against the supervision. All the Liberals supported it. Conservatives shouted in the streets around the Palace, and that night all the lights were ablaze in Chamorro's house and he spent the evening receiving the congratulations of his supporters. When Americans spoke to him next day of the events in the House he blandly expressed surprise and regret that the transitory provision had been defeated.

Minister Eberhardt and General McCoy were quite unruffled at the defeat and immediately set in motion an alternative plan for obtaining the authority to supervise the election. General McCoy and his assistants, with the help of Nicaraguan officials and lawyers, spent several days devising a presidential decree. It was cabled to the State Department for approval and then presented to President Diaz for his signature. It placed dictatorial power over the conduct of the election in the hands of General McCoy, and even provided that the Guardia Nacional, the armed force of the Nicaraguan Government, should be subject to his command until the Congress should proclaim the results of the election.

President Diaz signed the decree as submitted, except for minor verbal changes which he made, and it was proclaimed on the afternoon of March 21, in a picturesque Spanish ritual. A soldier of the constabulary, accompanied by the presidential brass band, moved from corner to corner of the city. At each corner they stopped, the band played a series of lively airs, and the soldier read the decree aloud to the assembled crowd. Liberals laughed at the overriding of the Chamorristas.

On the following Sunday the Liberals had a great pro-American demonstration. Two thousand of them met at the city hall and cheered themselves hoarse for Moncada, "la ley McCoy," and "los Estados Unidos." Headed by Mayor Zelaya, a nephew of the old dictator, they formed a column and marched to the American Legation. The vanguard was composed of mounted men who had fought in Moncada's army. A dozen banners, inscribed in Spanish on one side and in impeccable English on the other, blazoned the gratitude of the Liberals to the United States. Barefoot old women strode along shouting on the flanks of the column. Many of the paraders waved Nicaraguan and American flags made of paper, souvenirs of the reception to Lindbergh. One of the mounted men repeatedly fell off his horse. At the Legation where they stopped and cheered they found only a pair of embarrassed marine sentries and a mildly interested clerk, for General McCoy and Minister Eberhardt had gone to the country. Next day the principal Conservative newspaper made great fun of the "alcoholic demonstration" and said that the Liberal party, in its desire to curry the favor of the American Government, was acting "like a tame bear at a carnival."

CHAPTER XXI

A FREE AND FAIR ELECTION

THE issuance by President Diaz of the decree
establishing American supervision of the
election did not stop the efforts to sabotage
the program but called forth new and ingenious
schemes to set it at naught.

Despite the care and cleverness with which the decree had been drawn to place complete power in the
hands of General McCoy and his aides, there was one
joker of which they knew but which they could not
remove. That was a provision in the Nicaraguan Constitution for the election of the president and vice
president by Congress if no candidate received a majority of the total vote. Such a thing might happen if
there were more than two parties in the field. If it did,
American supervision would become a large and ex-
pensive joke. The Conservative majority in Congress
in all likelihood would elect one of its own party and
the United States would have failed to keep the promise it had made to the Liberals.

Opponents of the supervision immediately centred
their attack on this weak point and began spawning
extra parties. One of these was headed by Dr. Luis
Filipe Corea, a native of Nicaragua who has practiced

law in New York for many years and was a naturalized citizen of the United States until he returned to Nicaragua in 1924 to run for President. After that defeat, in which he polled 7,000 votes, he resumed his residence in the United States. He appeared again in his native land in the Spring of 1928 as the leader of the Liberal-Republican party. There was a strong suspicion in Nicaragua that his party had been revived by General Chamorro in order to split the Liberal vote. The National Board of Elections unanimously ruled it out on the ground that since it had polled less than 10 percent of the total vote it had lost its standing as a holdover party according to Nicaraguan law. A group known as the Republican-Conservatives appeared, and they also were eliminated.

In May the Autonomist, or Nationalist, party was organized by a group whose principal member was Toribio Tijerino, former Consul General at New York, former secretary to General Chamorro, former financial agent of Nicaragua, former director of the National Bank and the railroad, and reputed to be one of the most active sympathizers with Sandino. He made his home in New York. Others prominent in this group were Bartolomé Martinez, former President whose ambition to succeed himself had been forestalled by the United States; Alberto Lopez Callejas, who had recently ceased to be vice manager of the National Bank, and José Dolores Estrada, who had been President during the few days between the flight of Madriz and the accession of his brother

Juan in 1910. Its program demanded an end of American intervention; the withdrawal of the marines; and the restoration of Nicaraguan management of the Republic's bank and railroad, and of its fiscal affairs. It also called on Sandino to cease fighting and join other elements of the country in civic reform. The time between the issuance of the electoral decree and the closing of the party lists was too brief to permit this group to establish a party identity by means of petition, and it, too, failed to win a place on the ballot. So in July there remained only the two parties, the Conservative and the Liberal, and any danger of the election being thrown into Congress was past.

The Liberals got an early start in the campaign. Even before the defeat of the McCoy law in the Congress the Liberals had held their national convention at León and nominated General Moncada for the presidency. Many of the León group of Liberals would have preferred another candidate, but they recognized Moncada's strength among the rank and file of the voters and indorsed him because he embodied their best hope of victory.

The eloquent Moncada delivered before the convention which nominated him a reasoned defense of the general policy of the United States toward Nicaragua. There was fear in Latin America, not without reason, he conceded, that the United States infringed the sovereignty of the states bathed by the Caribbean. "But are there enough forces in all Spanish America," he asked, "to oppose this avalanche, this omnipotent evolution of North America?" Yet it was the United States which, by the Monroe Doctrine, had prevented Central America becoming another Balkan region by forbidding its colonization by the European countries which coveted it.

"We have no choice but to rely on this evolution, on destiny, on the development of the world forces in the direction of human idealism, hatred of war and regard for the rights of the weak," he declared. "I sincerely believe that for its own greatness and safety the United States of America will maintain the sovereignty of our Republic, and the worthier we become of surviving as a nation, the more the Washington Government will respect our independence. My Americanism has been firm since 1911, and I have known since then that our future is everlastingly attached to that of the United States."

The platform of the Liberals was quite as cordial toward the United States.

"The American Government may have committed errors in the methods it has employed to implant a constitutional régime in Central America," it stated, "but its expression of desire that a republic shall reign unrestricted among us is proof evident of its disinterest and its dedication to the solemn promise made to us by President Monroe 100 years ago that it did not intend to take possession of our lands or rob Nicaragua of its sovereignty."

While Moncada was actively campaigning for the presidency the Conservative party still struggled within itself. Chamorro, unable to be a candidate himself, advanced Vicente Rappaccioli, an elderly, wealthy man of little political experience, as his candidate. The moderates of the party, with whom Adolfo Diaz had identified himself, formed behind Dr. Cuadra Pasos. On April 12 President Diaz accentuated the schism in his party and broke politically with Chamorro by issuing a manifesto in his dual capacity of President and leader of the Conservatives calling upon the party to nominate Cuadra Pasos because of his friendliness to the American policy.

"I desire that all Conservatives shall understand clearly," Diaz wrote, "that the essential point in the program of our party must be the continuance of its political confidence in the friendliness of the Government of the United States, which has been so fruitful in good works and progress for Nicaragua. As a result of our relations with that great republic we have passed almost without pause from a bloody war to the civilized contest in which we are today engaged."

General Chamorro reacted to this characteristically. On May 20 the Conservative party held its national convention. The Diaz-Cuadra Pasos faction met in one hall. The Chamorro faction met in another. Each claimed to be the official convention of the party, and each nominated a candidate—Rappaccioli and Cuadra Pasos. Both factions tried in vain for a month to swallow each other, then gave it up and laid the quarrel before General McCoy's National Board of Elections. The Board ruled that neither faction was the historic Conservative party and appealed to the members to compose their differences so that the coming election would be a conclusive and undebatable test between the parties. Adolfo Diaz grew weary of the bickering and withdrew from active participation, and in another national convention held by the Conservatives, Adolfo Benard, a wealthy supporter of Chamorro, was nominated and Chamorro again had won control of the party.

By mid-summer the organization of the American electoral commission was completed. General McCoy had the services of technical advisers including such experts as Professor Dodds and Colonel Arthur W. Brown, of the Judge Advocate General's Department of the United States army. His immediate assistant was Colonel (afterward Brigadier General) Francis LeJ. Parker, who, as vice chairman, was second only to General McCoy. The executive officers and the chairmen chosen for the departmental boards included army officers who had seen many years of service in Latin American countries. Besides these, the Navy Department sent thirty ensigns chosen from among the recent graduates of Annapolis who stood highest in Spanish, to assist the departmental chairmen and to train the marines who were to be precinct chairmen. Schools were established to familiarize the marines with every detail of the election procedure and to prepare them against every trick which wily politicians might be expected to devise. Above all, there was to be no favoritism, or appearance of favoritism.

"All American personnel," said an order of General McCoy, "are warned to maintain a scrupulously neutral attitude between Liberals and Conservatives, and to remember that the slightest evidence of partiality toward individuals of one party will be magnified immediately by both sides as an evidence of bias. The hospitality of a group of Liberals must not be accepted unless similar hospitality can be accepted from a group of Conservatives, and vice versa. The ordinary phrases of courtesy and appreciation customary in all countries but especially necessary in Latin America must be equally divided by American officials between the two groups. The spirit of friendship and goodwill toward Nicaraguans is to be cultivated by all proper means, but in an exact equality with both parties."

General Beadle, who had striven since taking command of the Guardia Nacional to indoctrinate it with the novel idea that it was the army of Nicaragua and not of a political party and hence must be nonpartisan, sent his men through the country to inform the people that the coming registrations and elections would be free and just, that intimidation would not be tolerated, and that they were to vote according to their own wills and not according to the dictation of political leaders.

The registrations were held in September and October. At the request of General McCoy, President Diaz decreed a mild form of prohibition lasting until after the election. Padlocks were placed on the government liquor warehouses, whose contents often in the past had been used for purposes of corruption by the party in power. Even the shooting of fireworks also was forbidden by presidential decree for fear that their explosions might be mistaken for gun fire and precipitate disorder.

The marines, noncommissioned officers and privates who were to act as precinct chairmen, were sent to their remote stations. Some of them had to travel for days on muleback over the mountains and through the torrents of the rainy season, lugging ballots, ballot boxes and other election supplies. Some reached their precincts by dugout canoes. A few of the precincts were so completely isolated by flooded rivers that contact could be maintained with them only by airplanes, which dropped messages and supplies in response to requests signaled from the ground.

The campaign of the marines had brought a state of peace to the country more complete, probably, than it ever had known before, and this was reflected in the magnitude of the registration and the subsequent vote. The total registration was 148,831, some 35,000 more than had registered in 1924.

The Liberals and Conservatives campaigned actively but with a sportsmanship previously unknown in Nicaraguan politics. The conduct of the registration at last convinced them that the United States intended to be rigidly impartial, and before the election leaders of both parties pledged themselves publicly to abide peaceably by the results.

General Moncada and Adolfo Benard exchanged courteous letters in which each promised that in the event he was elected he would ask supervision of the next election by the United States.

"Let there be no more fratricidal wars and let freedom and order be established forever among us," wrote Moncada. "Now that we are witnessing the justice with which those in charge of the American supervision are proceeding, when with generous and praiseworthy earnestness they are extending us their hand in the development of republican institutions by means of a true and honest electoral liberty, we who desire an era of peace and industry for Nicaragua could agree to accept this same supervision for one or several periods more of constitutional government."

Señor Benard accepted the suggestion as a partial guarantee of lasting peace, and proposed also that the candidates agree to extend and perfect the existing financial plan "so that we may be able to carry out operations on which to establish a basis for the progressive development of our resources, indemnifying our citizens for the damages suffered in the past emergency and carrying out works of material progress for our country."

The registration and the election were carried out with only one incident of serious disorder, the wanton murder of eleven members of a Liberal group campaigning for Moncada in the Department of Jinotega by a gang led by Pedro Altamirano, a lieutenant of Sandino.

The election itself, on November 4, was a festival day for the cheery Nicaraguans. On the eve of the voting, a final air reconnaissance was made by twelve airplanes of the marine corps, whose pilots saw streams of people dressed in their holiday best on the roads of the northern departments where there so recently had been severe fighting. Hundreds of voters came out of their cabins in the jungles and mountains and spent the night before election day in the villages and towns where their precinct polling places were situated.

As each voter stepped up to the railing in the polling place to receive his ballot his finger was stained with a red liquid to prevent him voting again. President Diaz, General Moncada and Señor Benard submitted to this smilingly like the rest. There was only one interruption to the perfect calm of election day. A Liberal bull ran amuck in the town of Dario and was shot by a marine. His owner immediately dressed him and held a barbecue for members of his party.

The total vote was 133,663, 50,000 more than in 1924. Moncada won with a majority of 20,000.

Two days later, when it was evident that the Liberals had swept the election, *El Commercio,* the principal Liberal newspaper of Managua, published this banner across the top of its first page: "The

United States is Vindicated Before the World."

On the same evening *La Prensa*, the Conservative organ, headlined: "The American supervision has honorably observed its promise. The elections Sunday were honest, tranquil, correct and honorable. The Liberals obtained the victory."

The Conservative leaders accepted their defeat in good spirit and there was no murmur against the result. It was a miracle in Central American politics.

So on January 1, 1929, José Maria Moncada took office, displacing a Conservative régime which had obtained for eighteen years and had operated largely under the tutelage of the United States. And yet, in this leader of a party which so often had endeavored to block the American program, the United States had to deal with a new President of Nicaragua who had been only less outspoken in his professions of friendship for the United States than Adolfo Diaz had been.

In his inaugural address President Moncada referred to "the canal which will supplement the Panama Canal."

"Geographically situated in the centre of the New World, and having common interests and a common destiny with the United States and the other nations of this continent," he said, "we Nicaraguans are imperiously and inevitably obligated to open the heart of our country to civilization in order that we may contribute something of what generous nature has given us for the benefit of all the people of the earth."

CHAPTER XXII

PROFIT AND LOSS

THE United States has now come to a point of
pause in the long experiment which it has
been carrying out in Nicaragua, that perfect
laboratory of its Caribbean policy. It is by no means
the end of American activities there, for all that
peace and good feeling now seem to be triumphant,
for Nicaragua remains as much as ever a region in
which the United States has a paramount interest and
over which it will continue to watch. But there is a
rounding out of an epoch in the fall from power of
the party through which Washington has worked
until now that makes this moment peculiarly suitable
for considering the benefits and the costs of the guardianship which the United States assumed over Nicaragua nearly two decades ago.

In that long relationship the United States has obtained the definite objects which it wished: perpetual, exclusive control of the canal route and the eradication of stimuli to European interference in this
doubly strategic part of the Caribbean region. It has
obtained them at an unexpectedly high cost in lives,
money, trouble and humiliation.

Nicaragua also has gained definite benefits under

that guardianship. It is now stable and orderly; it is financially and economically healthy; it has more of justice and honesty; life—at this moment—is safer, and possibly happier. But one would wish that Nicaragua had forged farther ahead in the past 18 years. No one would wish it more than the North American statesmen who have affected its history. Nicaragua's gains, undeniable though they are, have not been in proportion to the effort, the money and the blood which have been poured out.

In one important respect dollar diplomacy has been disappointing in Nicaragua. The dollars on which Mr. Taft and Mr. Knox counted for the pacification of Nicaragua unhappily have not done away with the bullets—not even with American bullets. With all the anxiety of the North American Government that there be peace and order in Nicaragua, for the sake of its own interests as well as for the good of Nicaragua itself, the little Republic has been racked by two major revolutions in this period of American oversight. Moreover, the United States itself was a factor in both those revolutions. The Mena outbreak in 1912 was a stroke against the Americans as well as against the ruling faction of the Nicaraguans, and the disorders of 1926–1928 could not have occurred except for the premature weaning of the Republic and uncertainty as to what the North American Government would do.

It is impossible, of course, to judge whether Nicaragua would have had more or less peace if the United

States had not flung itself into the Republic's affairs 'in 1909. One can only know what has happened; never what might have happened if history had taken a different path at any fork in the road. But one may be pardoned for wondering if Nicaragua would have had to endure such devastating revolutions if left in command of its own destinies.

We can acquit the United States of exploiting Nicaragua, but it is inescapable that unwittingly and unwillingly it has worked to the confusion and sometimes the harm of Nicaragua. Paradoxically, the harm that has been done has often been the result of the very desire of the United States to benefit its ward. There has been a stiff-necked righteousness sometimes in the attitude of the United States toward its Latin American neighbors and specifically toward Nicaragua—an air that if they do not do as the United States does they are no better than they should be. Actuated to some extent by this feeling, and with the zeal of a reformer, Washington has tried to transform Nicaragua into a little United States. It has been only partly successful.

It is the fashion of Nicaraguan orators when they wish to compliment the United States to refer glowingly to the example in free government which was set in North America for the rest of the hemisphere. Yet that example has been the worst disservice which the United States has ever done Nicaragua, whose masses are so grotesquely and hopelessly incapable of governing themselves. Nicaragua, like other Latin

American states, modelled its constitution on that of the United States. But Nicaragua has had only the effigy of democracy. It is the powerful few who have ruled, usually with a dictator at their head who held his power until his hand weakened and another dictator, or an oligarchy, succeeded him, usually by force. This was not an ideal system by any means, but it was inevitable so long as Nicaragua endeavored to govern itself, and it worked fairly well. Often there were long periods of relative peace between the serious revolutions which drove one party from power and placed another in. The Outs bore the injustices which the Ins inflicted upon them with fortitude while they awaited their turn to govern.

But this Central American method of compromising with the outward form of democracy sometimes endangered foreigners and injured their property, with resultant complications unwelcome to the United States. The United States determined, therefore, that there must be an end of revolutions. It was not enough that Central Americans apotheosize the example of North America; they must follow the example literally as well. This determination took definite form in the Central American Conventions of 1907 in which the five republics agreed to withhold recognition from any government coming into power through revolution, and was further crystallized by Charles Evans Hughes in the Conventions of 1923.

This policy, so famously espoused by President

Wilson in his endeavor to force Huerta from the presidency of Mexico, was known as the policy of non-recognition, and its aim was to check the habit of violent change of government in Latin American countries by removing the rewards of violence. In practice it had the effect of setting up the North American Government as a censor of the eligibility of presidents. As Wilson himself spoke of it in a conversation with Sir William Tyrrell in the midst of the Mexican crisis of 1913: "I am going to teach the South American republics to elect good men."

A pungent discussion of the policy has been made available in "The Life and Letters of Walter H. Page." The American Ambassador, Mr. Page, and the British Foreign Secretary, Sir Edward Grey, were talking of Wilson's difficulties with Mexico.

"Suppose you have to intervene, what then?" asked Grey.

"Make 'em vote and live by their decisions," Page responded.

"But suppose they will not so live?"

"We'll go in again and make 'em vote again," said Page.

"And keep this up 200 years?"

"Yes," said the American Ambassador, "the United States will be here 200 years, and it can continue to shoot men for that little space until they learn to vote and rule themselves."

As thus expressed, and as carried out in Nicaragua, this policy has been one of democracy imposed from the outside. In Nicaragua the United States has said in effect: "You are going to have liberty if we have to run your government for you and put marines at every city, village and crossroads in your country."

It is a policy which has had beneficial results, for as embodied in the Conventions of 1923 it unquestionably has prevented several revolutions. At the same time, it tends to keep strong men out of office, as in the case of Emiliano Chamorro, and to drag the United States into intervention against its will, as it did so recently in Nicaragua. Even in the State Department opinion as to the wisdom of the policy has been divided.

Such an authoritative observer as Professor Dodds, who not only is versed in the theory of government but has an extended firsthand knowledge of Nicaragua, has pointed out the tendency of the present policy to multiply the occasions for intervention. In his view the policy as recently applied warns the Central American republics: "You must conduct your government in a manner recognized as constitutional under Anglo-Saxon theories of political science. Whether you like these theories or not, we believe them to be best for you and it is our duty to make you follow them."

"If this," continues Professor Dodds, "is really to be a consistent policy it will involve more rather than less intervention in the future, beyond that which has been in the past sufficient to protect our legitimate interests and fulfill our responsibility under the Monroe Doctrine. Undoubtedly the United States lives more peaceably under its conception of constitutional government than does Nicaragua. But does it follow that it is best suited to Nicaragua?"

If the present policy has its shortcomings and dangers, it will still be difficult to discover one which will answer all the requirements. Such a policy must at the same time safeguard what the United States regards as its own vital interests in Central America, uphold what the United States considers to be right and just, and be in accord with the desires of Latin Americans themselves. And the Latin Americans are, to a North American, an extraordinarily baffling people.

It is very well to talk of the "sister republics of the Western Hemisphere," of their devotion to common ideals of self-government, and of their natural unity of interest because of their geographical propinquity. These are excellent topics for speeches at receptions to goodwill ambassadors and at Pan-American meetings. Unfortunately they are nonsense. In the essentials of culture and character the people of North America and the people of Latin America are as far apart as the poles. They think differently, feel differently and act differently. Few Latin Americans understand North American psychology; fewer North Americans understand Latin psychology. In countries such as Nicaragua whose population is of mixed blood a racial factor enters.

"The half-breeds and their descendants govern the Ibero-American democracies," wrote F. Garcia Calderón, Peruvian diplomat, "and the republic of English and German origin entertains for the men of the tropics the same contempt which it feels for the slaves of Virginia, whom Lincoln liberated. In its friendship for them there will always be disdain; in its progress, a conquest; in its policy, a desire for hegemony. It is the fatality of blood, stronger than political affinities or geographical alliances."

Even between the North Americans and the people of pure Spanish extraction complete sympathy is rare, for they have different standards of value and conduct. These cultivated Latins cannot understand the preoccupation of North Americans with business, to the sacrifice of the soft enjoyments of life, and the North Americans have little patience with the relative inefficiency of the Latins.

Besides these basic differences of character and mentality, a certain lack of frankness, a certain hypocrisy sometimes, on the part of the Washington Government has afflicted its relations with the countries to the south. The aims of the United States in Central America have been simple and not heinous— the possession and the security of the means of swift passage from ocean to ocean—and these are well known and approved by most influential men in the countries concerned. Yet often the Washington Government has been loth to admit them, and when it has explained some enterprise by which it was trying to ward off a real or fancied threat in the canal region as "the protection of American lives and property," or as some benevolence for the Central Americans themselves, the Latins, knowing other considerations were present, have wondered just how far the United States was intending to go and have worried about their own security. This reticence of Washington has encouraged them to read into everything that the United States does the machinations of a scheming colossus. Thus Manuel Ugarte, of Argentina, could say:

"Never in all history has such an irrresistible or marvelously concerted force been developed as that which the United States is bringing to bear upon the peoples which are geographically or politically within its reach. . . . At times imperious, at other times suave, in certain cases apparently disinterested, in others implacable in its greed, pondering like a chess player who foresees every possible move, with a breadth of vision embracing many centuries, better informed and more resolute than any, without fits of passion, without forgetfulness, without fine sensibilities, without fear, carrying out a world activity in which everything is foreseen—North American imperialism is the most perfect instrument of domination which has been known throughout the ages."

But Señor Ugarte flatters the United States. There has been no such skilful and singleminded diplomacy as he has pictured, even when the goal has been easily in view as it has been throughout in Nicaragua. Instead, there has been a groping, an irresoluteness, a sidestepping, a backtracking, at many a point along the way. American progress in the Caribbean has been due partly to design, but more to what Isaac Joslin Cox calls the law of international gravitation "through which a larger nation attracts the smaller ones within the orbit of its influence." And this lack of coherent design in the acts of the United States, its hesitations at critical moments because of compunctions of conscience and timorousness as to what Latin America and its own people would say, have been more productive of trouble for the Nicaraguan and the American Government than have any of America's ambitions.

The reason for this lack of coherence and consistency seems to be evident. The United States is trying to do two mutually irreconcilable things in Nicaragua. It is trying to superintend Nicaragua's conduct and at the same time to preserve the Republic's political integrity. It has regarded its unimpeded command of the Isthmian canal and the elimination of instability in the region near it as a commercial and military necessity, yet it has sought desperately to observe the principle of the equality of all nations, great and small, in its hemisphere. It has violated the political integrity of Nicaragua while it made a fetich of the concept of political integrity. In this awkward dilemma it has squirmed like an unwilling sinner wrestling with the consciousness of guilt.

Latin America understands the wish of the United States to control the routes between the Atlantic and the Pacific, but it is skeptical of North American repudiation of territorial and political ambitions. It remembers William Walker, of the days of manifest destiny, and ignores the fact that the United States has rejected excellent excuses to extend its domain over Nicaragua more times than Cæsar refused a crown. The illogic of jealousy is sometimes evident in this eagerness of Latin America to believe the worst about the big republic in the North. There is an inferiority complex there—something of the universal instinctive dislike for those who are too successful.

In Nicaragua itself one finds surprisingly little distrust of the American Caribbean policy. There is indeed a widespread feeling among people of the higher classes that the United States should go further than it has gone in the guidance of their country; that since it obviously will be concerned in events in Nicaragua so long as ships sail through canals, it is better that it control the Republic through an avowed protectorate and forestall disorders rather than continue holding back until the country is prostrated by revolution before reluctantly intervening. Many Nicaraguans believe that under the present system Nicaragua has the disadvantages of vassalage without the advantages of a protectorate.

It was this consideration which moved Adolfo Diaz to seek a protectorate so persistently and to protest to the United States that the policy it was pursuing did not well serve either the United States or Nicaragua. On the Liberal side, President Moncada advocated a thorough-going protectorate as long ago as 1912, when the United States was putting down the Mena rebellion and there was unrest everywhere in Central America as to North America's objectives. Moncada has given indications in the past two years that his earlier view has not changed fundamentally, and on his election to the presidency in 1928 he requested that 1,000 marines be retained indefinitely in Nicaragua as insurance against disorder. Even Señor Tijerino, vigorous critic of the American policy and recent leader of the Nationalist movement, who was routed from his bed by American marines, has expressed a wish that the United States govern Nicaragua openly.

"I would like to see Nicaragua taken into the American confederation," he said recently across a restaurant table in New York. "Then we would have rights as citizens and not be subject to being ordered about by marines who are answerable to nobody."

At another table, in a club in ancient Granada, the writer heard the attitude of the United States likened to that of a dog in a manger by an elderly physician who professed only admiration for the United States and contempt for Nicaraguan politicians of whatever party.

"To my mind," he said. "there are only two possible solutions. First, the United States may take the country and govern it in accordance with military principles, as it has done so successfully in Haiti and Santo Domingo. Second, it may build the Nicaraguan canal, as it has built the canal at Panamá, whose prosperity and progressiveness may well be set up as an example of American efficiency and greatness. I have not the least doubt that the Nicaraguan canal would be a source of prosperity and happiness to my country.

"It is the duty of the United States to do something definitely good for this country. The Monroe Doctrine has been a great boon for Spanish America, in that it has insured its independence against European aggression, but it certainly has been a drawback in that it has kept the white man from civilizing these countries. Had it not been for the Monroe Doctrine England would have taken this country and we would today be part of the British Empire and far happier and more prosperous than we are today."

There is justice in the complaint of this doctor. The United States, by tying up the canal route, has blockaded Nicaragua's greatest avenue to wealth until the United States itself shall open it. When that canal finally is constructed, as it probably will be some day, it will carry into Nicaragua such riches as it never has known before. One may wonder whether in that era Nicaragua's Indians will be happier toiling on wharves and selling curios to tourists than they are today tilling their little corn patches and lazying in their hammocks, but by orthodox standards the country will be enormously benefited.

In that day, too, the problem of Nicaragua, so far as it concerns the United States, will have found a solution, for the strip of land and water which so many nations have coveted will then be an American military zone, safe from any ambitious rival and secure against disorder. Whether the achievement of that solution will be worth all the effort it has cost, whether all that effort has been necessary, whether indeed the security of the United States is as dependent on swiftly moving ships as the strategists believe, are questions which the author refrains from attempting to answer. He has been content to trace out the motives which have actuated the United States in Nicaragua and to reveal so far as he could by simple history the manner in which they have worked.

SOURCES

Much of the material used in this volume, especially in the later chapters, was obtained, as has been indicated, by firsthand observation or from persons participating in the events. Among other principle sources of information are Foreign Relations of the United States, State Department releases, reports of the Collector General of Customs and the High Commission of Nicaragua, newspaper files, especially The New York Times, New York Herald Tribune, New York World and New York Herald, and reports of testimony before Congressional committees. Of the Committee hearings, the most important are the following:

Foreign Relations Committee, U. S. Senate. Testimony on alleged invasion of Nicaragua by U. S. naval forces; investigation pursuant to Senate Resolution 385; October, 1912. Government Printing Office, 1913.

Foreign Affairs Committee, House (69th Congress, second session) Conditions in Nicaragua and Mexico; hearings on House Resolutions 373, 372, 368, 388, 389, 394, 376, 371, 357; January 12, 13, 28 and Feb. 1, 1927. Government Printing Office.

Foreign Relations Committee, U. S. Senate (69th Congress, second session) Hearings before subcommittee on foreign loans pursuant to Senate Concurrent Resolution 15; January 25, 26, 27 and Feb. 16, 1927. Government Printing Office.

Foreign Relations Committee, U. S. Senate (70th Congress, first session.) Use of U. S. navy in Nicaragua. Hearings on Senate Resolution 137; Feb. 11 and 18, 1928.

The following list of books and magazine articles is restricted to works in English bearing on the events and problems dealt with in this volume.

BIBLIOGRAPHY

Nicaragua and the United States, 1909-1927, by Isaac Joslin Cox. World Peace Foundation, Boston, 1927. [Excellent, impartial, brief view of period.]

A Brief History of the Relations Between the United States and Nicaragua, by the State Department. Government Printing Office, 1928. [Accurate so far as it goes.]

Latin America in World Politics, by J. Fred Rippy. Alfred A. Knopf, New York, 1928. [Comprehensive, compact, authoritative history of relations between North America and Latin America.]

The Recent Foreign Policy of the United States, by George H. Blakeslee. Abingdon Press, New York and Cincinnati, 1925. [Contains good general discussion of Caribbean problem.]

Mexico and the Caribbean, edited by George H. Blakeslee. G. E. Stechert & Co., New York, 1920. [Contains collection of authoritative opinions on American relations with Caribbean countries.]

Latin America, edited by George H. Blakeslee. Stechert, New York, 1914. [Collection of background studies by various authorities.]

Caribbean Interests of the United States, by Chester Lloyd Jones. D. Appleton & Co., New York, 1916. [General survey, economic and political, of North America's advancing influence.]

The Nicaragua Canal and the Monroe Doctrine, by Lindley Miller Keasbey. G. P. Putnam's Sons, New York and London, 1896. [Good historical background of present problem.]

The Monroe Doctrine, An Interpretation, by Albert Bushnell Hart. Little, Brown & Co., Boston, 1916. [History of Doctrine and its interpretations, with abundant illuminating quotations.]

Observations on the Monroe Doctrine, by Charles Evans Hughes. Article in American Journal of International Law, vol. 17 (1923) [Views on Caribbean policy by a Secretary of State.]

The Monroe Doctrine; Its importance in the International Life of the States of the New World, by Alejandro Alvarez. Oxford University Press, New York, 1924. [Balanced, authoritative study of its development into agency of North American hegemony, rich in quotations from statesmen and publicists.]

The Destiny of a Continent, by Manuel Ugarte, Alfred A. Knopf, New York, 1925. [Attack by distinguished Argentine publicist on what he considers ruthless imperialism.]

Latin America: Its Rise and Progress, by F. Garcia Calderon, tr. by Bernard Miall. Scribner's, New York; T. Fisher Unwin, London, 1913. [Latin American distrust of North American preëminence, as seen by conscientious Peruvian intellectual.]

Problems in Pan Americanism, by Samuel Guy Inman. George H. Doran Co., New York, 1921. [A moderate North American's view of Latin American sentiment.]

The Monroe Doctrine: An Ancient Shibboleth, by Hiram Bingham. Yale University Press, New Haven, 1913. [Argument by an American for its abandonment.]

Anglo-American Isthmian Diplomacy, 1815-1915, by Mary Wilhelmine Williams. American Historical Association and Oxford University Press, 1916. [Broad but concisely put background study.]

Survey of American Foreign Relations, 1928, edited by Charles P. Howland. Yale University Press, 1928.

America's Foreign Relations, by Willis Fletcher Johnson. 2 vols. Eveleigh Nash Co., London, 1916. [Two concise, lucid chapters on Nicaraguan canal route problem.]

The Interest of America in Sea Power, Present and Future, by A. T. Mahan (U. S. N.). Little, Brown & Co., Boston, 1908. [The strategy of the United States by a foremost naval philosopher.]

The Panama Canal and the Distribution of the Fleet, by A. T. Mahan. Article in North American Review, vol. 200 (1914) p. 406. [Extremely important exposition of Caribbean strategy.]

The Defence of the Panama Canal, by Henry L. Stimson. Article in Scribner's Magazine, vol. 54 (1913) p. 1. [Strategic importance of canal mastery by ex-Secretary of War.]

Report of the Nicaraguan Canal Commission, 1897-1899. Lord Baltimore Press, Baltimore, 1899. [Scientific findings of latest engineering survey, including study of danger from volcanoes.]

Report of the Isthmian Canal Commission, 1899-1901. Government Printing Office, Washington, 1904. [Comparison of Panama and Nicaragua routes; texts of pertinent treaties, contracts, etc.]

The Key of the Pacific: The Nicaragua Canal, by Archibald Ross Colquhoun. Constable & Co., London, 1895. [The route, Nicaragua and its people.]

The Central American Peace Conference of 1907, by James Brown Scott. Article in American Journal of International Law, vol. 2 (1908) p. 121.

The Peace Conference of Central America, by Luis Anderson.

Article in American Journal of International Law, vol. 2, p. 144.

Central America and Its Problems, by Frederick Palmer. Moffat, Yard & Co., New York, 1910. [Includes vivid picture of Nicaragua in Zelaya's time.]

The Revolution of Nicaragua and the United States, by José Santos Zelaya. (English version) B. Rodriguez, Madrid, 1910. [Fallen dictator's protest.]

With the Knox Mission to Central America, by William Bayard Hale. Article in World's Work, vol. 24 (1912) p. 179. [Eyewitness account of Secretary of State's nerve-racking goodwill visit to Nicaragua.]

The United States and Central America, by George T. Weitzel. Article in Annals of the American Academy of Political and Social Science, vol. 132 (1927) p. 115. [Compact review from American official standpoint by ex-Minister to Nicaragua.]

Nicaragua and American Intervention, by J. M. Moncada. Article in Outlook, vol. 147 (1927) p. 460. [Defense of marine occupation by Liberal leader.]

Imperialism and the Monroe Doctrine, by J. M. Moncada. Privately published by Aloysius C. Gahan, New York, 1911.

Social and Political Influence of the United States in Central America, by J. M. Moncada. Gahan, 1911. [Early expressions of pro-Americanism by new President of Nicaragua.]

Public Appeal of Nicaragua to the Congress and People of the United States, by Argüello, Lejarza and Martinez. New Orleans, 1914. [Early protest by Nicaraguan Liberals against intervention.]

The Economical Situation of Nicaragua, by Pio Bolaños. New Orleans, 1916. [Nicaraguan protest.]

The Five Republics of Central America; Their Political and Economic Development and their Relations with the United States, by Dana G. Munro. Carnegie Endowment for International Peace, Washington, and Oxford University Press, New York, 1918. [Comprehensive, sympathetic, unbiased, important.]

The United States and Nicaragua, by Harold W. Dodds. Article in Annals of the American Academy of Political and Social Science, vol. 132 (1927) p. 134. [Acute discussion of Nicaraguan politics by firsthand authority.]

American Policy in Nicaragua, by Henry L. Stimson. Scribner's,

New York, 1927. [His own account of his peace mission.]

Sandino and American Policy, by Carleton Beals. Articles in Nation, vol. 126 (Feb., Mar., April, 1928). [Interview with Sandino and charges of marine atrocities.]

The Central Americans, by Arthur Ruhl, Scribner's, New York, 1928. [Sympathetic present-day picture of countries and peoples.]

Nicaragua, an Economic and Financial Survey, by W. W. Cumberland. Government Printing Office, Washington, 1928. [Expert, impartial, exact, important.]

Dollar Diplomacy, by Scott Nearing and Joseph Freeman. Viking Press, New York, 1925. [Unflattering presentation of financial penetration.]

Nicaragua, a Commercial and Economic Survey, by Harold Playter and Andrew J. McConnico. Government Printing Office, Washington, 1927. [Report by American consuls of resources and markets.]

Central American Currency and Finance, by John Parke Young. Princeton University Press, Princeton, N. J. 1925. [Contains financial and monetary survey of Nicaragua.]

American Foreign Investments, by Robert W. Dunn. Viking Press, New York, 1926. [Contains texts of 1911 loan contract and of agreement for purchase of railroad and bank stock.]

Conquest; America's Painless Imperialism, by John Carter. Harcourt, Brace & Co., New York, 1928. [General discussion of economic penetration.]

Relations of United States Companies with Latin America, by Victor M. Cutter. Article in Annals of the American Academy of Political and Social Science, vol. 132, p. 130. [Industrial penetration viewed by president of largest North American interest in Central America.]

Monetary Reform for Nicaragua, by F. C. Harrison and Charles A. Conant. Report of experts to Brown Brothers & Co. and J. & W. Seligman & Co., 1912. Privately printed by bankers. [Dispensable because most of its material is published by Young, Dunn, et al.]

Filibusters and Financiers, by William O. Scroggs, The Macmillan Company, New York and London, 1916. [Careful, interesting, documented history of William Walker's expeditions.]

Nicaragua, Its People, Scenery, Monuments, and The Proposed Interoceanic Canal, by E. G. Squier. 2 vols. D. Appleton &

Co., New York, 1851. [Surpassingly interesting account of country in time of Manifest Destiny; a classic.]

The Naturalist in Nicaragua, by Thomas Belt. John Murray, London, 1874. (Also in Everyman's Library) [Interesting old book of travel, with studies of plants and animals, human beings and volcanoes.]

Old Panamá and Castilla del Oro, by C. L. G. Anderson, Page Co., Boston, 1914. [Spanish discoveries and conquests, and rise of English buccaneers; rich in color and anecdote.]

History of Central America, Hubert Howe Bancroft. 3 vols. The Bancroft Co., New York, 1902.

INDEX

A